Fiddling with
Disaster

CLEARING THE PAST

Fiddling with Disaster
CLEARING THE PAST

Ashley MacIsaac

with Francis Condron

Warwick Publishing
www.warwickgp.com

We acknowledge the financial support of the Government of Canada through the Book Publishing Industry Development Program for our publishing activities.

ISBN: 1-894622-33-2

Published by Warwick Publishing Inc.
161 Frederick Street
Toronto, Ontario M5A 4P3 Canada
www.warwickgp.com

Distributed in Canada by:
Canadian Book Network
c/o Georgetown Terminal Warehouses
34 Armstrong Avenue
Georgetown, Ontario L7G 4R9 Canada

Distributed in the United States by:
Weatherhill, Inc.
41 Monroe Turnpike, Trumbull, CT 06611 USA

National Library of Canada Cataloguing in Publication

MacIsaac, Ashley, 1975-
         Fiddling with disaster / Ashley MacIsaac ; with Francis Condron.
Includes index.
ISBN 1-894622-33-2

         1. MacIsaac, Ashley, 1975- 2. Fiddlers--Canada--Biography.
I. Condron, Frank II. Title.

ML418.M149A3 2003   787.2'092   C2003-902461-X

Photos courtesy of the MacIsaac Family; The Halifax Daily News
Front Cover Photo: Donald Weber
Printed and bound in Canada

Contents

1 New York 7

2 Creignish 27

3 Music 51

4 Biz 71

5 Rich and Famous 95

6 Drugs 127

7 Media 159

8 Sex 177

9 Happy Fuckin' New Year 201

10 Poor and Famous 235

Epilogue 259

Discography 273

Index 275

New York

It turned out the lady on the answering machine did know me. Well, sort of knew me. When I called her back, she told me that her name was JoAnne Akalaitis. She and her husband had come to Cape Breton just that past July on a holiday and had seen me perform at a square dance in Mabou. She was impressed, I guess, because she wrote my name down so she wouldn't forget it when she went back to New York.

JoAnne explained that she was the theatre director of a "folk opera" they were putting on in New York called *Woyzeck* and this famous composer Philip Glass was writing all the music for it. I guess she just assumed I knew who he was, because she didn't offer any details — and I wasn't going to make a fool of myself by asking.

It was a very popular show, she said, although I had sure never heard of it. It was the last work of some composer who died before he could finish it, so every time it was produced, it came out a little different. Philip Glass's version was going to be a totally "new age" treatment of the original story, JoAnne explained, and there was a real buzz about it in New York. Everyone had high hopes for it because it had a really good director, and good actors, and was being put on in a big theatre. It had already got quite a bit of attention in the papers, including the *Village Voice*, which I knew well.

The reason they were interested in me for it, she said, was because the show was based on an old folk opera full of traditional music from Europe. The idea was to take the play and replace the original European folk music with folk music from all over North America. I would have a small part where I would come out and play my fiddle while the cast members step danced — I would be basically representing the North American connection to Celtic folk music.

"When I saw you perform in Cape Breton last summer, I just knew you'd be perfect for it," JoAnne gushed.

So, in addition to teaching the cast how to step dance, I would be expected to do a show a night for four nights a week, then two shows each on Saturday and Sunday. For that I'd get $1,000 U.S. a week and my room and board paid for three months.

"Sounds good," was all I could say, but my heart was practically jumping out of my chest. Sure it all sounded exciting, but it was also scary as hell. I mean, I knew I was pretty good, but good enough to go from square dances in Cape Breton to playing for a New York theatre crowd?

"Sounds good," I said again. I didn't know what else to say. I think JoAnne sensed that and quickly tried to allay my fears.

"Well, why don't you think about it and talk it over with your parents and call me back in a couple of days," JoAnne said. "But I would really appreciate it if you could tell me for sure then, because if you can't come, we have to make other arrangements."

That was it then. I thanked her and we said goodbye.

I was stunned at first, but the possibilities this opened up for me quickly spread out before me, and not just the professional possibilities. *This was my chance.* Without hesitation, I looked at my mom and said, "Can somebody get me on a plane, please?"

She stood leaning against the stove with her arms crossed and a look of suspicion in her eye. "Not so fast," she said.

When my dad got home, my parents and me sat at the kitchen table to talk it over. It was a huge opportunity, for sure, but it also meant going to a lot of trouble. I would miss the first half of my last year of high school for starters, and what was that going to do to my chances of graduating in the spring with my class? Then I would be alone — my dad couldn't get that much time off work and my mom had to look after the house and my little sister. If I went, I would be on my own.

The whole concept of New York City was way too much for my parents to take in. So their first reaction was to go to my teachers and to the priest and to their relatives and ask each one of them what they thought about it.

My teachers were all pretty excited for me, but then most of them had been away to university and were a little more worldly wise than the locals. Still, they were all a little leery of me going to New York by myself for so long.

A couple of them had even heard of Philip Glass. With the help of one of my English teachers, I did a little research and found out he really was quite a big wheel in the high-brow music world and had written big orchestra and dance pieces, operas and film scores. I figured he must have been pretty old compared to me, because he was putting out albums back in the early 1970s. He really made his name, apparently, when he wrote the music for an art film called *Koyaanisqatsi*, which, surprisingly enough, my brother Henry had seen in one of his high school English classes.

"What was it about?" I asked him.

"Not much," he said. "Just lots of pictures of buildings and people and cars and mountains and clouds all running together. I don't think anybody in it says a thing."

"What's the music like?"

"Well, you couldn't dance to it, I'll tell you that," Henry said. "It kind of goes round and round like a busted record. Nothing like fiddle music at all."

That sounded accurate enough, given what I'd read about Glass's music. In some of the reviews that I'd managed to find, people talked about Glass's "minimalist compositions," and "hypnotic circular rhythms." People seemed to like it though. In some of the magazine articles I read, Glass was described as "the avant-garde's best known composer," and "post-modern music's most celebrated and high-profile proponent." One magazine even called him "the most innovative and influential composer of the 20th century."

I also found out that he'd collaborated on projects with a whole bunch of people who I'd at least heard of; people like David Byrne of the Talking Heads, Ray Manzarek (the keyboard player for the Doors), Paul Simon, Suzanne Vega and the film director Martin Scorsese. "And now he wants to work with little Ashley MacIsaac from Creignish, Nova Scotia?" I thought. It was almost too ridiculous to be true.

As for my relatives, their reactions were predictable, given the place they were coming from. When you said New York to them, all they pictured was TV New York, the city they knew from *The French Connection* and *Baretta* and *Kojak*. "New York — are you crazy?" "You want to get on a plane — are you crazy?" "Stay in New York by yourself — are you crazy?" So that was the consensus within about 24 hours of that phone call: I was crazy.

There was one voice in the wilderness though, and it belonged to a guy my dad knew who worked as a janitor at the plant in Port Hawkesbury. It turned out this guy, I think Archie was his name, was actually from New York, but he moved up to Cape Breton in the early 1970s to dodge the draft for the Viet Nam War and had never left. Now Archie may have worked as a janitor, but he was college-educated and a hell of a lot smarter and well-travelled than most folks round about.

When my dad described the opportunity to this guy, he said my parents would be crazy not to let me go. "Once-in-a-lifetime chance," Archie told my dad. He also assured him that I would be staying and working in a good part of town, and that theatre people were not the low-life types you tended to see on the cop shows. I would be surrounded by intelligent, talented people, he said, and most of them would have lots of money.

"Sure New York looks like a big, scary place to go to when you're from Cape Breton," he assured my dad. "But there's 10 million people living there, and they aren't all cops and bad guys. Most of them are people just like you."

My mom and dad thought about it for a little while, then they finally decided that the opinion of someone who was actually from New York was probably more valid than the collective opinions of a bunch of people from Creignish. They decided to let me go.

The next day my dad called JoAnne back and it was all arranged for me to go to New York. I didn't have much time to change my mind, if I was ever going to. About one week after we confirmed things, a plane ticket arrived at the door by courier. Two days later, I was on my way to the airport in Halifax with my parents.

* * *

I flew into Newark Airport on a Monday at about 10:00 in the morning. The weather was wet and foggy, so I didn't get a really good look at the skyline from the air, and I was on the wrong side of the plane anyway. But I did catch the odd glimpse of buildings that appeared familiar through the window across the aisle as we turned in, and I felt my excitement level rise for the first time since I left Halifax. I had had a pretty tearful goodbye with my parents, as you might imagine; it's not every day you send your own little man off to Broadway I guess.

Customs took a while because I was coming into the States on a special work visa. After finding out how to retrieve my one bag of clothes — my fiddle case, of course, never left my arms during the flight — I headed out to the terminal, bursting with excitement now and full of real fear of the unknown for the first time.

Actually, to be honest my biggest fear at that exact moment was finding my ride. JoAnne, the theatre lady, had told me there would be a driver waiting for me when I got off the plane, but I found that a little confusing, seeing as she was the one who had seen me in Cape Breton in the first place and knew what I looked like. As I rode the escalator down into the terminal, I remember being really worried about how I was going to get downtown if the driver couldn't find me. Just then, above a crowd of people beyond the gate, I saw a pair of hands holding up a sign that had "MacIsaac" written on it in black marker. "Of course," I thought, "just like on TV."

The driver was a large black gentleman who told me his name was William. He took my bag and led me out to a big white airport limo that was even bigger than my Parisienne. The drive from Newark into Manhattan, where I would be staying, took about 45 minutes, so I had lots of time to take in the scenery and wrap my head around what was happening to me. As I got closer and closer to New York, it really began to sink in that I wasn't in Kansas anymore, as the saying goes.

What struck me the most, I think, in that first half hour in the car, was that there didn't seem to be a patch of available dirt that didn't have a building on it of some description. Another thing I noticed was the black people. I easily saw more black people in that ride from the airport to my hotel than I had seen in my whole life to that point. In fact, after making some small talk with William, I had also said more to a black person during that car ride than I had in my life to that point.

Eventually we hit the bridge linking New Jersey to New York and I got my first really good glimpse of the Manhattan skyline from ground level. I searched out the buildings I knew from the movies and the TV — the Empire State, the Chrysler Building, the World Trade Centre, of course, was there then. As we rumbled across the bridge, the theme music to *Taxi* was playing in my head as I struggled to take it all in. It was like an out-of-body experience, like I was watching myself in one of those New York cop shows.

All kinds of thoughts were going through my mind. I thought about Creignish and how far away I was from it, both physically and emotionally. I though about how small my hometown really was, and how small Cape Breton was, and Halifax for that matter. I thought about how in awe I was as a kid when I would meet Buddy MacMaster and how I thought of him as a god. Now I was going to meet "the most innovative and influential composer of the 20th century."

"Nope," I thought to myself. "Sorry Buddy, but this is much, much bigger."

It also hit me how I was, for the first time in my life, completely alone. Here I was, in one of the largest, most exciting and dangerous cities in the world, and there was no one there from my family, or from my school, or from my hometown, no one from the same cultural background as me (nobody I knew at least). I was completely stripped of everything, other than my fiddle, that was familiar. Christ, I'd never been in a limousine before; now I was on my way to start a job where I'd be getting paid $1,000 U.S. a week. *And I was only 17 years old.*

Eventually we got right downtown and ended up pulling up not in front of a hotel, like I expected, but in front of the theatre where the play was going to be on. As I stepped out of the limo, a woman came out the front door and walked quickly up to me smiling with her hand extended. "Ashley MacIsaac, welcome to New York," she said. "I'm JoAnne Akalaitis."

From her voice, I immediately recognized she was the lady from the phone. I can't say I recognized her from the square dance back during the summer, but I pretended to anyway; it was important for me to know somebody, anybody, just then.

She took me in for a quick tour of the theatre. It was big enough, all right, but not Carnegie Hall big, and that was a comfort. I was pretty nervous about the whole thing, you can imagine, but at least I knew I wouldn't be intimidated by the hall. True, this was New York, but I'd played a lot of shows by age 17, and often in hockey rinks or community centres that could hold a lot more people than that theatre. I began to feel a little more sure of myself after that.

When we got backstage we bumped into some of the actors in the show, and that's when I was first introduced to the person who would end up becoming one of my best friends in New York, Camryn Manheim. Of course, she's a big star now, and I make a point of watching her on *The Practice* every week, but she was just another struggling actor back then, taking any work she could get and looking for that one big break. We made some small talk and she promised to show me around the city, and then she was gone.

We soon got back in the limo and JoAnne took me to the place I'd be staying. It turned out to be this gorgeous little one-bedroom apartment in a small building off Central Park West. It was in one of those beautiful walk-up apartment buildings built in the 1920s that you always see people like Woody Allen living in in movies. JoAnne introduced me to the landlord but said she couldn't stay with me because she had something she had to do, and off she went. I was alone again.

The landlord took me in and showed me around. I guess he could tell that I was pretty young, because he pointed out that it was a very expensive building and a young guy like me should feel lucky to have such a nice place. He didn't ask me any questions, but I'm sure he was wondering what this kid was doing moving into a Manhattan apartment all by himself.

After I got my bag unpacked I remember sitting on the ledge of one of the front windows of this apartment and looking out at the city. The feeling of awe had kind of subsided by then, as had any feelings of fear I might have had about my living arrangements and where I'd be working. That had all worked out better than I could have ever expected. I knew I was safe then, and that this was going to be a great experience. I finally felt totally relaxed and free, the same way I felt the first time I took my fiddle and drove off on my own in the Parisienne to play a gig.

It was only about 7:00 in the evening then, and I didn't have to be at the theatre until noon the next day, so I decided to look around a bit. With some directions from my landlord, I made my way to the subway and decided to see where it would take me. Looking back now, it was a stupid thing to do, but I just picked a stop at random and went up to the street.

I can't remember the name of the place I got off — somewhere around 8th Avenue and 42nd Street — but it might as well have been Oz. When I got up to the street, I walked right into the middle of one of the worst sections of the city. I was surrounded by peep shows and XXX movie shops and bums and porn. I couldn't go 50 feet in any direction without someone offering me drugs or without some hooker offering me sex. On top of that, there seemed to be black people every- where, but not a white face in the crowd, save for mine. It was like I'd just landed on another planet.

You have to remember, when I was growing up in Creignish, there were no black people or people of colour at all in my community. The only black people I ever saw when I was a kid, until I started to travel to cities like Halifax later on, was a single family that lived in Port Hawkesbury. They were the very definition of "visible minority" on Cape Breton. That was my entire exposure to non-white, non-Scottish culture growing up, so you can see why the diversity of cultures hit me like a nuclear explosion when I got to New York.

For a couple of seconds, I must admit, I panicked. As I moved quickly along the sidewalk to I didn't know where, I thought, "This is great, your first night in New York and now you're going to die and you never even got a chance to be in the stupid show."

Then I stopped dead in the street. I took a few deep breaths and tried to relax. I said slowly to myself, "Ashley, what are you running for? Nothing bad's happened to you yet. This is just New York. This is where you live for the time being, so you better get used to it."

It was then I started to notice that not every person walking past me looked weird or scary, and I also noticed a few cops standing on the cor- ner just a few yards away. Then I realized that, in a place like New York, you tend to see what you want to see, and while it's true the nasty stuff is there, there's lots of cool, interesting stuff as well. As I calmed down, I began to notice there were whites, and Orientals and Indians and all kinds of people other than blacks.

But the more time I spent in New York, the more I understood that stereotypes just scratched the surface. From that first night on, I wanted to learn about as many other cultures as I could — and what better place to do that than New York. Imagine living for years thinking there was only one colour of paint and then going to a store where there are hundreds of shades of every colour; that's what New York was like for me from a cultural perspective.

As I became more of a "New Yorker," I actually started to seek out people from different cultures to have conversations. I saw it as kind of a project as well, just to get rid of some of my upbringing in a place that was very one-culture-oriented. And as I became more comfortable with the fact that I was gay, accepting people who were different from me became sort of a duty.

I ended up walking all the way back to my apartment that first night. I dropped into some neat stores, sat in a coffee shop, bought some gay porn and my first current copy of the *Village Voice*. I even stopped and got into conversations with people I met along the way, hookers and dope dealers included. I stopped fretting about my situation as well, I think, because I saw that there were lots of people in that city who were a lot worse off than me.

The truth was, I'd never really seen what real poor people looked like before New York. Sure, there were some families I knew in my little corner of Cape Breton who maybe weren't as well off as some others, including my own. But everyone had a home at least, and family nearby to help them out, and a job most of the time. As I walked the streets of New York for the first time though, I looked into the faces of people who were desperate in every way: no home, no money, no family, no job — and no hope of ever having a job, probably addicted or insane.

It was a real shock to my system to see just how low a human being can sink and still be alive. I remember thinking to myself, "How the hell do these people end up like this?" I couldn't have even imagined finding myself in a similar situation. But the truth is, it can happen to anybody; and I would find that out the hard way.

As I say, though, in a big city like New York, you tend to see what you want to see. And for someone like me, a young musician with money and complete freedom, the cool things about living in the Big

Apple quickly covered over the negative things. After the shock of that first night, the bums and the addicts, the dealers and the hookers just faded into the background. They were just a part of the scene, part of what makes New York New York. "Once you get that," Camryn told me, when I told her how shocked I had been that first night, "then you're a New Yorker."

Camryn and I got along really well, I think because I brought out the mother in her; well, the big sister, at least. We were both kind of at the same point in our careers then as well, and that gave us something in common. She had been in a lot of smaller local things before, but this was the first "big" production she had been on at a big downtown theatre and with a big-name director and composer involved.

She was living in a small one-bedroom apartment on the Lower East Side at the time, and it became like a second home to me. She installed herself right away as my official "New York" mentor.

"If you're going to live in New York," she said, "you have to learn to act like a New Yorker. And I'm going to teach you."

She showed me how to get around town on the subway and took me to all the tourist spots, "just to get it out of your system," she said. She showed me around the cool neighbourhoods in the city, like TriBecA, Soho and Greenwich Village, and took me to the trendy clothes stores and the coffee shops and restaurants where the artists and actors hang out. She also taught me to do cool "New York" things that you just couldn't do in Cape Breton, like order really good Thai take-out at 2:00 in the morning. I figured out pretty fast that eating out in New York could be cheaper than going to the grocery store.

I don't know if she felt sorry for me because she thought I was lonely, but Camryn was just a really wonderful person to me. She taught me crazy things too, like how to pretend to do sign language to freak people out in restaurants and how to pretend to speak Chinese. She was an awful lot of fun, but I could also see that she was a fabulous actress even then. It would take a few more years before the rest of the world found that out.

With Camryn's help, it didn't take me long to become completely immersed in my new life. I got used to it so fast, in fact, that my life in Cape Breton became a distant memory; like something I'd dreamt, but didn't really happen.

In fact, I think Camryn was one of the first people I ever told I was gay. It was just a few days after I'd arrived in town and she took me out for dinner one night in Greenwich Village and was asking me all about Cape Breton and my family and what I did for fun, which, of course, wasn't much. Finally she asked the big question: "So, have you got a girlfriend back home?"

"No," I answered. Then, half lowering my voice, "and I don't exactly want one, if you know what I mean."

Well, Camryn had been around the theatre crowd long enough that she didn't need to be told twice. But, of course, it was nothing to her, and that made it all the easier for me to say it. Taking my hand, she said, "Listen kid, in this business, it's more about who's *not* gay than who *is* gay." Then she started to list off all the people working on the play who were gay, men and women, and there were plenty. Over the course of the next few days and weeks, Camryn introduced me to all of them and they sort of took me under their wings as well. Before I knew it, I was making the rounds of all the best gay clubs, parties and coffee houses in Manhattan.

When you're a naturally outgoing person, as I am, you're very seldom lonely. Hell, on my first night in New York I managed to meet people and have conversations with them. They may not have been the best people to talk to, but I got along with them all right.

Well, I can honestly say that I wasn't lonely for even 10 minutes in New York. As soon as I found my bearings and knew how to get around, I made a beeline for that world that I'd been reading about in the *Village Voice* and seeing in the gay porn magazines I picked up in Halifax. The gay nightclub scene soon became my new home and the people I met in the clubs became my new family. I was underage, obviously, but my gay theatre friends had connections, and there was always room in the club for an eager 17-year-old with a kilt and a cute accent. The fact that I didn't drink helped me too, because the bar wouldn't get in trouble for serving me if I crashed a car or something.

Drugs, of course, were everywhere, but I managed to avoid them as well. I was just high on being free, and in New York, and exploring my sexuality for the first time. I guess there were so many other things I wanted to experience then that drugs just didn't have any attraction for me. Months later, when I wasn't nearly so happy and had basically nothing else around to draw my interest, drugs would look a lot different to me. But in New York, I had better things to do.

There were a lot of "firsts" for me in New York, both personal and professional, but especially sexual. All I can really say about my first gay sexual experiences was that I got them over with fast so I could get right on to the next, and the next … . I was green as the grass from an experience standpoint, but I had had years of practice in my fantasies and I knew what I was after. And, unlike at home, there was no shortage of willing partners. The best way to describe what I was in the New York club scene was a boy-toy. If you've ever seen the TV show *Queer As Folk,* I was like the blond high-school kid who hangs around with all these gay guys in their 20s and 30s, getting passed around from person to person on a weekly, or even nightly, basis.

The clubs were a musical awakening for me as well. I was in the clubs almost every night, surrounded by the thumping club music. I was listening to RuPaul and Madonna and the Pet Shop Boys. What I was doing, really, was immersing myself in a new culture, the gay culture. I'd come from a place with its own music, and its own forms of dance, its own traditional clothing and its own language, just like any culture anywhere in the world. And when you think about it, the gay culture is no different. It's just like-minded people coming up with ways to feel a part of something, like they belong somewhere. My culture always made me feel that way in Cape Breton, and becoming immersed in the gay culture of New York made me feel that way too.

Ever since then I've felt like I have two cultures within me. I'll always be a Cape Bretoner, and I'll always feel at home around Cape Breton music and around other Cape Bretoners. But the same thing goes for the gay culture I adopted, or that adopted me, in New York. That same culture exists in places I lived later on, like Halifax and Toronto, and I was able to blend right in with it.

I know this is probably hard for anyone who isn't gay to understand, but being in New York and actually having access to a community where there were people who shared my sexuality was like a dream to me. It was the fantasy world I had been imagining for years come to life. For the first time, I was free to really acknowledge who I was as a person and not feel self-conscious about it. As a matter of fact, you were strange if you *weren't* gay in a lot of the places where I hung out. You have to remember, I was coming from a place where, if there were any gay people, they sure as hell weren't talking much about it. And that feeling of knowing you're different from everyone around you, and fearing they'll reject you if they knew — that's true loneliness.

I know that for a fact, because true loneliness was exactly what I experienced when I finally came home from New York. The irony wasn't lost on me: I had spent 17 years of my life being so much a part of a place and a community and a culture, but I never felt like I really belonged anywhere until I left. That's not to say I felt like I belonged in New York specifically, although I could live there full-time, I think. It's more like, New York was the first place I ever felt at home in my own skin. Like I say, it's hard for anyone who isn't gay, or at least some kind of socially unacceptable minority, to fully understand.

It really was like I was living in the perfect world — music all day, clubs all night. For the first six weeks I was in New York, I was in the theatre from 9:00 in the morning until about 6:00 at night in rehearsal. I'd either be playing my fiddle for the director or working on the music with the band or teaching the actors to step dance.

The whole dancing end of it was particularly interesting, because it elevated me from being merely a bit player to making a really serious contribution. The director decided to include a square dance sequence in the production, and he quickly decided after he saw me dance that I was good enough to learn from. That's how I became a sort of assistant choreographer. I had given step-dancing lessons to younger kids in Cape Breton, but now I was teaching a group of professional actors, all of them older than me, to perform a square dance they came up with just for this production.

When I got there, I was just a kid from a tiny village in Cape Breton who could dance and play the fiddle. But by the time the show was done, I was a choreographer, an actor and a professional musician rolled into one.

Meeting Philip Glass for the first time was scary. I had been in New York for about a week rehearsing the music before I actually met Philip. When I first got there, the director basically handed some music from the play over to me and told me to learn it as quick as I could. That was no problem — it was straightforward violin music that had a few twists and turns and maybe a more modern sound to it. That was the "new age" part I guess. Thanks to my fiddle teacher Stan Chapman, though, I had a good enough grounding in reading music that the director was quite happy with me after only a couple of days.

Before I met Philip, the most famous person I'd ever met "up close" in my life was Buddy MacMaster. Of course, I'd played the fiddle in Halifax for the Pope when I was a kid, and he's obviously more famous than Philip Glass or Buddy (except on Cape Breton), but I didn't go out for coffee with him afterwards. It helped, though, that I didn't know what Philip looked like. I've met lots of famous people since then, and I find it always freaks you out more when it's someone you already have an image of in your head.

When we finally did meet, it was at the theatre, and Philip walked right up to me with his hand out. After the initial "hello" I just stood there nodding my head as he asked me questions about how I liked New York and how the apartment was and everything. I was expecting him to start asking me about the music when he said something I wasn't expecting at all:

"I bet you didn't know I was a Cape Bretoner," he said, and my jaw dropped.

Well, he was and he wasn't, as it turned out. He wasn't actually from Cape Breton, but he had spent a lot of time vacationing in Inverness, just a quick trip up Route 19 from Creignish. He knew all the towns I knew. He knew all about Cape Breton culture and music and was familiar with Buddy MacMaster and a lot of other local musicians I knew. We chatted for about 20 minutes about Cape Breton, and it put me right at ease with him. Then, all of a sudden, he said, "OK, let's get to work."

He started by giving me some music he had written specifically for me to play as my solo. I tried it two or three times reading it right off the sheets, but I just couldn't seem to get it right. (In fact, I still try to play the same piece of music to this day the way he wrote it and I still can't get it.) I think the problem was that some parts of the piece were just too classical in nature and really needed a classically trained violinist to play them well. I could play the notes close enough, but some of it was too difficult for me; the sound just wasn't in my vein of musicality, is the only way I can describe it. It's like asking a really great honky tonk piano player to play Debussy; he can, but he can't. The same holds true going the other way too.

Anyway, instead of jumping on me or getting impatient, Philip asked me how I would approach the parts I was having trouble with. I took a few minutes and came up with something of my own that he liked that was along the same lines, and that was it. We worked that way from then on, with me playing what I could as it was written and us compromising on the rest.

I know the only reason I got away with that is because Philip is a really down-to-earth, nice guy, as well as being a fabulous composer. I was really young and raw and dealing with being away from home for the first time, and he knew that. I suppose if I had been a professional musician from New York, he wouldn't have been so flexible. Anyway, I really appreciated the fact that he was willing to work with me, and we became fast friends.

Much to my initial disappointment, my little apartment off Central Park West turned out to be a temporary thing. Eventually I moved out and went to stay with Philip and his family at his house. I guess it was costing too much to keep me in the apartment, but at any rate, staying at Philip's made it easier for us to work on the music for the production and it gave me a little company.

I didn't realize it at the time, but getting a chance to spend so much time with one of the world's great contemporary composers probably had as big an impact on me musically as living in New York did personally. I got a first-hand look at how a true professional goes through the various steps of writing, arranging and playing a piece of music, refining it all the time, until it's exactly the way he wants it. All I really knew at that point was how to take my fiddle out of the case and play music. But watching Philip work, I realized that playing music and creating music are very different things; creating music takes a lot more care, and thought, and discipline. That knowledge would prove very useful to me when the time came for me to go into the studio to record my first major record.

When the time finally came for the show to open, it was kind of anti-climactic for me, to be honest. I knew my part and I had the music down cold because I'd been playing nothing else for weeks by that time. Of course it was cool experiencing "opening night" in New York, but I don't think I was half as nervous as most of the rest of the cast. When you think about it, playing my fiddle in front of people was about the only thing I did in New York that *wasn't* new to me. When I walked out on the stage and looked out into the sea of faces, I could just as easily have been in some community centre in Cape Breton. And when I put my fiddle under my chin and raised my bow, the music came just as natural as breathing.

Once the show got rolling, it soon began to feel just like any job would. You go in on time and do what you have to do, but you're really more concerned with what you're going to do when you're not at the theatre. In fact, I actually had more time on my hands once the show started than I had when it was in rehearsal. More time to explore the city, meet interesting new people and even have my first real relationship.

Meanwhile, New York was also opening me up to a tidal wave of new musical influences. For the first time in my life I had black friends and Puerto Rican friends, and I was getting to hear their music. I was listening to all kinds of dance music in the clubs. I was hearing rap and rock from boom boxes in the street. When I got to New York, I could read and write music and play music, but I found out in a hurry that I didn't know very much about it at all. But that was just one more voyage of discovery for me.

That wasn't to say I was completely devoid of Celtic influences in New York. In fact, I was invited several times to play at some big Irish clubs in the city by people who had seen me playing in the show. That was a welcome break for me at the time; I was so into the whole artist scene and the gay scene by then, I had almost forgotten what it was like to play Cape Breton fiddle music to a room full of people from the same basic culture. It worked out well professionally as well, because I met and played with some musicians at those gigs that I would play with again years later as a professional touring musician.

More often than not, though, my fiddle was the furthest thing from my mind in New York, and that was another first for me. The reason, of course, was that I had developed a life away from my Cape Breton culture and away from the music and away from my instrument. I'll admit my attachment to all those things hasn't been the same since. I think because I spent my first 17 years surrounded by nothing but Cape

Breton music and culture, I spent the next 10 trying to experience anything *but* Cape Breton music and culture.

I don't think that's necessarily a bad thing, because I think I got a good enough grounding in my own culture early on in my life that I'll never have to worry about losing it. It's like people who learn a language when they're babies: Even if they grow up and move away and learn another language and don't speak their mother tongue for years, they always have that first language in them just as fluent as ever. Sure, I still practise the fiddle, and I still don't know every single Cape Breton fiddle tune there is, but I don't have to practise as much as I once did. In New York I realized I could relax a little, walk away from my culture for a while and do something different, confident in the knowledge that it would all be there when I decided to go back to it again.

While it is true to say I was never lonely in New York, I did struggle at times with homesickness. I was busy all the time and had lots of new friends and new things I wanted to experience, but that didn't mean I didn't miss my parents and my brother and sister.

The homesickness got worse as Christmas approached. I'd been away almost three months by the time December rolled around, but it didn't hit me until I started to see the decorations going up in the store windows and the lighting of the tree at Rockefeller Center. The play was scheduled to run right through to the New Year, so I had originally planned to spend Christmas in New York. The closer Christmas got, though, the more I missed my family. Finally I couldn't take it any longer; I decided to make a quick trip home to surprise them all for Christmas.

I made arrangements to get a few days off during the week and bought a plane ticket home without telling anybody. Then I called a friend a few days before I left and got him to pick me up in Halifax, making sure not to tell anybody what he was doing. I got into Halifax about noon on a Monday and my friend was there waiting for me. As we pulled out of the airport, I asked him to make a quick pit stop at a big mall on the way out of town so I could pick something up. My friend figured I was just going to run in and pick up some last minute Christmas gifts, but when we got there, I headed right to the appliance department of Sears.

"I hope you're not looking to buy a washing machine or anything," I remember him telling me, "because we're not going to get it in the car."

He was almost right. What I wanted, actually, was an appliance box. Nobody at my house knew I was coming home, so my plan was to get a huge box and climb inside it and have my friend ring the doorbell. I ended up talking the salesman into giving me an empty washing machine box, although he would have preferred it if the washing machine had been in it.

When we got to Creignish, we pulled the car over around the corner from my house and got the box out of the trunk. Because it was winter, it was already dark by dinnertime, so we had no trouble sneaking up to the front of the house. Trying not to laugh, I climbed in the box and my friend rang the doorbell and ran around the side of the house. A few seconds later, my mother stuck her head out the door and from inside I could hear her say, "What the heck is this, now?"

Then she called my dad, "Angus, there's a washing machine box on the driveway."

A few more seconds passed, then he came out. I could hear them coming down the steps and walking on the crunchy snow toward the box. Just then, I burst out of the top of the box and screamed, "Surprise! Merry Christmas from New York!"

My plan worked perfectly; nobody knew a thing. My mother almost fainted when she saw me, and a bunch of the neighbours came out to see what all the fuss was about. I spent a really nice couple of days with my family, telling them all about New York and about the play. Relatives and friends dropped in and made small talk. Luckily, I had to get back to New York in time for the Thursday performance, so my parents didn't have time to tackle a whole bunch of tricky questions I knew were lurking just under the surface. It was just kisses and hugs all around and I was gone again: I didn't know it then, but that would pretty much sum up my relationship with my family for years to come.

It really hit me on that return trip to New York that I had probably left Creignish behind for good, on an emotional level anyway. As I rode into Manhattan in the cab I felt the way I should have felt driving home from Halifax, like I was back on my own turf and looking forward to seeing all my friends. But other than my family, there was nothing about Creignish that I missed particularly. In my head and in my heart I had a new home, although that would be gone as well a few weeks later when the show wrapped up.

And wrap up it did, with the big closing night party and the hugs and kisses goodbye from the cast and crew. It was especially sad for me because I was the youngest and it was my first show; the rest of the people had been through this many times before, and they already knew that that's the nature of the business. Besides, most of the other show people were moving on to other productions, either in New York or in Chicago or even Los Angeles. Only I was heading for the isolated outpost of Creignish, Nova Scotia. And only I was a completely different person than I had been when the show began.

So, after spending four months living in New York, making friends, having lovers, performing almost every day, and making lots of money, by mid-January I was back in my high school class in Judique, talking about John A. Macdonald or some damn thing. I mean, for Christ's sake, I'd just discovered the lost city of Atlantis, as far as I was concerned; I guess you could say my heart wasn't in it

It's not every day people from that area jet off to work on a play in New York, so you could say I was a minor celebrity when I got back. All my friends from school wanted to know all about New York, and what did I do for fun, and did I meet any famous people, and was it like it is on the cop shows on TV. I warmed right up to the celebrity thing, natural attention seeker that I am. I had picked up quite a taste for fashion hanging out in the clubs, so I really dressed the part as well. On my first day back at school, I wore red suede shoes. On the second day, I wore blue suede shoes.

Along with the curious ones, there were also quite a few people when I got home who resented the fact I'd gone at all. They resented the fact I'd made some money there. They resented my new clothes. I cut my hair different in New York, and they didn't like that. I think more than a few people thought for sure I was gay, and they sure as hell didn't like that. As I walked down the halls in school, I could hear them talking:

"Oh here he comes, the queen himself."

"Who the hell does he think he is — Elvis?"

Keep in mind, all my schoolmates were exactly the same as I'd left them. The timeline in their lives hadn't been interrupted by four months and they hadn't been exposed to anything different that was as absolutely life-altering as the things I'd been exposed to during my time in New York. They were all just Cape Breton Scottish kids — some of them played hockey or whatever, and some of them were into music, and some were cooler than others. But none of them had ever had an experience like the one I'd just been through. I did some crazy things in New York. Imagine it: while they were at home doing their homework for the next day at Judique High School, I was being a judge at a "Biggest Package" contest at some club in Manhattan. And when they where going to bed, I was heading home with one of the contest winners. I was a long, long way from home.

After the joy of seeing my family and the excitement of being the centre of attention wore off, the full impact of returning home really hit me. And when it did, it was a totally jarring physical event for me, like childbirth. It was a tragedy for me, really. That's the only word that I think adequately describes the feeling I had when I settled back into my room in Creignish after four months on my own in New York City — tragedy.

~ 2 ~

Creignish

My goal in life has been the same right from the beginning: to become a Cape Breton fiddle player. And if you were to ask someone on the street who Ashley MacIsaac is, I think quite a few people would describe me as just that — although some would probably insist on tacking on a few extra things, like "crazy" Cape Breton fiddle player, or "gay" Cape Breton fiddle player, or "stoned" Cape Breton fiddle player. I guess I can't complain though, just as long as they remember the fiddle player part.

The truth is, I started my life on this planet not in Cape Breton but off the island, in Antigonish, Nova Scotia. Antigonish is a pretty well-known university town, and a very Catholic one at that, but then the whole of Nova Scotia is pretty Catholic. People in Nova Scotia tend to see Antigonish as kind of a halfway point between modern civilization and what I would call the almost medieval land that is Cape Breton Island. Cape Breton's the kind of place where the very odd individual might choose to have an outhouse instead of an indoor toilet out of personal preference. In fact, the plumbing is one of the few things that have changed over the years.

I was born in 1975, the second child in my family, the first to my dad and mom. I found out afterwards that I wasn't the first to my dad actually and that I have some brothers somewhere that I don't know very well. I came along after my dad married a lady who had already had a child four years before — my half-brother Henry. So I'm the second and the first, if you know what I mean. I guess we know now how that birth order affects behaviour later in life.

As I say, I was born in Antigonish, but I didn't come home to Cape Breton until a month later. I would have made the move earlier, but I had some lung problems and I just found it too hard to breathe. It's always struck me as unfair that a baby can come into the world with health problems; I mean, whose fault is that? At least if I end up with lung trouble at the other end of my life, I'll know who to blame.

Anyway, I eventually went home to Cape Breton and became a Creignisher. A Creignisher is what you call a person from the village of Creignish. It's a very prestigious title, too, because there's only about 300 Creignishers in the world at any given time, which must qualify them for some kind of endangered species list.

Creignish is a space on the map of about a mile. Not a mile square mind you; more like a mile from sign to sign. It's just a bump in the road really, along the coast. It's very like a village you might pass through in Ireland or Scotland if you left the big city and went off driving along some coastal highway. You're flying along the coast highway surrounded by fields and fabulous views of the sea and then you come around a bend and *bang* — you're in Creignish.

With only about 300 people in town, you can imagine I went to a pretty small school. Actually, a few years after I left it they turned it into a craft centre because there weren't enough kids around. That's how small Creignish is. By the time I left, the population had sort of levelled off and by now it's probably going the other way. I won't be surprised if one day I go back to find the place gone altogether.

I know it's common to hear horror stories about unemployment on the East Coast, but I can honestly say I never really saw much of that growing up. My father, Angus, was, and still is, an electrician, and my brother ended up going into the same line of work. People do all kinds of things to make a living there. Some are still fishermen, believe it or not, or lobstermen. Many Creignishers, my dad included, work in a major plant in the next big town, Port Hawkesbury. My mother, Carmelita, worked before I was born, but I only ever remember her as a typical stay-at-home mom.

I don't know why but we never moved to Port Hawkesbury, even though my father worked there. Not that I wanted to — to me, as a kid, Port Hawkesbury was the "big" town, and I guess that kind of scared me then, coming from such a tiny place. For me, moving from Creignish to Port Hawkesbury would have been the equivalent of someone moving from the Northwest Territories to Toronto. It was only a few miles away, but it was that separate a community from mine, at least to the mind of a child.

When you come on to the island of Cape Breton, across the causeway from Nova Scotia proper, if you turn right you go into Port Hawkesbury, then on to Sydney and all the towns and villages along the east coast of the island. But if you turn left after you leave the causeway, the first place you hit is Creignish. Although Creignish itself probably doesn't ring a bell for most people, the region it's located in, along the west coast of Cape Breton, has quite a few claims to fame. Creignish is one of the first villages you encounter along what they call Route 19, or the coast highway, which is quite a familiar tourist spot for Americans and Canadians alike. It's all quaint villages, beautiful beaches and ocean vistas from one end to the other.

Cape Breton is generally thought of as a place with deep Scottish roots, and it is. But along the west coast of Cape Breton is probably the most predominantly Scottish area on the island. Not surprisingly, the centre of it all is a place called Inverness County, named after the homeland of the original settlers. It's in the villages along Route 19 that you feel the culture the most, and it's from these villages that much of Cape Breton's musical heritage has sprung over the years.

Of course, the music has always been there, but now quite a few of the local musicians have managed to take it on to the national, and even international, stage. There's yours truly from little Creignish. There's Natalie MacMaster, my distant cousin, from a town close to mine called Troy. If you go farther down the road, you hit places like Port Hood, Inverness and Mabou, where the Rankin Family are from. If it's diversity you're looking for, Route 19 is not the place to find it; the people are Scottish, the music is Scottish, even the language you hear is sometimes Scottish — well Gaelic anyway. That was my whole world growing up.

My even more immediate world, the house I grew up in, consisted of my parents, my brother Henry (or half-brother, although I never considered him to be anything other than my brother even when I was old enough to understand the difference), and eventually, three years after me, my little sister Lisa.

My first real memory of my childhood was probably the birth of my sister. I don't think I remember my own birth; that would be insane, although I have met people who swear they do. (There are people who'll tell you that I've regressed at points back to that time in my life, but I have no clear picture of it.) My sister was born in 1978, and I was born in 1975, and I can remember when my mother was pregnant with her, so that would make me about two and a half. I remember everything about my life from about then on, at least to the point when I started erasing chunks of time from my memory with chemicals, but we'll get to that later.

We had a good Catholic upbringing and nobody ever had cause to think we were anything but a good Catholic family. I remember swearing was a bit of a problem. I had a pretty dirty mouth as a little kid. I guess I was looking for an audience even then, but when I was at school it was always "F… this," and "F… that," "You prick," "You fucker …" I was non-stop.

My parents certainly didn't speak like that, so the only thing I can figure is my relatives must have sworn quite a bit, because I did spend quite a lot of time with my relatives as a very small child. I get quite a hard time now over my foul mouth, but at least that's one of my many vices I can put down to my upbringing.

Relatives played a huge role in my early life. Of course, I had the whole strictly Catholic and Scottish side, that was my dad's side. But, unlike most kids in Creignish, I also had a French side, Acadian French, which came from my mom. She was a Port Hawkesbury girl, so she didn't grow up in the exclusively Scottish area. Plus Port Hawkesbury was a bigger town, so it was a whole different world from my dad's village upbringing. My mom also grew up very poor, and I think that in itself probably had a lot to do with my slightly, shall we say, coarse manner, because her family were a tougher crowd. Her father was an old Bluenose-style, swearing sailor himself, so I guess it's a family tradition of sorts.

The whole French, Port Hawkesbury end of my family was just

such a different experience from the totally Scottish environment of Creignish. I mean they lived in apartment buildings, some of them; that was downright exotic compared to my father's side, who all lived in the woods. But my father's side always remained the most dominant influence because that was where my connection to Cape Breton music really came from, so I tended to be drawn more that way. The musical bloodline goes back a long way in my father's family. My grandfather on my dad's side, and his father before, were pipers. There were a few fiddlers in there too, and many of the older folks were Gaelic speakers.

That's not to say my mother's family wasn't musical, because most people on Cape Breton tend to have some musicality in them, whether they're musicians, or singers, or step dancers. But I think just the fact that I had some French background was vital for me as far as the development of my musical style went, because it opened me up to the Acadian influences in Cape Breton music as well as the Scottish.

Of course, I didn't really become aware of the nuances between the Scottish and Acadian music until I was pretty much a fully developed fiddle player, say around the age of 14 or 15. It was around that time that I really started to play a lot of dances and things all over Cape Breton, so I had to learn some French tunes for that audience. It was only then that it dawned on me that one of the instructors that taught me Scottish music was a Frenchman. That seemed odd to me at the time, but it began to make more and more sense as I became a more proficient player myself.

That instructor had told me the story of how when he was young, he had lived in a lighthouse in an Acadian region of Cape Breton, near Cheticamp, and had practically no English at all. He learned to play the fiddle, he said, by listening to tapes of this old-time fiddler playing Scottish tunes and then copying them note for note. But as he grew and started playing his fiddle with other Acadian musicians at functions in the French community, that influence gradually crept into his playing. The result was, whenever he played a Scottish tune later on, he put an Acadian spin on it.

That's when I started to notice the subtle differences in his style compared to the traditional Scottish fiddlers I knew. It's hard to describe, but you know it when you hear it, a sort of jaunty quickness. You can hear it in traditional French Canadian music and in Cajun music from Louisiana. I realized then how his playing sort of matched the way he spoke French — very fast to the English speaker.

From that point on, I became very interested in the whole French side of my family and in the Acadian music specifically. My own playing style started to become more consciously up-tempo in terms of the melody line and the rhythm. I believe that whole process of feeling my French blood has made me more of a true "Cape Breton" fiddle player, rather than a purely "Scottish" fiddle player. Then again, that's what Cape Breton music really is, a mix of the Scottish and French influences.

Both my mother's and father's families were shining examples of Catholic restraint. I'm not exactly sure of the number, but I know I have more than 70 first cousins on my dad's side. My mother's family was the same; she had 18 brothers and sisters, and they all had big families. If you add it all up, you get probably close to 300 close relatives — brothers, sisters, aunts, uncles, first cousins — all living, say, within 40 miles of each other. Hell, the entire population of that whole 40-mile stretch of the coast of Cape Breton couldn't be more than 10,000 people total. No matter where you went, it was tough not to run into a relative.

Actually, it's all a little too close for comfort from a genetic point of view, if you get my meaning. I'm not saying there's inbreeding going on, but let's just say the apple never falls too far from the tree on Cape Breton Island. I remember my mom saying to the neighbour over the fence one time, "Well, you know his dad's sister is married to her second cousin, and her kids have big teeth because of it."

Still, it's wonderful being surrounded by relatives when you're a kid. It's an endless string of birthday parties and anniversary parties and graduation parties and just plain old "party" parties. I remember there was always tons of food and huge games of baseball and tag and hide-and-seek with my cousins.

The best time of year wasn't Christmas but springtime, when the lobsters were in season. When I was a kid, lobster season was almost like a four-month Christmas celebration, with all kinds of parties and dances and everybody in a good mood. Obviously a lot of that has to do with the financial repercussions in the communities of the lobstermen going back to work. Lobster season in Cape Breton is when a lot of people would buy their new vehicles or make additions to their homes or buy their kid a new bike.

While it's true lobster season brought money into the community, all I cared about as a kid, and still care about today in fact, when spring came around was getting my hands on a heaping helping of the delicacy that is Cape Breton lobster. Lobster to a Cape Bretoner is the same as caviar to a Russian.

Actually, not eating lobster all the time is one of the things I miss the most about Cape Breton now that I don't live there permanently anymore. Living in Toronto now, where you can pay as much as $33 a pound for fresh lobster in a good restaurant, I'm a little ashamed to tell people how much of the stuff I ate as a kid. We used to bring it to school for lunch, for God's sake; at night you'd see people on *Lifestyles of the Rich and Famous* drinking champagne and eating lobster, and the next day you'd have a pound of it wrapped in tin foil in your A-Team lunch box. I've been all over the world, but Cape Breton's the only place I've ever been where lobster's cheaper than hamburger at the grocery store. Cheaper than Kentucky Fried Chicken too.

Anyway, the lobsters and those 300 relatives on that 40-mile stretch of coastal highway served as pretty much my entire universe until I was about 12 years old. Oh, I got to Prince Edward Island a few times on holidays before that, and maybe once or twice to Halifax, but that was it.

My early years in school were traumatic. Not for me, mind you; for everyone else involved — teachers, classmates, small animals. I was a foul-mouthed, obnoxious little boy (*So what else is new,* says you).

I remember when I was in, I think, grade two, being on the playground and teaching some of the other kids bad words. There was a whole pile of kids around and I had this one boy up against the wall, trying to explain to him exactly what a "blow job" was. It all seemed funny at the time, but when I look back on it now it does seem like I had a bit of an unhealthy interest in sex for a seven-year-old.

I know I didn't think I was gay as a kid because I remember once going out of my way to tease another kid everybody thought was gay. Pretending to be this other kid, I took my T-shirt off and ran around the schoolyard showing off my beautiful body and shouting, "Look at me, I'm gay! I'm gay!" Now, I don't exactly know what that was all about, except to say that it meant I was gay and didn't know it yet. But that's another one for the therapist.

While it is true I was a foul-mouthed, obnoxious little boy, I was a foul-mouthed, obnoxious little boy who also happened to be a great step dancer. No doubt about it, little Ashley was hard to love from Monday to Friday, but I quickly found my talent for dancing made me quite popular on the weekend. There was always something happening on the weekend, be it a wedding, or a music festival, or just a local dance, and there I'd be, decked out in a bowtie, tartan vest, white pants, and patent-leather shoes with my mop of curly hair bouncing on my shoulders. I was the perfect MacCauley Culkin-esque image of Cape Breton.

I don't know if culture is learned or if it's just in you, but I was drawn to it like a magnet. Sure, I played baseball and hockey and swam like any kid, but I was just as eager to step dance. Of course it helped that I was surrounded by Cape Breton music constantly. I would hear my dad sing with people that came to visit the house. I would dance while various relatives played the fiddle, the guitar or the piano at family gatherings.

My first real step-dance teacher was my Aunt Geraldine. I got started with her because my cousin Wendy MacIsaac told me that her mom was giving lessons at her house for any kids that wanted to learn. When I got a little better, I progressed to another relative, my cousin Mary Janet MacDonald. By the time I was seven, I had become so good that it was decided I should get more formal training. For the next two years I trained under Harvey Beaton, who was then, and still is, one of the most beautiful step-dancers in Cape Breton.

Going back even before I got involved in step dancing, I had always been fascinated by the musicians playing the traditional music at the various gatherings. Because of that, the desire to learn to play music was building in me right from my very early childhood. There was always a piano in my house, and like any kid, I would scramble up on the seat and bang the keys. My father had a violin, but I never really attempted to play it because it was much too big. But I saw the instruments around the house, and I saw people playing them and I guess I just assumed that playing music was just what people did naturally. Playing Celtic music that is.

Come to think of it, I didn't hear much in the way of other kinds of music. I remember my brother had some Twisted Sister records and some other heavy metal stuff. I also remember my mom having Beatles and Beach Boy records. So I heard other kinds of music around my house but I was never immersed in it like I was immersed in Cape Breton music. I must have liked it though, because I think some of those early influences came out later in some of the music I produced.

Looking back on that time now, I think I can say that the day Destiny tipped me once and for all to be a musician came when I was only about six, and I danced while the great Buddy MacMaster played the fiddle at a square dance at our community centre. The name Buddy MacMaster probably doesn't ring any bells for most people in Canada, but to East Coasters, and especially to Cape Bretoners, it's a household name. Buddy MacMaster was the first really big "star" of Cape Breton music that I remember. He was actually a train conductor; that was how he supported his family. He built his musical career the hard way, playing wherever he could around Cape Breton. He didn't put out his first record, I think, until about 1986, when I was 11 years old. I still get chills when I think about putting that record on the turntable for the first time in my own room, and trying to match him note for note.

I remember I was really nervous that night at the community centre because it was the first time I had really step danced at a big public event. Buddy just put his fiddle up to his chin and winked at me and said, "When you're ready sonny." I'll never forget, he came right up to me after I was done and shook my hand. He might have said "Good job, sonny" or something like that, but I was too overcome with fear to hear him. It was the same feeling you had as a very small child when you met Santa Claus for the first time — like meeting God. Buddy was always a mythic figure to me after that, and I think I probably decided then, deep down inside, that I would be a fiddle player.

When I was eight, my brother Henry started taking piano lessons. After a while, it got so he could play the piano while I step danced in the living room. I saw that my brother was enjoying piano lessons and I wanted to play as well, so my parents got me going on the piano. My piano teacher was strict to a certain degree, but she was open to creativity and recognized that I had a natural affinity for music. My brother eventually quit, but I stuck with it and ended up earning my Royal Conservatory Grade One on the piano at age ten.

The real turning point for me musically, though, came when I was nine years old. One day I was sitting in a piano lesson and there was still about 10 minutes to go when my dad came into the room and said I had to leave a little early that day. I put my coat on and we went out and got in the car, but my dad didn't start it up right away. Instead he pulled a piece of paper out of his pocket and handed it over to me.

"Know what that is?" he said.

I unfolded it gently because it was well worn. "It looks like an old lottery ticket, so what," I answered.

"It's a lottery ticket, but it's not just any old lottery ticket," dad said. "It's the *winning* lottery ticket…"

Unlike me, my dad is always very calm, cool and collected, very controlled in his emotions about everything. Maybe it has something to do with being an electrician; obviously you can't hurry or get upset working with live wires or you could get killed. My dad is very strong and sturdy; a working man. Although he's only about five foot eight, he weighs about 200 pounds, and I'm sure if he had to, he could lift 500 pounds over his head.

My dad has an even temperament all right, but he could be stern when he got mad enough. He would settle disputes with you by having a one-to-one sit-down discussion where you told him why you did what you did and he told you why you couldn't do it anymore — in no uncertain terms. Needless to say, I had more than my fair share of "talking-to's" growing up, but that hasn't had a major effect on our relationship, not as much as other things have, things he couldn't control.

He could be stern, but I wouldn't say that my dad was what you might call a disciplinarian, at least not in the punishment sense. I certainly don't ever remember getting spanked or struck in any way, in spite of the fact I deserved it more often than not. But he was disciplined in the way he went about his life and his work, and I think that must be where I got the discipline to work so hard at my music. I suppose it was discipline in the sense that you learn discipline in the military; how to get up in the morning and get going and how to be organized and complete all the things you have to do each day so you can do the things you want to do.

My dad just went to work every day and came home in a good mood usually. I remember sitting around the dinner table and he'd be telling stories about work and the good times he had with the people he worked with. He seemed to enjoy his job so much that I guess I learned early that I wanted to come home feeling good about my work as well. He always stressed that if you work hard and give your best, at the end of the day, you should get something back out of it. At least it should work that way; I learned later on from bitter experience that it doesn't always.

Anyway, about the lottery ticket ... You know how you hear about people winning huge sums of money in lotteries and you always want to say, "Who the hell are these people?" Well, my father, the electrician from Creignish, actually won $150,000 in 1984 in what was then called the Atlantic Lotto, or the "A-1."

Dad made us all keep quiet about it until he had a chance to actually get his hands on the money; like the rest of us, I think he didn't really believe it was true. The next week the whole family piled in the car and drove to Halifax to pick up the cheque. I remember all of us being totally wild with excitement the whole way, and we got to stay in a hotel and the whole bit, which I think may have been my first time doing that.

The morning after we arrived, we all went together to the lottery office and stood in line with all the people cashing in their $5 and $10 tickets. I remember my dad leaning up to the lady behind the counter and sort of whispering as if he was embarrassed.

"Have you got the numbers for March 13?" he asked her.

She looked at him sort of confused. "For what date sir?"

"March 13," Dad said again, a little louder.

"No, it's only February sir," she said, kind of irritated. I think she thought he was joking around.

"I mean *last* March," said Dad, so loudly this time that it caused everyone in the office to look over.

It turned out he'd had the ticket for 10 months but had never checked it. He told us the story afterwards that he'd found this old book of tickets in a coat pocket the week before and went to the variety store in Creignish to check them. At first, the lady in the store told him she couldn't check the numbers because the tickets were too old and my dad was about to tear them up. Then she said she could call the office to get the old numbers if he wanted to wait until the next day. So, the next day he took me to my piano lesson and went back to the variety store to check the numbers while he was waiting for me.

Anyway, the woman at the lottery office pulled out the numbers from the previous March and, sure enough, my dad had a winner. Within an hour the office was full of balloons and there were pictures taken with the cheque and the whole bit. In fact, winning the lottery was the first time I got a taste of what it was like to be a celebrity. Obviously, the A-1 was a very big deal on the East Coast, where so many people spend half the year on unemployment. It was so big in fact that CBC Radio even showed up to cover the handing over of the cheque. I remember the CBC guy with the microphone talking to my dad and everyone smiling and laughing. Then he leaned over to my little sister, who was only about six then, and asked her what she wanted my dad to buy her with the money.

Lisa thought about it, and then said, "I want some balloons and a chocolate bar."

Of course that brought the house down, and I felt a little jealous when the man didn't ask me what I wanted.

I know 150 grand doesn't sound like much, but from then on, my father was a rich man, certainly in Creignish terms, and now I could have just about anything I wanted. Well, if you ask any nine-year-old boy what he'd like if he could have anything he wanted, he might say a minibike, or a BB gun, or some kind of computer game, but I guess I wasn't like most nine-year-old boys. When my chance came, the only thing I could think that I wanted was a fiddle, and that's exactly what I got. My father went right out the next week and bought me a little tiny fiddle of my own, and the week after that I took my first fiddle lesson.

I have to admit, if you're not born rich, there's no better way to guarantee a pleasant childhood than to win the lottery. Now, my family had lived pretty well before the lottery money came, I thought, compared to some other families in Creignish. I mean, we got to go off to Halifax occasionally, and we ate in restaurants quite often. But I'm sure just before he won the money my dad was thinking, "OK, the kids are getting older, I've got to start putting some money away for college, but I've just got enough to pay the bills now. Oh shit, how am I going to do this?"

When he won the money though, it was like that whole burden of worry for the future was lifted off his shoulders. He paid off his mortgage. He built a new garage and bought a couple of new cars. It wasn't enough for him to quit working, but it sure made things a lot easier around the house. I quickly developed a taste not so much for money, but for the feeling of security it can buy. Also, I soon found out that having no money worries makes for a pleasant atmosphere in general.

If anything, Dad became even more careful with money when he finally had it. Because he had lived for so many years with just enough money to get by, my dad was a great one for saving rather than spending, and he drilled that into me and my brother and sister early on. I learned that lesson so well that by the time I was old enough to drive I had saved so much money I really didn't need to save that much anymore. But just a few years later I stopped thinking about saving money altogether, and a few years after that, I had no money saved at all. It's amazing how easily you forget the lessons your parents work so hard to teach you.

Obviously my dad's good fortune was big news in Creignish. I remember going back to school for the first time after we picked up the money and feeling like Richie Rich. Here I was, surrounded by all these little kids from this tiny community who didn't know anything about anything — $150,000 might as well have been $150 million in their eyes.

In terms of the community, the money didn't really change the way people treated our family. In fact, there were families there that were better off than ours before we won the money, and they were still better off than us afterward. But then every family in Creignish pretty much had a decent house, and decent cars, and parents who worked, so it wasn't like we were living like kings in this desperately poor Maritime outpost.

The best thing to come out of the whole lottery experience for me was that fiddle. The small fiddle my dad bought me originally only lasted a few months before I sort of outgrew it. When it looked like I was going to stick with the fiddle lessons, my dad bought me a proper violin off of my instructor that I still have to this day, although it's pretty much worn out now. My first fiddle went to another student who was starting out and then changed hands several times again after that.

I progressed quickly on the fiddle because I was blessed with a real sense of discipline when it came to music. I never needed my mother or anyone to drag me to lessons or scold me into practising. I would say from the ages of nine to fifteen, I was playing about four or five hours of music a day, between lessons, practice at school, practice at home, and playing at various events. On a Saturday or Sunday, it wasn't unusual for me to play music 12 hours in the day, depending on what was going on. By the time I was 13 and playing for money, I might get up and play at a funeral in the morning, a wedding in the afternoon, and a square dance that night. The time just flew for me though, because music was what I did for fun.

It also helped that there weren't a lot of distractions in Creignish when I was a kid. We didn't have Nintendo, or the Internet or a video arcade or anything like that, and we only had two TV channels most of the time. I was on a hockey team for a few years, but then my music started to take up all of my spare time.

From a very early age, I always found it very easy to make money. I was always selling things; I would sell lobsters or seashells to tourists, whatever. I did any little job I could find. And there was one other thing I did, in between all the fiddle playing and going to school and going to lessons — I went to Bingo. That was a big big part of my life as a kid in Creignish; that's where I learned, even before my dad won the lottery, that it was cool to have money.

I started out going to the Bingo at the local community centre with my mother, who was a fiend for it, and playing a couple of cards myself when I was about nine. A little later, I actually started helping out at the Bingo by selling cards or Bingo dabbers. I eventually ran a canteen there, selling pop and bags of chips, when I was about 13. I even called games on the odd occasion, anything that would pay.

I won my fair share of Bingo games as well. I remember when I was just 13, in grade eight, I went to a fortune teller in Port Hawkesbury with some friends and she told me to buy a lottery ticket that day and I'd win. Instead of buying the lottery ticket, I went to Bingo and ended up winning the big prize, $1,600. I remember I went to school the next day with the whole $1,600 in my pocket. I didn't show it to anybody; I just sort of kept my hand on it and took it out a few times in secret to count it.

Because I was always looking for ways to make money, I ended up having a lot more money than most kids usually have, especially in Cape Breton. Luckily, my parents made sure I didn't go wild with it.

They were always encouraging me to buy bonds whenever I had a nice chunk of money built up in the bank, and by the time I was 14 I had $7,000 or $8,000 in bonds.

Plus, I was never the kind of kid who spent a lot of money on things like clothes or records. In fact, when I won the $1,600 playing Bingo, my mother took me into Port Hawkesbury to buy my first really nice pair of jeans. I paid $80 for them, and on the way out of the store I told my mother I wouldn't be doing that again any time soon. I wasn't sure at that point why I wanted to make so much money and what I wanted to spend it on, but I figured out pretty early that you can piss money away in a hurry if you're into things like designer clothes, jewellery and cologne.

Looking back on that time now, I suppose it was possible to see the various aspects of my adult personality taking shape even then. On weekends and in the evenings, my world revolved around the music, and the culture, and my dancing, and the Bingo. I lived in a basically adult world where I felt very comfortable and got a lot of praise for what I was doing — not to mention money. At school, on the other hand, I would be swearing and chasing little girls around with live lobsters, trying to set other kids' hair on fire and going into the dugout at the baseball diamond to play doctor.

On my report cards the teachers would always refer to my behaviour as "rambunctious," but they were trying to put a positive spin on it, I suppose, for my parents' benefit. The thing is, what teachers call "rambunctious" at six turns into "obnoxious" by twelve and "antisocial" by twenty-one.

Ever since I was a kid though, I've just had this tremendous energy within me, constantly looking for a way out. Dancing to Celtic music and later playing it provided a perfect outlet for that energy for me as a kid. But when I wasn't expressing myself through the music, the energy inside me came out in a negative way, more often than not. That's true to this day.

I guess my dad was one of the first people to notice how Cape Breton music seemed to have the ability to burn up the excess energy banging around inside of me, so he encouraged me to "play with passion."

"Get mad at it," he'd say. "Play as hard as you feel."

With my dad spurring me on, I started to bring my body into my playing a lot more, eventually step dancing while I played, and that playing style ended up becoming a kind of trademark for me.

Considering the way my personality was as a kid, and in many ways still is, I don't know where I got the desire that was necessary to learn to dance and play music as well as I did. All I can think was it came from a deep inner need to express what I felt inside. I don't like to put it any other way than that, because if I do I'll risk going down that road that says your talent is "God-given," which I don't like to hear, and I've heard a lot.

The problem is, when people talk about individuals having God-given talent — like a Wayne Gretzky in sports, or a singer like Celine Dion — they tend to forget the work and discipline required to reach that level and the real passion for the sport or the art required to maintain that discipline. No one becomes really good at something if they don't love it, and you can't stay good at anything if you don't work at it.

Surprisingly enough, when it came to doing my actual schoolwork, I was just as disciplined as I was at my dancing and music lessons. Actually, the one probably helped the other, because my mother wouldn't let me practise my dancing or my music until my homework was done, and I always had to have my schoolwork sorted out before I could go off and play a dance or something at the weekend. But at all points along the line, my behaviour problems at school aside, I was always an above-average student.

Of course, as I got up into high school and the demands of my music career started to build, school slowly but surely began to get pushed into the background. Luckily, I went to a high school that really nurtured my talent and made a hell of a lot of allowances for me.

When it came time to go to high school, which in Cape Breton is grade seven, kids in Creignish had to go to a school in the neighbouring village of Judique, about 10 miles down the road. Now Judique was bigger than Creignish, but not much. There were only about 30 kids in my grade level, and only about 200 kids in the whole school, from grade seven to twelve.

The great thing for me about going to school in Judique was the fact it was a totally Scottish community. My teachers and the other kids understood the music and what it meant to me and they all tried to help me along as much as possible. I would sit during recess and lunch and play tunes on the piano. The school would often hold concerts with Celtic music and dancing that I was very involved in.

As I got older, I was also often allowed to miss school so I could travel with my dad to gigs around Cape Breton. The first chance I got to really travel came when I had just turned 14 and I got the chance to play my fiddle on St. Patrick's Day in Detroit.

The whole thing came about because my family was taking a trip to Windsor, Ontario, to visit an uncle of mine. St. Patrick's Day was coming up, and my uncle knew I was a pretty good fiddle player so he mentioned to a few Irish friends of his that I might be willing to play a few tunes at this club they all went to. It was all set up, and I didn't mind, of course, because I was well used to playing at all kinds of little events down home and this was like my first "tour" gig.

When I got there it turned out the place was this big pro-IRA hangout full of wild-drunk Irish-American guys in Notre Dame shirts and real Irish guys, also wild drunk, working in the U.S. illegally. The atmosphere was in full swing by the time I got there, and everybody was in the mood to sing and dance. I didn't have time to feel nervous, because as soon as my uncle introduced me to the manager he dragged me up on the stage and said into the mike: "OK folks, we have this young fella here, Ashley, from Nova Scotia, Canada, and he's going to play the fiddle for you."

That was it — he jumped down and left me standing there by myself. Without saying a word, I ripped into the giddiest Celtic jig I could think of and had them all clapping right off the bat. I only played a few tunes, but I turned out to be the hit of the night.

After it was over, I had a real sense of satisfaction, not just because the people had liked the music and had had a good time, but also for the first time I realized Cape Breton fiddle music could really take me places. By the age of 14, I had already played to packed halls and dances at home, so that was nothing new. But before my gig in Detroit, I had always been playing for people who knew the music already, had grown up with it, and had a deep cultural connection to it. This time, at my first "out-of-province" show, I felt like I was introducing the music to a new audience, and they loved it. I got my first glimpse of my own future that night.

That wasn't the only revelation I would get in Detroit, though. After I was done, the manager "paid" me with an Intellivision video game, which was useless to me because I didn't have an Intellivision system. Of course I didn't say anything because that would've been impolite, but it taught me a valuable lesson about being a professional musician: people will always be willing to give you nice gifts for all the good work you do, but none of them are any good if you can't spend them. I even wrote a tune later called, "If You Can't Spend It, It Ain't No Good."

It was another year before I hit the road again for another "tour" gig, and that wasn't really even a scheduled gig like the one in Detroit. I travelled to Toronto when I was 15 to attend a big square dance being held just outside the city in an area called Bramalea. I wanted to go because John Morris Rankin was doing the music for the event, and I knew him well from playing around Cape Breton for the last few years at similar events. I ended up playing a square set at the dance, even though it was really John Morris's night. I made a good impression though, because the organizers of the event booked me in right then and there for a dance the following year.

That's basically how I spent my high school years — travelling all over Cape Breton, sometimes over to Antigonish, sometimes farther away, to play weddings and all kinds of square dances, or funerals, anything that would come along I'd play at it. Having learned my lesson in Detroit about getting paid with something you can spend, it wasn't long before I was making a nice little bit of pocket money from my fiddle.

My teenage years weren't typical. The typical teenager is going to school and hanging out with their friends and going to parties and thinking about who's going out with who and that kind of thing. I didn't really have time for any of that, I was so busy working and practising. I can only really remember going to two or three of your standard teenage "house parties." One of them I only remember because they had *The Exorcist* on the video machine and it scared the hell out of me so bad I left early. I still can't watch that movie; I guess it's the Catholic in me.

I remember another, in particular, because I tried to fondle a girl's breasts at it; it was my big "first sexual experience" party. I think I was about 14 and this older girl had passed out drunk on one of the beds upstairs. Myself and several other guys went up and went into the bedroom one at a time to have a feel. It came to my turn and I went in. It was dark and I could just make out her shape lying on the bed, breathing loud like passed-out people do. I stood there in the dark for a few seconds, trying to work up my nerve.

I remember being excited about the prospect of touching my first breast, but not exactly "turned on." It was more the excitement you feel when you know you're doing something bad, rather than the excitement you feel when you're horny. But at 14, I wasn't even sure what "horny" meant, and homosexuality was just a kind of mysterious concept I wasn't even sure existed. So I can't say I really wanted to touch her breast, and I can't say I didn't. I guess it just seemed like the thing to do at the time, and like all teenagers, I wanted to fit in as much as anybody else.

I decided to go for it. But just as I was going in for the kill, the girl woke up and started screaming at me: "Bastard!" "Pervert!" "Sonofabitch!" I think she called me a "faggot" as well, and that was kind of mind-boggling when you think about it. Anyway, I ran out and, of course, all the other guys were long gone.

Up until I was 16 and got my driver's licence, my dad drove me to any gig I couldn't get to on foot or on my bike. As soon as I got my licence though, I was determined to take some of the money I'd saved up from playing and get myself some wheels. And I knew exactly the wheels I wanted: a Pontiac Parisienne.

Once when I was a kid, I had seen Buddy MacMaster arrive to play at a square dance driving this huge white Parisienne. It was one of those really wide ones from the early '70s with spoke wheels and whitewalls, the kind they turn into low riders in L.A. Well Buddy looked just like Elvis to me getting out of it, and I never forgot it.

I had had my eye on this particular '85 Parisienne for a while that was sitting at a car dealership in Port Hawkesbury. My parents didn't take much convincing when the time came. After all, I had my licence, and I had the money, and my dad was getting just about fed up driving me all over hell's half acre to play gigs. So it was decided — that Saturday, me and my dad drove over to Port Hawkesbury to get me a car.

It's a strange sensation walking on to a car lot for the first time actually intending to buy a car. I had been to this particular dealership lots of times in the past with my dad, before we had money, just looking at cars and dreaming. I guess the salesman inside had us pegged for window shoppers too, because he didn't jump off his chair to come out and talk to us. Finally he wandered out and, half sarcastic, asked my dad, "Looking for a car or just looking?"

"No, no," my dad said. "My son's looking for a car."

The salesman looked me up and down and kind of smirked. A 100-pound 16-year-old with a mop of curly hair; he obviously wasn't impressed.

"Oh yeah, really," he said. "I guess he'll want something sporty then."

With that he started to lead us over to the compact section of the lot where there was something like a Pontiac Tempest and a little red Z24 sitting. That's when I piped up.

"What about that Parisienne?"

"Nah, nah, nah," he smirked again. "You don't want that car; that's an old man's car."

"Maybe so," I said. "But does the old man got cash?"

I ended up paying $3,200 and I had my wheels.

That was it for me and the school bus. Starting in grade 11, I cruised the 10 miles between Creignish and Judique in my 1985 Parisienne, looking like some 50-year-old gentleman floating down the highway in a 40-foot cabin cruiser.

I remember a few days after I got the car, just driving off down Route 19 with no particular place to go. After a while, I pulled over and got out and sat on the huge hood, just looking out at the sea. I remember thinking, "OK, now I've got a car. I've got the ability to play the fiddle. I can go out and make as much goddamn money as I want."

For the first time in my life I felt truly independent. I had always had a knack for making money, and with my own transportation, I knew I didn't need anyone's help to survive anymore. That revelation turned out to be a blessing and a curse. On the one hand, I never wanted for work or money for a long time after that. On the other hand, at 16 I started a stretch of about 250-plus dates a year that lasted for about the next eight years and almost killed me.

Musically, and financially, life was good for me in high school. Of course, I couldn't have done any of it, and learned a damn thing, without the cooperation of my teachers. That's why I think I was lucky to go to school in Judique. It was the perfect place for me to mature as a musician, even if I didn't mature much as a person.

Unfortunately, that school is closed now, but there must have been something about it, because I went to it, my cousin Wendy MacIsaac, who is also a musician, when to it, and so did Stephanie Willis, who has made a living playing the fiddle, and I can probably think of three or four others who went to that school and went on to work as professional musicians. Pretty near every kid in the school was involved in music in some way. Who knows, if my family had moved to Port Hawkesbury when it came time for me to go to high school, which was a distinct possibility, I may not have been able to develop as a musician in the same way.

Eventually though, you have to leave the nest. In my last year in high school I was only there for the second half of the year because I spent most of the first half of the year off playing my fiddle in New York. Usually when you're in your last year of high school you're trying to figure out what it is you want to do and are maybe working hard to make sure you have the marks to get into university or whatever. But I knew what I wanted to do long before I reached my final year of high school, and it didn't have anything to do with higher education. I liked school, but you can see why it began to matter less and less to me as my music career began to take off. Unfortunately, in the end, school started to become little more than a nuisance.

I'd like to say it all ended well, but it didn't. As the end of my last year of high school was coming up, my teacher asked me to do an additional exam because I had missed so much time at the beginning of the year due to my time in New York. And this was in spite of the fact I had done all the regular work that all the other kids had done.

They had scheduled this exam for the very last week of school and, lo and behold, I couldn't be there because I had a gig. They wanted me to cancel it, but I couldn't because it wasn't just a local dance or something, this was a "major" gig for me. I was going to Newfoundland on what was going to be my first real touring act.

There was a Mexican standoff for a few days: I refused to blow off my gig to write the exam and they said if I didn't write the exam they wouldn't let me graduate. Eventually my parents got involved and the school finally agreed to let me write the exam before I left on the tour.

I did all right on it too — 15 out of 20. Not great, but I graduated, and I probably made more money that year than my teacher did as well.

The end of high school pretty much marked the end of the line for me as a full-time resident of Creignish. In reality though, after I bought my car and could get myself around, I was only really a part-time resident anyway. I was travelling all over Cape Breton and into Nova Scotia to play during the summer and on holidays, and I was out of town most weekends during the school year playing gigs. And after New York, well, … how ya gonna keep 'em down on the farm, right?

But, although I eventually grew out of it, Creignish will always be a special place for me. I can't think of any better place to spend your childhood, that's for sure. We were cut off from the rest of the world out there on the coast of Cape Breton. We had our culture, and the music, and the Catholic Church, and we weren't affected by trends that may have been happening in Toronto or New York or California. You just didn't see things like pregnant 14-year-olds or crack dealers on the corner in Creignish. It was a place maybe not literally frozen in time, like an Amish community, but just as frozen in its philosophy about how to live. Now, I may have ended up paying a bit of a price for that early isolation later on, but as a kid, it made things safer, and simpler, and probably happier.

In fact, now that I think about it, my childhood on the west coast of Cape Breton Island wouldn't be one most writers would use in a story about the trials and tribulations of a "controversial" musician — unless, of course, it was the truth. There's no broken home, no alcoholic parents, no grinding poverty, no sexual abuse at the hands of the parish priest. No, all it was was music, and dancing, and family, and school, and lobsters and Bingo — that's it. Now I may have a few screws loose, and I'm not saying I don't, but whatever I do have wrong with me can't be blamed on Creignish, Nova Scotia, or anybody in it.

But that's what people tend to do though isn't it, try to find some kind of link between a person's childhood and the way they act as an adult, especially if they have some problems. People, the media mainly, have been doing that with me for the past 10 years, whether it was my language, or my music, or my performing style, or my personal life. I never thought about things like why I play the way I play, to tell you the truth, before I started to live in the public eye; I just always did what came naturally. But I suppose if people ask questions you can't answer enough times, you begin to ask questions yourself.

I'm no psychologist, and I don't know how much stock I put in all that Freudian crap anyway. But, if you insist, I guess I can remember a few experiences I had between the ages of about two and about five that may have played some role in making me perform the way I perform and act the way I act.

When I was very small — I think I was only maybe two going on three — I can remember going to some kind of show for the first time. It was Santa's Land, but all I can remember about it was that there were monkeys on the stage. I have this image burned in my mind of these monkeys in little tuxedos going around in little cars. I was sitting on my mother's lap watching this bizarre scene, and the next thing I knew, I was on stage with the monkeys in another little car following them in a circle. As I followed the monkeys around the circle in my little car, my parents suddenly appeared beside the line of cars trying to take my picture. Imagine having that image knocking around in your subconscious — everything is Christmas and flashbulbs and you're riding around in a little car with a monkey in a Santa hat. Tell me that wouldn't have an effect on you.

Another image from my childhood that I can't seem to shake relates to an experience I had maybe a year after the monkey thing, so I was probably still recovering from the trauma of that. I remember stopping by the side of the road on some family trip to see this massive pink Easter bunny; it must have been about 45 feet tall. Once again, I remember being forced to sit on its foot to have my picture taken — that was a standard family traumatization technique I guess — and being totally overwhelmed by the sheer massiveness of it. I also remember being terrified for the next several years that this huge beast was going to try to slip into our house to leave chocolate eggs for me and my brother and sister. I was a teenager before I could eat chocolate again.

If that wasn't enough to twist me up for life, when I was about five I remember seeing this picture of a "wanted" poster of a really rough-looking cowboy behind bars. I remember it said, "Wanted Dead or Alive — $3,000 reward."

The guy had a scar and a mean look on his face, but it was actually supposed to be a fun thing. I don't know why, but that poster really appealed to me as a kid, and after I saw it, I think I thought differently about what it meant to be a bad guy. From then on I think I associated, to a certain degree, "bad guy" with "wanted." I guess, on a subconscious level, I've let that association creep into my personality and my career.

As I say, I never really thought a lot about my childhood experiences until I was much older and other people started to look for excuses for my "behaviour" both on stage and off. It was only when I became an adult — say age 21, although there are people who will argue that point — and smoked a lot a pot, and had time to reflect on my childhood that I realized how these three experiences had stuck with me: the Monkeys on Parade, the Gigantic Pink Easter Bunny and the Wanted Poster. I don't know what they mean exactly, but those three images have been hanging in the back of my head as long as I can remember. I don't worry too much about them, but I'm sure there's enough there to keep an army of head shrinkers busy for a few months anyway.

~ 3 ~

Music

My first fiddle was a basic, beginner's Suzuki model that cost about $125. We went to look at it in a shop in Antigonish one Saturday shortly after we got back from picking up Dad's lottery winnings in Halifax.

I took fiddle lessons from a few different teachers when I first started, but then I settled on a guy named Stan Chapman. There were other teachers, like Kinnon Beaton for example, sprinkled in for a few weeks or months here and there, but it was basically Stan Chapman one hour a week for about four years straight.

The great thing about training under Stan Chapman as a young person just picking up an instrument was that he was a real student of the fiddle himself. I suppose that's because Stan was a school teacher by trade, and not so much a performer; in fact, don't think I've ever seen him play in public more than four or five times in my life. But while he wasn't much for standing up in front of a crowd and belting out a tune, he was probably more versed in the music and more technically skilled than most musicians you find out playing for money.

Ironically, Stan wasn't from Cape Breton at all; he was actually from New Glasgow, which is on the mainland of Nova Scotia. He had learned from his uncle, and apparently the Chapman family were quite well known as musicians on the mainland. They played in the style of Don Messer, which many older Canadians know well from watching

Don Messer's Jubilee on the CBC years ago. He could play anything — jigs, reels, polkas, waltzes, you name it.

Although Stan wasn't born into the real Scottish, Cape Breton musical style himself, he mastered it as well as almost anyone. He started picking it up when he moved from New Glasgow to Antigonish to take his teaching job. Antigonish is very close to Cape Breton and is loaded with Scottish people and culture. In fact, it's known as the "Highland Heart" of Nova Scotia.

Stan started giving fiddle lessons in Antigonish and built up quite a reputation in the area as an instructor. And if you look at the list of Stan's former students who went on to play professionally you can see why: there's myself, my cousins Natalie MacMaster and Wendy MacIsaac, Dwayne Cote, Dougie MacDonald, Kendra MacGillivray, Troy MacGillivray ... a who's who of young Nova Scotia fiddle players. He eventually started giving lessons in my primary school in Creignish, where he ended up teaching none other that Buddy MacMaster's daughter, Mary Elizabeth. That tells you right there what kind of music teacher Stan Chapman is — that's like Wayne Gretzky sending his kid to a particular coach to learn to play hockey.

I remember my first lesson with Stan like it was yesterday. I was with a bunch of kids, including my cousin Wendy. Stan took us in the classroom and immediately set about tuning everybody's fiddle, because kids had come with broken old fiddles and basically anything they could find. After that, he showed us all the parts of the violin, where the A string was, the D string, the E string, the G string. Then he wrote some staffs on the board to show everybody what fiddle music looked like written down. Then he started us off playing notes one at a time. We sounded like a bunch of alley cats warming up for a fight — *screeeech, squoooooonk.*

The first night was supposed to be just an hour, but it turned into almost two hours. At the end, he went around the room and checked to make sure everyone was holding their fiddle right. When he got to me, he saw that I was holding my fiddle in my right hand and my bow in my left. He looked confused for a second, then said, "I don't know if this is going to work for you or not."

He had a point. After all, the strings were in the opposite order on the right side.

"Why do you want to hold the violin on that side?" he asked.

The truth was I didn't know. It was more comfortable for me and just felt more natural. The only excuse I could come up with, though, was that that was the same way I held my hockey stick.

"Well, we don't want to mess up your hockey, do we," Stan said. "OK, I guess we can figure it out; I'll pretend I'm looking in a mirror when I show you."

With that he went back to the front of the room and said, "OK, now we're going to play the tune you'll have to learn for next week, if you come back. You can play along with me because you know what all the notes are now."

He played this short fiddle tune a few times so we had it in our heads, but he didn't really take the time to teach us the tune. And that was that; we went home that first night knowing all we needed to know to learn that little fiddle tune. But Stan knew that only the kids who were inspired to learn would practise that tune and have it down pat for the next week. The others would either come back having made no progress from the first week, or they wouldn't come back at all. That was Stan.

Well, obviously I "heard the muse" that first week. I practised that tune and had it going pretty good when I went back for my next lesson. A few kids from the first week had disappeared, just like Stan expected. He started off the next lesson with that tune, but this time he went around the room and went to each student one-on-one to help iron out the rough bits. By the end of that second lesson, the whole group was playing it pretty darn well. I was well and truly hooked then; one week in and I already knew how to play a song on the fiddle. I don't know how many relatives' houses I was at throughout the following week playing that tune.

It was evident right off to everyone that I had a bit of a knack for the fiddle. Within a couple of months of my starting lessons with Stan, I was playing my first "live gig" at a step dancing festival at the mall in Port Hawkesbury. I remember, right around the same time, I used to see that video on TV of that long-gone pop star Tiffany singing "I Think We're Alone Now" at malls all over the U.S. I figured that made me the Tiffany of Cape Breton in some weird way. Anyway, I had the bug.

The hook was driven home permanently just a couple of months later when myself and a whole bunch of Stan's other fiddle students got to go to Halifax to play for Pope John Paul II himself. The Pope was on a tour of Canada at the time, and they were putting on a whole big display of Maritime culture for him. I was going to get all dressed up in my little tartan dancing outfit — Cape Breton's MacCauley Culkin again — and play a Cape Breton fiddle tune with about 20 other kids of all ages. My parents were thrilled. Stan taught us the tune we were going to play about two weeks before and I practised it over and over every day up until the time came to go.

I don't remember very much about the day itself, except that there were tens of thousands of people there. We waited for a long time backstage while the Pope said mass and addressed the crowd. When we were finally herded out to do our little tune, the Pope was sitting at one side of the stage about 30 feet away; he looked just like he did in all the pictures I'd seen of him on the walls at school, smiling and dressed all in white.

Before I even had a chance to look around or get nervous, Stan sounded the starting note that was the signal to get ready. Then we were off. It didn't really matter how well I played, because when you play with a big group like that, you tend to get carried along and lost in the mix, but I remember I concentrated very hard and tried my best to keep up.

In what seemed like a few seconds, we were finished, and a huge roar went up from the massive crowd. It was only then that I looked out from the stage and realized what a huge audience we'd just been playing to. I was fascinated by the sea of faces and the sheer noise of the applause. I remember thinking, "This must be what Buddy MacMaster feels like after he plays a fiddle tune."

We never got to meet the Pope — they ushered us right off after so some highland dancers could come on — but he did clap and smile and he made the sign of the cross in our general direction. So I was blessed at least, but I didn't care much either way. Just being in front of that huge audience was a big enough thrill for me, bigger than even if I'd got to sit on the Pope's lap. Stan couldn't get rid of me after that.

Not only was Stan great at communicating the technical aspects of fiddle playing to his students, he also really stressed the cultural aspects of the music and the Cape Breton style. On top of the music, you learned all about how the first Scottish and Irish settlers came to Cape Breton and Nova Scotia and how they lived.

When it came to the music, we learned both the traditional Scottish tunes that were written hundreds of years ago as well as tunes written by Cape Bretoners in more recent times. All Stan's students really learned to read and understand the notes in the old tunes and the new tunes; that way we could see how the music had evolved over hundreds of years into the distinct form it is today. What's that saying? "You can't know where you're going if you don't know where you've been." Stan communicated that musically.

I'd have to say Stan was the driving force behind me making such a strong and lasting connection to my own culture. It was inspiring for me to learn from someone who knew so much about Cape Breton culture and Cape Breton music, in spite of the fact he wasn't from Cape Breton himself.

Something else Stan gave me, and anyone else who had the good fortune to study music with him, was a really good grounding in the technical fundamentals of music. These are the essential elements that are at the core of all music, from Cape Breton Scottish music to reggae to classical. Basically it's about learning to read music and play it as you read it, just like if you were reading a book out loud, keeping in mind things like time, rhythm and tone.

The way Stan did it was by introducing his students to the work of a guy named James Scott Skinner, who was a very well-known fiddle player back in the early part of the 20th century. Skinner was a classically trained violist, but he made his name by taking very old traditional Scottish fiddle tunes that had been passed down for generations, by ear essentially, and actually writing them down in formal arrangements. He was like an anthropologist making a dictionary of some ancient language so it wouldn't be lost to time.

It was really cool to study Skinner's work if you were right in to your music and culture, like I was as a young music student, because it was like looking through a window back through hundreds of years of musical tradition. Stan spent a lot of time telling us about Skinner and his relevance to the history of Scottish fiddle playing. He would show us Skinner's arrangements in written form and play us very old recordings of the same tunes. Finally, he would get us to learn the tunes ourselves, note for note, and practise them until we sounded just like the old recordings. His goal, I realized later, was to make his students skilled and disciplined players first, before trying to flex any creative muscles.

Once you had the essentials of playing Scottish fiddle music down pat, and Stan thought you were ready, it was time to move from simply "reading" the music to really "feeling" the music. Scott Skinner's fiddle tunes were a great starting point for this exercise as well, because Skinner provided a solid basic arrangement that players who came along later could put a more modern swing to, and there was no better fiddler for that than Buddy MacMaster.

Without a hint of hesitation, I would say that there isn't a single musician who has come out of Cape Breton since the 1950s who hasn't been influenced in some way by Buddy MacMaster. I don't care if they're a fiddle player, or a piano player, or if they just have a guitar in the house and they don't know why; it's because of Buddy MacMaster. I'm sure if you even asked Rita MacNeil why she became a singer, she might say because she saw Buddy at a square dance in her youth and wanted to be like him.

For that reason, Stan used Buddy, and various other fiddle players who came along over the course of the last half century, as an example of how you can take the traditional tunes and put your own stamp on them while still maintaining the traditional integrity of the music. In fact, Stan felt that fiddle players like Buddy MacMaster would ultimately have more relevance to what my generation of students were going to turn out to be in the world of fiddle players than the traditional players of the 19th century. That's because he knew that although the traditional underpinning will always be important, the music had to evolve and move with the times if it was going to survive.

Stan also taught me and his other students to take pride in the musical heritage that we were born into. He talked about the great musical families on Cape Breton and showed us how the music was passed down from generation to generation. I also remember hearing Buddy MacMaster tell a story at a square dance about how, when he was just a child, his mother would sing old Gaelic songs to him when she'd be hanging out the laundry. In that subtle way, the seed was planted in our heads, when we were just kids, that it would be up to us to pass along the traditions when our time came.

I was always fascinated to learn about how the traditions were passed along from a genealogical point of view, because I was so close to it. Natalie MacMaster, for example, lived just down the road from me, and her father is Alec, Buddy MacMaster's brother. Natalie's mother, Minnie, was a Beaton, which is probably the other main musical family on Cape Breton. So you can see how Natalie MacMaster was bred to the music through and through.

The Beatons came out of a town called Mabou, which is best known now-a-days as the home of the Rankin Family. What Mabou offers is what you could call a "direct route" back to Scotland. It is still, to this day, a great centre for Gaelic speakers on Cape Breton. The original settlers from Scotland — who came over in the 18th century after being driven out of the Highlands — were all Gaelic speakers, and somehow the language still survives in Mabou. My father's family had Gaelic speakers in it, and he knew quite a bit, but I'm only good for the odd word or phrase, which sadly is the case in most parts of Cape Breton. In fact, very few young people of my generation and younger speak Gaelic now (except in Mabou).

Still, if you agree with Stan Chapman's philosophy of a culture that evolves, as I do, then the Gaelic language can live on in a way in Celtic music. If you've ever heard Gaelic spoken, you know that it has a sort of poetic lilt to it that's very light and musical. Also, the flowing pace at which Gaelic tends to be spoken — as opposed to the very quick pace of French or the sort of jerky pace of German — can also be heard in the music. So I'm an English speaker but I know that Gaelic lilt, having heard it all my life, and I incorporate it in my music, as do other Cape Breton fiddle players.

Now, when you get really close to the music, as only somebody who has studied and played the music probably can, you get so you can hear various accents in music that are associated with various regions. The Beatons, for example, have their own lilt, which tends to be different from the lilt of the MacMasters.

The MacMasters come from Judique and Port Hood, and they're known as a very Catholic, upstanding, respectable family, and well-to-do by Cape Breton standards. As a result, their style (and I say "their" style because family members tend to teach other family members to play music) is more refined and polished — prim and proper you could say. And that's one reason Buddy MacMaster became such a respected fiddle player, because he had such a disciplined upbringing. He's the kind of guy who wouldn't say a mean thing about anyone.

The Beatons, meanwhile, have a whole different accent to their music because their lifestyle was different from the MacMasters. They were still a respectable family, of course, in the Catholic sense, but they had a much harder go of it, as far as I could see. Most of the Beatons were coal miners, and had been ever since the first one of them got off the boat from Scotland. And they lived in Mabou, where you were a lot more likely to associate with miners than with lawyers or bookkeepers. So in the music of the Beatons — the music that John Morris Rankin and all the Rankins learned to play because they grew up in Mabou — you can hear the accent of those strong, hard-working people.

It's very subtle, but when you hear Buddy MacMaster play a tune, you'll notice his style is very pleasant and easy on the ear and very technically precise, with a definite pulse between each note. But when a Beaton would play the same tune, you'd notice a rougher, sort of angrier approach, where the notes drag one into the other, sort of like the way a drunk person would slur his speech. As the country music folks would say, there's more "hurt" in the Beaton style, even in a happy tune.

Stan Chapman was the first person to point out these subtle nuances in Cape Breton music to me, and the role that genealogy plays in the evolution of the music. As I became a more sophisticated musician myself, I really began to understand the elements that went into creating the various styles — things like your financial circumstances, and your bloodline, and who you learned from, and who you listened to as a kid.

I was lucky, I guess, in that I wasn't really born into any particular style of music. I grew up listening to Buddy mainly, because he was my dad's favourite, but later on I took lessons with Kinnon Beaton as well. And growing up in Creignish, I was sort of between the various regions, each with their own particular musical styles.

So along with teaching us music, Stan really made his students aware of all the culture living and breathing around them. Obviously, it's easy to get distracted as a kid, by TV and movies and popular music, to the point where your own cultural heritage becomes incidental to you. But once you're made aware of how cool it can be, it's easy to be inspired as a musician. I had all the bloodlines right there in front of me; all I had to do was take an interest and I could be a part of it all as well. When I understood that, there was no stopping me. From about the age of 10 on, I was consumed with listening and learning and being involved in the whole cultural scene going on around me. Thanks to Stan, I was totally tuned in to my environment and wanted to learn everything there was to learn about Celtic music.

I'm very thankful for that now, because I know there were kids I grew up with who weren't into music or dancing and kind of ended up hanging around the fringes of the community until such time as they could leave for good. I think that's really sad, because I know they really missed out on so much. The same goes for anyone who doesn't get to know their culture, no matter where they come from.

Becoming immersed in your culture, or music, or sports for that matter, can save you from a hell of a lot of boredom and trouble as well when you're growing up. I remember when I first started taking fiddle lessons from Stan Chapman, my dad would drive Wendy and me and some of the neighbour's kids to the lessons in the back of his truck. One kid in particular — I can't remember his name — didn't stick it for too long. I remember seeing him around town for years after that and not really knowing anything about him. Anyway, he finally left Cape Breton as a teenager and ended up living out west.

I think it's true to say that the kids I knew growing up who were into music seemed to have a lot fewer problems than the kids who weren't. That may sound funny coming from me now, but even the problems I encountered later in my life were the result of things I got into away from the music.

So I give a lot of credit to Stan Chapman for helping to make me and Wendy and others into the skilled professional musicians we are today. There's no denying the fact he inspired his students. We learned a lot, and we learned it quickly. But the desire to be a fiddle player, and the motivation to practise and improve, that didn't come from Stan, and he knew that. No, I believe my desire to become the best Cape Breton fiddler I could was hatched, if not in the womb, then before I was even out of diapers. And it's love at the root of it — love of music, love of family, of community, of culture. Stan just showed us how to channel that love into the fiddle.

I took lessons with Stan Chapman from the age of eight-and-a-half right up to about 14-and-a-half. Then I stopped. I stopped because there was really nothing more Stan could teach me, and it was time for me to go out into the world to meet and learn from other musicians. I also stopped because that evening spent at fiddle lessons was another evening I could spend actually making money with my fiddle.

I would have made a lot more money too, if it wasn't for people trying to put me out of business. Most of my gigs in my early teens were square dances and weddings and funerals, family stuff. But I also got a lot of offers to play pubs.

Now my parents didn't have any problem with me playing in pubs because my dad was always with me and I was too young to drink anyway. There was one guy though, another fiddle player as a matter of fact, who didn't like the idea of a kid horning in on his business. This guy would call the liquor licence people any time I played a gig at a pub or anywhere there was drink served and complain about my being a minor and all. Eventually, it got so the pub owners didn't want me because it was too much of a hassle.

Naturally, I was pissed off about the whole thing because I wanted to make money, and I would complain bitterly about it to anyone who'd listen. One person who was sympathetic to my cause was my French teacher at school, who was himself a fiddle player and a beautiful Gaelic singer (married to a Beaton, I might add). It just so happened that, at that time, he was also the MLA for our riding in the provincial government. And, as it turned out, I wasn't the only one having a problem.

My teacher told me that quite a few young musicians in the area, including Natalie MacMaster and Wendy MacIsaac, had complained to him about not being able to play in the pubs, even though none of us drank. That gave him an idea; I guess being a musician himself he saw an opportunity to make a contribution to the culture of the region and win a few votes at the same time.

A little while after that, with the support of people like my dad and the pub owners, this MLA put a proposal forward in the provincial legislature to amend the liquor laws to allow for underage performers in establishments where drink was served. He argued, correctly I think, that the law as it stood only discouraged young people from trying to make a living as professional musicians. And that, in turn, threatened the very cultural heritage of Cape Breton and the province of Nova Scotia itself. Well that got people's attention all right: in Nova Scotia, culture brings tourists, and tourists bring money.

Just like that, I was back in business. From then on, every time I wanted to play at a licenced place, I had to fill out a form and have my dad sign it. I actually went out and bought a fax machine so I could send the form to the Liquor Board office in Halifax. They'd approve it then and fax it over to the bar so they'd have it if anyone questioned me playing my fiddle there.

Now while the new rules made it OK for me to play in bars, it didn't mean I could go to gigs unsupervised, even after I had my own car and could get myself around. As long as I was underage, my dad or some other adult had to accompany me to the gig and see to it that I didn't get into any trouble. Another rule was underage performers weren't allowed to "hang around" the pub, either before or after their set. You were just supposed to get there in time to set up your equipment, which for me was nothing, before you started playing. After you were done, whether it was one set or two, you were supposed to pack up your gear and get the hell out of there.

Between sets you had to stay out of sight. I remember one New Year's Eve when Natalie and I played together at a dance at a Knights of Columbus hall near where we lived and when we weren't playing we had to hang out in the kitchen.

Come to think of it, I spent quite a lot of time with Natalie playing the fiddle when we were kids. We took lessons together, played at dances together, and family gatherings. We always just thought of it as fun, sort of a change from playing solo all the time. But there were always people, especially when our careers started to take off, who wanted to play us off, one against the other, in a *Family Feud* kind of thing. But that sort of thing never interested me, and I am pretty sure Natalie feels the same, because it was just not the way we were brought up. I played at all kinds of events growing up, but I don't remember ever playing in any music competitions, per se. That's because the culture of Cape Breton is never used in a competitive sense, and people who aren't from Cape Breton don't really get that.

See, in Cape Breton, the focus is all on creating music and keeping the culture alive, building it up as much as possible. But when you think about it, competition is as much about tearing down as it is about building up. In a competition, there has to be a winner and a loser, everyone is judged and you're either good or you're shit. Well that's fine for the best dancers and musicians, but it doesn't offer any encouragement to the average person to learn to play or dance just for fun.

When you're judging something, you have to base that judgement on what went before and was considered good or acceptable. That approach works for the long jump, but the goal of music and culture is not necessarily to improve, but to survive and grow. And I believe, in order for a given culture to breathe and thrive, it has to be embraced by everyone, not just the ones capable of winning a competition.

Cape Breton music and step dancing is the social glue that holds the community together. And when you think about it, competition is really anti-social. Anyway, it's not something I, or my cousin, or most any Cape Breton musician spends a lot of time thinking about. We were always more interested in playing well and making sure everyone had a good time — and getting paid, of course.

Looking back now, I think having to deal with all those rules in the bars as a kid may have had something to do with my never taking up drink. Unlike most kids, I started going into bars and clubs regularly as a 14-year-old, but never to sit and have a drink and a chat. I always associated those places with working — going in, doing your set, getting paid and getting out — so it never really occurred to me to try liquor.

Anyway, with the blessing of the Liquor Licence Board of Nova Scotia and the enthusiastic support of the provincial government, I quickly turned myself into a fiddle-playin', step-dancin' Cape Breton money machine. One or two gigs a week at 14 became two and three gigs a week at 15, then four and five at 16.

As I say, I was so busy, between playing and travelling and keeping up with my schoolwork, I hardly had time to spend even a portion of what I was making. My mom would deposit money for me regularly at the bank, usually on Mondays after I'd been playing all weekend. I also got in the habit of throwing any extra money I had in my pocket or fiddle case in the top drawer of my dresser, and after a few years of that I had a nice wad going in there too. Early on I kept pretty good track of what I had, just because it was exciting to be making money as a musician and having so much more money than any other kid my age. As time passed though, and the money piled up, I got so I didn't know how much I actually had at any given time. My dad always said that when you didn't know how much money you had, you probably had too much for your own good. Once I got to that stage, I decided to do something about it.

In the winter of 1992, when I turned 17, I finally decided to put all the money that had been building up at the bank and in my dresser to some good use. I'd been a working musician for a good few years by then, and I got to thinking about the hundreds of people that had come up to me after various gigs and asked me if I had any kind of recording they could buy. Of course, I didn't, and I was really too young in the early days to even know how to go about making a recording. It made me sick to think about it: here were people with money in their hand ready to give it to me and I had nothing to give them. "Jesus," I thought. "Getting even $10 out of them after a good square dance would have been no problem."

I remember pulling a note pad out and doing the math at the kitchen table. I figured if I could sell even five hundred CDs in the course of a year, that would be a nice chunk of cash in addition to my gig money. And that's the way I looked at the idea of making a CD as well, as just another way to make cash. I still wasn't thinking in terms of taking my "career" to the next level and making a CD to help move that process along. As far as I was concerned at 17, my career had gone just about as far as I ever expected it to. Making a CD just seemed like a neat thing to do.

So, after the usual kitchen table discussion with my parents, I decided to spend my own money to make a CD. I knew quite a few people in the "industry" by then, so I asked around, made some calls, and quickly found out where I could do it and how much it was going to cost. I made out a budget for a short six-track CD of traditional Cape Breton fiddle tunes. I would have to hire a few musicians, and pay for rehearsal time and studio time with an engineer. Then I would have to pay the manufacturing company in Halifax to press the minimum one thousand copies and package them up for me. All told, I figured the whole project would cost me between $5,000 and $6,000.

"Even if I can only manage to sell the thousand for $5 a piece," I reasoned, "then at least I'll break even."

I recorded my first independent CD at a place called Solar Audio in Halifax. It was the only real major professional recording studio you could record in in Halifax that wasn't owned by the CBC. In fact, Solar Audio was probably the mainstay recording studio for the East Coast music industry for many years, until new digital recording equipment made it cheaper and easier for people to set up small recording studios in other provinces.

I went out and hired myself some musicians for the session, guys I had known all my life from playing around Cape Breton. One was Joey Beaton, a renowned piano player out of Mabou and a member, of course, of that great musical clan the Beatons. The other was a guitar player from Cape Breton named Dave MacIsaac, who I believe is my cousin but I'm not sure. (Dave played with me again several years later on the second traditional record I made called *Fiddle Music 101*.)

We rehearsed the tunes every day for about a week, then we went to Halifax and knocked the whole thing out in about a day and a half. When I listen to it now, it sounds a lot rougher than it did at the time, but then we didn't really have the time to keep working on it and working on it until it was perfect. At the time though, I thought it sounded pretty damn good. When it was finished, I put the master in a box and drove it over to the manufacturer. Then I went home and waited.

Two weeks went painfully by. Finally, one thousand CDs of my first recording arrived at my parents' house in a big box, shipped to me by courier from the manufacturer in Halifax. They were waiting for me in the living room when I got home from school.

I'll never forget the feeling I got when I broke open the box and held the shiny case in my hand — with no cover, mind. It gave me a real sense of accomplishment to know that I put the whole project together myself and handled the money and the scheduling and everything, and now I had the result of all that work in a neat little package.

My family was just as thrilled as I was, of course. My mom got busy on the phone and pretty soon all kinds of aunts and uncles and cousins were coming over to see it. It ended up being quite a scene: maybe 40 family members gathered around to listen to my CD in my parents' living room. I had to get tough defending the box so half of them didn't walk out with my profits.

Anyway, talk about a good idea: when I started selling them, I went through that first thousand CDs like they were potato chips. I found I could sell as many as a hundred copies after a big square dance. I think the whole box was gone inside of two months, and the summer hadn't even got going yet. Then there was the money; between getting paid to play three or four times a week and selling CDs after, I might walk away with $1,000 for the week. I'd finally found some use for the money piling up in my dresser, and now I had twice as much.

As soon as I sold the last CD out of the original shipment, I called up the manufacturer in Halifax and ordered another thousand copies, and they went just as fast. I would have ordered more, but fate sort of sidetracked me before I got the chance.

✻ ✻ ✻

At first glance, I didn't really have any reason to be discontented with my life when I was 17. I was playing the fiddle like I always wanted to, I had my own CD, I had the car I always wanted, and I was making more money than my dad was after being employed for 30 years. Then a combination of things suddenly made me realize that I had to get out.

The first thing I realized about that time was that I was tired. I played maybe a couple of hundred gigs in the four months leading up to my last year of high school and wore a path up and down Route 19 the width of my Parisienne. I went from playing someone's wedding and somebody else's funeral to playing everybody's wedding and everybody's funeral; I think I knew damn near every family in Cape Breton after that four-month stretch.

I actually pulled the car over by the side of the road on the way home one night and cried. I was selling my CD out of the back of the car, I was playing weddings and dances. I had a dresser full of cash. But I was freaking out because I didn't know what I was doing. If money was my goal earlier on, I had achieved that. But I never had a clear vision that I wanted to be this big star selling tons of records and playing these huge shows, like someone like Madonna always had. Growing up in Creignish, I think I wasn't even aware that that kind of success was possible for a Cape Breton fiddle player. My image of the pinnacle of success for a local musician was Buddy MacMaster, loved by everybody and making all kinds of money playing square dances and driving a Parisienne. Well I had all that, and I was 17. But I knew inside that something was missing.

Looking back, I guess my music preferences at the time could have given me a clue about what it was I was missing. School dances were another one of those teenage things I basically skipped, as much out of choice as out of necessity. I did get to one or two though, and to tell you the truth, the music is what turned me off the most. The dances at the high school were very different from the square dances I was playing at. Square dances were strictly Celtic music, while the school dances played popular music on record players. There was U2 and Nirvana and REM, and it was OK, but it just didn't have the same effect on me that Celtic music did.

I was so into Celtic music as a teenager that I even listened to it on my stereo at home when I wasn't playing it. In fact, I can remember the first time I went into a record store and bought a tape of popular music, it was such a rare event for me. I was 13 and it was in a record store in Halifax; I went in and bought "99 Luftballoons" by Nena. I bought it because I'd seen the video on *Videoclips* or some show that week and I thought it was cool to hear someone singing in German.

I didn't buy a non-Celtic recording again until three years later when I was back in Halifax and bought a RuPaul dance music CD. The next time I went back, I bought a CC Peniston dance remix. So by the age of 17, my personal music collection consisted of three dance pop CDs and a stack of Buddy MacMaster and other Celtic music from the East Coast and some from Scotland and Ireland. And of the three pop CDs, two were very gay, and the other was borderline gay. Not your typical 17-year-old's music collection, I think most people would agree. Forget the childhood experiences, that record collection alone could have told a psychiatrist all they needed to know about me in high school: "Obsessed with Celtic music; has homosexual tendencies." Now I just needed to figure it out, and that's where my Parisienne came in.

Aside from making it possible for me to travel around Cape Breton to play my fiddle, another thing having my own transportation did was finally give me the freedom to explore the sexual feelings that had been lurking under the surface and were just starting to make a real push to break out. With the car, I could take off on my own and hang out on distant beaches where I could see and talk to guys, tourists mostly, without fear of being seen by anyone I knew. I still didn't know for sure that I was gay then, but I was beginning to get a pretty clear idea of what it was I was interested in sexually, and I was also pretty sure I wasn't going to find it in Cape Breton.

It was about that time that I bought my first gay porn magazine on a trip to Halifax to play a gig. Once I flipped open the pages, I experienced what I can only describe as complete shock. It was not the shock of disgust, obviously, but more like I was dumbfounded. It was a sort of unbelieving feeling you might get if you looked under the steps of your house and found a whole civilization of tiny people living there.

Seeing that magazine was the first time I had ever really seen what gay sex was like and what the gay scene was like. Sure I had heard about the gay club scene and imagined what it must be like to go there, and I had had sexual feelings for guys that I had known and fantasies about them, but this was the real deal. It was like I was looking for the first time through a small window into a place I wasn't sure even existed. It must have been a lot like Columbus must have felt when he sighted North America after wasting away for weeks at sea; I'd just discovered the new world. I knew then that I had to get out of Cape Breton to some place where I could experience the lifestyle I saw in that magazine.

It's even hard for me, today, to believe just how naïve I was back then. The truth was I had had no exposure to press that wasn't Nova Scotia press. Never read books and magazines really, and there was no such thing as the Internet; had there been, I'm sure I would have wanted to leave Creignish even sooner than I did.

Growing up, television was my only real outlet to the rest of the world. But back in the early 1990s, TV still hadn't got to the point where it was ready for open portrayals of the homosexual community — Ellen DeGeneres and *Will and Grace* were still a few years off, and they wouldn't have allowed anything like *Queer As Folk* on the TV in Cape Breton anyway. So the whole idea of a gay lifestyle was just an idea without any substance for me. I couldn't imagine there being places where people led openly gay lives in a vibrant gay community and had friends and relationships just like straight people. Deep inside though, I had a notion that was the kind of place I needed to be.

Then, on one of my many trips to Halifax, I picked up a copy of the *Village Voice*. I'd heard of it, and I knew it was a newspaper from

New York, but I wasn't sure what it was. I saw a copy in a bookstore and decided on a whim to check it out.

Reading that paper was the first time I had the realization that the kind of community I had imagined actually existed. Porn was one glimpse, but really a fantasy that only dealt with one aspect of that lifestyle, the sex aspect. Porn is porn, gay, straight or in between. I went to confession over looking at porn, but I didn't have to go to confession for reading the *Village Voice*, although I might have thought about it.

The *Village Voice* made me see that, in big cities like New York and San Francisco and Toronto at least, there was a gay community that was, yes, having sex, but they were also running businesses and having art exhibits and staging plays and festivals and being politically active. It was a whole lifestyle, a whole other world that I wanted desperately to see.

After that, every time I travelled to Halifax I would make a point of stopping to buy the *Village Voice*. It would come a week late to this one newsagent who specialized in foreign newspapers like the *New York Times* and the *Sun* and *Mirror* from London.

It came as a shock for me, given my very limited vision of the world. I got to see the ads in the back for prostitutes, male and female and otherwise and companion ads with men searching for other men. I even got into Michael Musto's column on the nightlife in Manhattan. It was a wonderful picture of a sort of fantasy world that was waiting just over the southern horizon. And it wasn't the New York I knew from TV, all cops and bad guys and skyscrapers and slum apartments and courtrooms. This was a New York of music and art and culture and food and clubs and beautiful people and, yes, sex, gay sex. Everything that Cape Breton was not.

I had a dilemma. There was no doubt about it, by the time I was 17, I was already an integral part of the culture of the region where I grew up. Practically everyone on Cape Breton had heard me play somewhere or other by then, and people knew my name. I had achieved, if you like, "local" celebrity status and built a bona fide career. My future was laid out before me if I wanted it; I knew by then that I could stay in Cape Breton and spend the rest of my life doing exactly what I was doing, and making a decent living doing it.

At the same time, though, I knew inside that it wasn't going to be enough for me, and I was overwhelmed by feelings of guilt. I don't know whether it was because of the whole Catholic upbringing or what, but I felt terrible because I knew I was never going to be content if I stayed in Cape Breton. It was like these people had given me the gift of my rich culture and my music, and now, just as they were embracing me with the promise of a good life and a good living, I was looking for a way out. It was so ungrateful, so selfish. I knew exactly what people would say: "Oh yeah, look at the prima donna; too good to play for Cape Bretoners."

That was on the one side. But on the other side, I could see where it was all leading. I already felt, at 17, that I owed all the success I had enjoyed to that point as a musician to the people of Cape Breton. But I also knew if I didn't find a way to take my music to a larger audience, my whole life and career would end up depending on those same people. Cape Breton would own me, and if the people of Cape Breton ever turned on me, where would I go then?

It was fine for people like Buddy MacMaster and fine for the Rankin Family; they could spend the rest of their lives playing gigs around the island and making good money and never have to worry about seeing the work dry up. Why should it? They represented everything that's good and attractive about Cape Breton music and culture. So did I, or so everyone thought. But by the time I was 17 I knew better. Yes, I was talented and lively and an exciting performer, but I was also pretty sure I was gay. And that extra piece just didn't fit the puzzle.

As the summer before my last year of high school wore on, my gruelling work schedule started to wear on me and I started to fret more and more about my future, both personally and professionally. I tried to convince myself I could keep doing it, playing lots of gigs and hoping to run into prospective partners by accident on the beach. I was pretty sure one of my old piano teachers was gay, so I knew there had to be some around; and then there were the tourists.

But try as I might, in my heart I knew it was never going to work. There was just something pulling at me, just an urge to get out and learn about the rest of the world. It was also an urge to be myself, truly, and experience things I wanted to experience, without feeling obligated to be a certain way. I knew I'd always feel obligated to my birthplace for my culture and the musical heritage I was given, but I had no say in that. I was born into it and, through my own hard work, had become a part of it. But when it came to my personal life I had a decision to make: would I go out and see the world and live the kind of life I wanted to lead, or would I become a victim of my environment?

That's a hell of a lot to put on a 17-year-old, but that's what I was facing as my last year of high school started. Little did I know, though, that a Parisienne-sized piece of shit was heading straight for one very big fan.

The tourists went home and I went back to high school for my last year, just about as confused as a kid could be. Because I wanted to recover a bit from my crazy summer and get my head together, I had no gigs planned for the first few weeks of school, and I was just beginning to enjoy the easy pace. Then one day, about halfway through the second week of September, I got home and my mom played a phone message for me:

"This is a message for Ashley MacIsaac, the fiddle player. My name is JoAnne Akalaitis and I represent a theatre company here in New York. I am calling because we would like to know if you would be interested in taking part in a theatre production this fall in New York being staged by the composer Philip Glass. If you would, please call me back as soon as possible."

I stood dumbfounded for a few seconds. I probably looked exactly the same as my dad had when he sat in his car outside my piano lesson that night eight years before and realized he'd won the lottery. Finally my mom broke the silence.

"Who's Philip Glass?" she asked.

I didn't know. I didn't know the lady on the phone message either, but she obviously knew me. I did know one thing though: whatever this was, it was big.

~ 4 ~
Biz

My time in New York in 1992 had been a coming out for me in a lot of ways — sexually, personally. But it was also a huge step for me in terms of my career as a musician. After my experience working on the play, I finally knew for sure I was going to make my living as a professional musician. I had already been doing that, in fact, on a local scale. But before I went away, I had always thought of my musical career in local terms: playing square dances and events around Cape Breton and maybe the rest of the East Coast and selling CDs out of the trunk of my car, just like Buddy MacMaster. Now that wasn't enough.

Going to New York had given me the confidence to dream of a musical career on a much larger scale. I figured if I was good enough to go to the biggest stage in the world and work with a great composer like Philip Glass, then there was no limit to where I could take my music. Why couldn't I take my Cape Breton fiddle music and play it for people across Canada and around the world? Why couldn't I make a record that radio stations would play and people would buy in the record store? I'd realized my dream of becoming a Cape Breton fiddle player, and now the dream had outgrown Cape Breton.

The bottom line was, my time in New York was just like Pandora's Box for me. For the first time, I'd let a whole bunch of things out — dreams and feelings that I'd ignored or kept locked inside. And now that they were out, there was no bloody way I was ever getting them back in the box.

Given the way things were, you can see how, if I had culture shock when I went to New York, I had it much worse when I went back to Cape Breton. I wasn't really going home, you could say, by the time I headed back to Creignish. The break had been made, once and for all. There's no doubt that the culture of Cape Breton inspired me to become everything I was up until I left for New York. Since that trip though, I think I can truthfully say that my influences have come from anywhere but Cape Breton, both musically and personally.

In fact, I'd go so far as to say I wouldn't be anywhere near the same person I am today if I'd never gone to New York and stayed living in Cape Breton; it would have been impossible. And I'm not denying there's quite a few people who'd say that would've been a good thing. But like I say, I wasn't really and truly happy with my life at home by the time I went to New York, and there's no reason to believe that would've changed at all if I stayed.

I had these tremendous feelings of loss and loneliness when I got back from New York. I missed the feeling of working full-time, which is a feeling of freedom all its own, and having the freedom to meet people and have relationships. I was also gripped by a real craving for the freedom of the city streets; the freedom you get when you're surrounded by millions of people but you still feel like you have privacy. It's the exact opposite in a small town. I didn't really know living in a big city was having such an effect on me when I was actually in New York. But after I got back, it really hit me hard. Christ, I couldn't scratch my ass in Creignish without everybody in town knowing about it.

My answer most of the time was to retreat to my bedroom to sulk. It was on one of those occasions, sitting in my room in my parents' house doing schoolwork because I was suspended from school for something again, that I finally grabbed myself by the collar and gave my head a good shake.

"What the hell am I doing here, sittin' in my bedroom in Creignish freakin' out?" I remember asking myself. "I'm still playing the fiddle, playing it really good. I'm not getting any enjoyment out of school. I know I can make a living making music full-time. I know it because I just did it. There's nobody around here, except musicians, that I want to hang out with. There's no one here I can have a relationship with. OK, I had this great experience. But I just can't let it go to waste. I just can't let it become this great thing that happened to me once and file it away somewhere."

I had to face facts: I had had a taste of the life I had only imagined, and I wanted another. I knew then that I had to come up with some way to get myself back to New York, or to a reasonable facsimile; Christ, Halifax at least. I thought about all the great friends I'd made in New York, of my first Halloween parade, going to the Macy's parade, going to Broadway shows, of the boyfriend I had just before I left. Then I made a decision: I was going to live in a place where I would be able to do these things, and that was it.

The guilt was finally gone. I knew Cape Breton had made me what I was as a musician, but I knew I couldn't sit there in Creignish and feel obligated to Cape Breton my whole life. In fact, I was feeling more obligated to New York at that moment, for showing me what I could become both as a musician and a person. I felt instinctively, even though I'd only been there for a few months, that I could live in New York and become as much a part of the culture there as I was in Cape Breton. After all, I thought, Manhattan is kind of an island, and the people are basically friendly when you get to know them, and the crime isn't as bad as everybody thinks. Plus, I'd met the lowest of the low there and seen the seediest side of the city, and hell, I was still alive. I just had to get off the island I was on.

The key, of course, was financial freedom. I'd worked for years and just piled money in my dresser because I never knew what I wanted to do with it. I'd always just played music to play it, because I loved it. Now it finally dawned on me that the financial freedom I could earn with my music would give me access to the personal freedom I knew I had to have.

From that moment on, music took on a different role in my life. It became my business, as well as my passion, and the thing that could make the lifestyle I desired a reality. Money was always just something I got for playing music, up to that point. But from then on, by God, money was going to be the reason I played music.

I'd been around the music scene long enough by then to know the first thing I had to have if I was going to be a real professional musician was a proper manager. Enough of this word-of-mouth crap and waiting for the phone to ring and selling CDs one at a time out of the back of the Parisienne. I needed someone to go out and sell me to people as a big-time musical act, then line up more work for me while I was playing gigs. Most of all, I needed someone to get me a record deal. Starting right that minute, I was working on "Operation Get the Fuck Out of Creignish."

I put the word around the bars and such that I was back looking for work, and it wasn't long before I got a call to do a gig. Then I got another, and another. Pretty soon I was back doing three or four gigs a week, just like the previous summer, and the money started rolling in. Still, all the work in the world couldn't drive away the loneliness that had dogged me since I got on the plane to come home. That loneliness, in turn, drove me to spend more and more time in Halifax, where I had at least a chance of meeting a few gay people. I eventually got involved in a relationship there, and the sting of leaving New York subsided a little.

As fate would have it, my sexuality played a part in taking my music in a new direction. Because of my new boyfriend, I began working in Halifax as much as I could. That was a good thing, career wise, because Halifax is basically the hub of the East Coast music scene, and I got a chance to meet other professional musicians and "industry" people. It was around that time that I met the person who would give me that final boost I needed to take my career to the next level. Her name was Sheri Jones, and she is a well-known agent and promoter in the music business on the East Coast. We would spend five years working together, and see my career grow from a regional act with lots of potential into a bona fide international success. We only parted company after years of hard drug use and endless touring culminated in me and my tour manager, who happened to be Sheri's husband, brawling on a hotel-room floor. But I'll get to that later.

Like with all great partnerships, Sheri and me got together by accident. I had been having this ongoing business relationship with this guy in Halifax who ran a small record manufacturing/distribution company. He was the guy who printed my first independent CD back before I went to New York. About a month after I got back, when I was getting back into the routine of playing gigs again, I realized I needed more copies of my CD because I'd sold out the second batch of 1,000 long before I left for New York in September of the previous year. When I called the manufacturer in Halifax to order more, he suggested I come in and see him, seeing as I hadn't spoken to him in months. We made an appointment for the next week.

I drove to Halifax the following week and got to the manufacturer's office about 10 minutes early. When I went in, I saw there was a woman sitting in the office with the guy I came to see, so I just sat down in the foyer to wait for them to finish talking. Just then, he must have spotted me through the door.

"Hello Ashley," he said. "Come on in, I want you to meet someone."

I went in and said hello and shook hands with everybody. The distributor introduced the woman: "Ashley, this is Sheri Jones, she works with lots of musicians you know."

We talked a bit about some mutual acquaintances, then the manufacturer guy asked me what he could do for me.

"Well actually," I explained, "the reason I came was to get you to print me off another 3,000 copies of my CD. I figure that should do me for the year. I have the money to pay for it right here."

With that, I took out a wad of bills and put it on his desk. They both hesitated for a couple of seconds, a bit stunned by both the order and the money, then Sheri piped up.

"You're ordering 3,000 copies of your independent CD and you're paying cash for it?" she asked, half laughing.

"Yeah, I figure I could sell that many," I said, a bit put out that she didn't seem to believe me. "I already sold 2,000 copies last year in just three or four months."

Sheri looked over at the manufacturer guy and he just smiled and nodded his head to confirm the numbers — he had printed them after all. Then Sheri just looked at me with wide eyes, still not really believing a 17-year-old kid had recorded his own CD with his own money and sold every copy he had in just a few months — and I hadn't even mentioned I sold them out of the back of my car.

Then Sheri just smiled and said slyly, "Maybe we should get to know each other a little better."

Sheri was a music industry pro, and she took one look at me and saw a potentially hot commodity — which I was. I just needed some help letting everyone else know it. I found out then that she was an agent for lots of East Coast musicians I knew, and that was it. I met her at her office a few days later and she spelled out what she thought she could do for me in terms of getting gigs and getting exposure and working towards getting me a record deal.

Of course, Sheri was selling exactly what I was looking for at that exact moment, so I didn't need a lot of convincing. She had a good reputation, so my parents weren't that concerned when I told them I'd got myself an agent. Besides, by that time, my music career had already grown beyond anything my parents were capable of dealing with. They had got me my fiddle lessons and drove me around to play at weddings and square dances for years, but once the conversation turned to things like agents and record deals, they were out of their depth and they knew it. I was 17, I was a professional musician, and I was on my own.

My new business relationship with Sheri Jones didn't exactly get off to the start I expected it to. I thought she would begin lining up big gigs for me and introducing me to record company executives. Meanwhile, Sheri was just interested in finding out if I was full of shit or not. She knew I was a good musician and was obviously good at making money on a local scale. But I think she wanted to find out how bad I wanted to make it in the "real" music industry; did I expect things to just happen for me, or was I willing to learn and do the work necessary to make it to the next level? To find out, she put me to work selling CDs.

Sheri got me a part-time job with a company called Atlantic Distributors. For the next two months, any time I was out playing my own regular local gigs like I'd always done, it was my job to peddle CDs to local music stores and book stores, pharmacies and souvenir shops and any other place Atlantic figured I could sell them. With boxloads of CDs filling the back seat and trunk of the Parisienne, I think I hit every conceivable community on Cape Breton Island, and a hell of a lot more in northern Nova Scotia.

My CD was included, but there were a lot more besides. All the East Coast artists distributed by Atlantic who were hot and had a CD out at the time were there: there was a Laura Smith CD, and I think Declan O'Doherty had something out, Theresa Malenfant, and maybe a Rankin Family CD.

The job with Atlantic was only available because the guy that had been doing it died suddenly. His name was Marcel Doucette, and he was himself a fabulous Acadian fiddle player famous for writing a popular tune called "Space Available."

I was never lucky enough to meet him, but Marcel was a real character by all accounts. In one of the greatest acts of shameless self-promotion I've ever heard of, Marcel showed up on the steps of the church at Wayne Gretzky's wedding to Janet Jones in Edmonton in 1988. He wasn't invited or anything, but when the bride and groom came out, there was Marcel playing his Acadian fiddle music.

Of course, Wayne and Janet didn't know what to make of it, but the crowd gathered outside were loving it, so I guess security got the nod to "let the man play." He ended up getting in all kinds of wedding pictures in newspapers across Canada. For years after that, Marcel told people that Gretzky had asked him personally to play at the church, which was a bold-faced lie. But what the hell, he thought, who's worse off for it?

Anyway, I flogged East Coast music the hard way for a couple of months until I got to the point where it got to be too much. After all, I was still trying to finish my last year of high school, and my own playing schedule was almost back to the level it had been at before I went to New York. Eventually, I called Sheri up to quit.

She answered the phone like she'd been expecting me to call, probably for a long time.

"Look, I can't be doing this," I told her. "This was not what I was looking for when I said I wanted to get into the music industry. All I wanted was to sell my own CDs. I don't want to be a distributor. I don't want to work for a record company. And it seems like I've spent a lot of time doing just that. I don't feel like I'm really getting anywhere."

I stopped and waited for her to come back with some argument about paying my dues or something like that, and I had my comeback all ready for her. But I got no argument.

"OK," she said. "I'm working on something for you. I'll call you in a few days."

That was the end of my career in record sales, or so I thought. The fact was, I hadn't even begun to sell records yet, not on the level Sheri was thinking about. It was only later that it dawned on me how much my experience with Atlantic had taught me about the business of selling CDs.

When it comes to big-time musical acts, I learned that making the music was just the beginning. After the artist leaves the studio, there's all kinds of work to be done to print the recording, package it, distribute it to the retailers, and promote it before you can hope to get people to actually buy it. And all the money required to do all those things has to be spent before you sell Copy-1, and that's probably what Sheri had in mind when she hooked me up with Atlantic in the first place. Even then, in spite of all the talent, and all the work, and all the money, it just doesn't happen. Once Sheri knew that I knew that and was still eager to try, she was ready to take the next step.

By the time I met Sheri, I was already a pretty old hand at lining up gigs for myself, and I was well known enough around Cape Breton by that time that I was never without work for long. I guess the main thing Sheri did for me in the beginning was hook me up with the "right" people. Whenever I played a gig in Halifax, she would call around her contacts and make sure prominent musicians and industry people knew about it. The bottom line is, there has to be a "buzz" about you in the music business, or you're going nowhere. I played the fiddle; it was Sheri's job to provide the buzz. And it wasn't long before my new buzz turned into a break.

Through Sheri's connections, I ended up getting an invitation to go on a real tour of the East Coast with a full band. The tour band was being put together in Halifax by a guy named Ron Hynes, who is a well-known performer Down East out of Newfoundland. It was going to be a pretty big deal, Sheri said, and would even have some financial support from Deane Cameron, president of EMI Canada in Toronto. The tour was being put on in support of Ron's album, *Hynes' Paradise.* "It's not a 'big time' rock and roll tour," Sheri said. "But it's big enough for the East Coast. And if you can get out and travel, and get seen, and make a buck, then maybe you can keep doing music full-time."

Obviously, I jumped at the chance, and not just because it would mean I'd be on the road making a living as a musician again. Playing with a band meant I could break out of the mould of just playing Cape Breton music; it would be something new and different, a chance to stretch my musical muscles.

I had played in bands before a little bit, so it wasn't an entirely new experience. I had played a few shows in Halifax with a few guys from

Cape Breton, and I played a little bit with the Rankin Family too, in Cape Breton, as a sort of sideman/opening act. But it would be great for me, because I would get the chance to see how professional tours work, rather than just one-off gigs like I'd been playing. Plus, I'd get to learn how record deals work and meet the guys from "the label."

The tour covered almost the whole East Coast. We started in Halifax, then went round Nova Scotia, then PEI, then over to Newfoundland and all over the place there, then finally over to New Brunswick. In all, it meant we would be playing one day, travelling the next, for six weeks — playing, travelling, playing, travelling.

The only problem was, the tour started before school ended, which meant I would have to miss my final exam as well as my graduation. Now, I had no problem with that, but of course the school had something else to say about it. That's when we got into that whole thing I mentioned before about the school insisting that I skip the tour and write my exam or they wouldn't let me graduate. Of course, my parents got involved and we worked it out so I could write the exam and graduate and all, but I didn't care; I was going on tour with Ron Hynes come hell or high water.

❉ ❉ ❉

Having seen the worst that drugs can do, both to myself and to other people, I do *not* advocate drug use to anyone for any reason. That being said, if someone made up their mind to get into drugs, and asked me the quickest route possible to maximum involvement, I'd tell them to join a band.

Other than the time my older brother got caught with some pot when I was about 13, I was never really close to drugs at all until I went to New York. I tried pot a few times in New York with some of my theatre friends, but even then, it wasn't something that caught my imagination or really became what I would call a part of my lifestyle. Sex was my big discovery in New York, and frankly I was too busy experimenting with that to think about experimenting with drugs.

When I got back to Cape Breton, of course, the sex outlet was gone. That gave me more time to think about getting into something that might help me forget the fact I wasn't in New York anymore. So, having tried pot a little bit in New York and having had a positive experience, I started to indulge on what I'd call a semi-regular basis — maybe once a week or so with my friends or after a show. I bought a little bit my first time, maybe a gram, and it lasted for ages. It was when I hit the road with that touring band, though, that pot became an integral part of my daily ritual.

I don't know if it's just the music business, or musicians in particular, or creative people in general, but drugs seem to be everywhere when you're touring with a band. It probably has something to do with being on the road for hours, and staying in lousy hotels in small towns far from home. Face it, drugs provide an escape from boredom. And, believe it or not, except for the shows themselves, being on tour can be just about the most boring thing a human being can do.

It's funny, but I can pinpoint, even down to the moment, when I embraced drugs as something I wanted in my life. I'd only been touring with the band for about a week, when we landed up in this little hotel in Corner Brook, Newfoundland. It was our first night off since we set out from Halifax and the weather was brutal. There was an absolute gale blowing outside and the whole band and the few roadies we had were stuck in this hotel room watching the one TV station we could get — CBC, of course, in French.

I was sitting there in the corner of the room, just shaking my head. This was definitely *not* what I had pictured when I found out I was going "on tour." If Corner Brook wasn't the end of the Earth, I thought, it was close to it.

"My God," I said to myself, "I thought Cape Breton was nowhere, but this is *really* nowhere. A few months ago I was in New York City, for Christ's sake, playing my fiddle for Philip Glass."

Then I started to think about the decisions I'd made. Maybe hooking up with Sheri Jones was a mistake, I thought. Maybe coming home from New York at all was a mistake.

"What the hell am I doing?" I thought. "I'm a Cape Breton fiddle player, and here I am on tour with a rock/country band. This is never going to get me a record deal of my own. What the fuck am I doing?"

Just then, I felt a tap on my shoulder and turned my head to see a long hash pipe held out before me, a thin trail of smoke rising slowly from the bowl.

"What the hell," I thought, "I have to do something to break this monotony." I took the pipe and took a long drag.

Now up to that point, I'd only ever smoked pot. Pot had had an effect on me, sure, but nothing like that first drag I took off that hash pipe. I think the fact that I just really wanted to be anywhere else that moment but where I was may have had something to do with it, but I really caught a buzz. It was like a gust of wind came up from behind me and lifted my chair about three feet into the air, then held it up there, just bobbing happily on this imaginary pillow of air.

I took another drag.

If you've ever indulged, you'll know what I mean when I say from that point on, the room took on a whole new perspective. Every person in that hotel room was suddenly really interesting and really funny, and every conversation was just fascinating. I giggled and talked and talked and ate anything I could get my hands on — chips, cheesies, Smarties, anything. Where I was meant nothing to me then; I could have been sitting in a hotel room in Hong Kong and it wouldn't have made a difference to me. The whole experience only lasted about an hour, then I passed out dead away in the chair and didn't wake up until the next morning — back in Corner Brook, safe and sound.

When I did wake up, the room was empty. I remember sitting there motionless for a minute, just going through the events of the past week or so in an effort to figure out why I was in a hotel room and not back home in Creignish. Finally, I figured it out and went into the bathroom to splash some water on my face. I remember thinking, "Holy shit … what the hell was that?" It was probably the same reaction that you'd have after getting kicked by a horse and waking up a few hours later on the floor of the barn. I looked at the clock and realized I'd been out of it for almost 10 hours. Then it dawned on me: that was 10 hours I spent in a shitty hotel in Corner Brook that I didn't really spend in a shitty hotel in Corner Brook. And I still had the whole day to go until the show. I knew then that drugs were going to come in pretty useful on that trip.

Within an hour of waking up, I had tracked down the rest of the guys and got high again. I stayed high for the rest of the day. I was high for the show. Then I smoked some more hash when we got back to the hotel. I can remember bobbing around the hotel pool at around four in the morning and just laughing uncontrollably. Nothing bothered me from then on; I was never bored, never homesick. Time and place had no meaning anymore because I could control both with the drugs. If I wanted to kill time, the drugs made time move faster. If I didn't like where I was, the drugs took me somewhere else. It was obvious to me then: "Of course musicians use drugs," I thought. "If you didn't, you couldn't do this for a living."

The tour was nothing but fun after that. I got along with everybody and the shows went well. Aside from my fiddle, I got a chance to play the mandolin and the keyboards, which was cool. If it ever occurred to me for a second that I wasn't enjoying myself, I just smoked another joint and I was laughing again.

Talk about your life-altering events. Out of the roughly 3,000 days that have passed since that night in Corner Brook, there's probably only been about 30 when I haven't smoked at least one joint. Take this whatever way you like, but I think it's no coincidence that I've only had a handful of what I'd call "bad days" in my career over that same span of time, and most of those bad days also happened to be days when I didn't have any dope.

Like my short-lived distribution job, playing in a band turned out to be a great learning experience for me. First of all, I learned to play "in" a band, not just "with" a band, which, for a musician, is a very different skill than just learning to play an instrument. Up until that tour, I'd had eight years, since I started playing the fiddle, of being basically a solo artist and a front man, so I knew that role pretty well. By the end of that first tour, though, I think I was a more complete musician.

In fact, I didn't realize how important learning to play "in" a band was until a little later in my career when I got the chance to play with really top-flight musicians. Maybe 50 or 60 different times since that first tour experience, I've had the chance to sit in with bands or with other great musicians, and it was on that first tour that I got the skills to do that and make the process seamless.

For example, I've had a couple of opportunities in my career to play with the Irish band the Chieftains, probably the greatest traditional Celtic music band in the world. But sitting in with musicians of that calibre can be terrifying, simply because, let's face it, if anybody on stage is going to fuck up, it's going to be the new guy. In that situation, you have to remember that every person on that stage is a soloist, capable of taking the lead and carrying the tune. You have to play your part, no matter what it is, and play it well, because you know darn well everybody else is going to play their part well. In a band you learn that music is "built," piece by piece, and if one piece is stronger than another, the structure won't stand up.

That first tour experience was also great because we played to all kinds of different audiences in all kinds of venues, and I learned to adjust my style to suit the situation. That skill came in very handy for me later on when I was touring on my own and started to get larger gigs in auditoriums and theatres. No matter where I played later on, I knew how to make the sound fill the room; not too much, not too little.

But as cool as it was to be in a band and be "on the team" and everything, that first tour also taught me once and for all that I was not born to be a sideman. Being in a band is a lot about taking instruction; I remember being in rehearsal with the other guys in the band and them teaching me the mandolin line for the show, and the keyboard line for the show, and the fiddle line for the show, and thinking to myself, "Jesus, this is a lot to take in. I'd rather be spitting it out." When you're the front man in your own band, you tell everybody else what to do musically and you build everything around what you know you're good at. So while I could do the sideman thing, it wasn't where I wanted to be.

When the tour finally ended, after two months of running from one end of the Maritimes to the other, I went back to Creignish for the last time. My high school graduation had gone ahead without me, and there was no denying that the time had come for me to move on. I immediately started thinking about my next move, which I knew had to be a full-blown studio album and a tour with my own band to back it up. By the end of the tour, I knew the music business was my element, and I couldn't stop thinking, "I've got to make this happen."

I also had a pretty good idea how the Canadian record business worked. The bottom line was, you had to get to Ontario, because that was where all the money was coming from. As an East Coast musician, you could pretty much always count on the East Coast fans to buy your records and go to your shows. But I figured out pretty fast that if you could make your mark in Ontario as an East Coast musician, that was the key to making the big bucks. So, although I didn't know it then, I set about putting together the pieces of a puzzle that would eventually catapult me from my parents' house in Creignish to the Juno Awards.

❋ ❋ ❋

Now that I knew how a band worked, and how a tour worked, I felt confident enough to put together a band of my own. I called up several Cape Breton and Halifax musicians I'd got to know over the years, and within about a week, I had my band and had started rehearsing. It was pretty easy for me to get some good players, because I was a pretty well-known commodity in the region by then, and these guys knew that I'd have no trouble getting gigs and making money.

Sheri Jones, meanwhile, got busy lining up one-off gigs for us, as well as a few mini-tours of some provinces on the East Coast. On top of that, Sheri also managed to get Universal Music interested in my indy CD, which they re-released on the East Coast with a few extra tracks. So between the band gigs and the money coming in from sales of the first CD, I was building up the war chest I was going to need to get my "big" CD project off the ground.

I was on my way, for sure, but I probably thought I knew more about the music business than I actually did at that point. Nothing illustrated that better than a mistake I made at one of those early head-lining gigs with my new band that Sheri set up in Halifax. I don't tend to dwell on decisions I made in the past, but I didn't know, at the time, that that decision could have had such a big impact on my career and maybe sent me down a different path from the one I ended up on.

It just so happened that a record executive from Warner Brothers dropped in to see one of my first band gigs in Halifax. After the show, this guy came backstage and told me he thought I had a bright future and the whole bit and offered to support me in getting a recording contract with Warner Brothers. My reaction: "Oh yeah, well leave your card with me and I'll get back to you."

Obviously, I shouldn't have let him out of my sight. But I didn't fully comprehend who he was and what was happening. He did give me his card, but I never did get back to him. To this day I can't explain why, since a big-time recording contract was exactly what I was working towards that summer. It was the reason I formed the band and started touring, and there it was, right in front of me. The only explanation I can come up with is that it happened too soon. I had a plan that I'd been following ever since I got back from the Ron Hynes tour: put the band together, play some gigs, get some money together, rehearse the music for the CD, record it, then sell it to a label. Here a big label was knocking and I'd just got the band together.

Besides, I think Warner Brothers scared me. It was just such a huge label. I was thinking I'd sign with some Canadian label that'd want to start promoting me just on the East Coast. This was the big time right off the bat, and I choked.

On top of that, I don't think I really believed that my talent was significant enough that a busy guy from a big label would take time out of his busy schedule to come see me play at a club in Halifax. Either that or I was just too high to understand what the man was saying to me.

When I did end up signing my first recording contract, later that same year, it was with A&M Records. A&M was still a big label, but it was a lot smaller than Warner Brothers, and I think I felt more comfortable in the smaller framework. In the end, I think I made the right decision in spite of myself.

As the summer progressed, I started writing down a list of tunes I wanted to include on my first big CD. I wanted a mix of traditional fiddle music and some of the modern, hard-edged Celtic music that was coming out of the East Coast at the time and riding the wave of the whole *Riverdance* craze for all things Celtic.

I took care not to make the record "just" a Cape Breton record. I considered traditional tunes from Ireland, and tunes from Scotland, as well as some written in Cape Breton. The more contemporary tunes came from all over.

By the time the fall rolled around, I was feeling pretty good about how things were going. My relationship with Sheri was working out great, the band was getting lots of good gigs and we were making a lot of money.

The band itself had been together for a few months now and was sounding really clean and tight. I pretty much knew what music I wanted to record when the time came to go into the studio and we were getting interest from several local record labels.

On top of all that, I was living in Halifax full-time by then, and my personal life was making a comeback as well. Then, just when I thought things couldn't get any better, they did.

I'd been going hard at it since I left to go on the Ron Hynes tour the previous spring and I was getting about fed up with playing music all over the goddamn East Coast. I decided what I needed was a break, a change of scenery so I could slow down and take stock of everything that had gone on in my life and career in the past year.

I had a nice wad of cash saved up by then from all the dates I'd been playing, so I made up my mind to make a hotel reservation and fly down to New York for a week. I knew plenty of people, and I knew my way around, and who knows, I thought, maybe I can scare up a gig down there in one of the Irish pubs to pay for it all. Within a week of making the decision to go, I was on my way to the Big Apple for the second time in a year.

I felt a lot different coming into New York the second time. Obviously, when I arrived the first time, I had just been in awe of the place and had no inkling of the new life and the new person I was going to discover inside myself. The second time though, it was like I was coming home. Everything seemed so familiar and beautiful. The nasty things that jumped out at me the first time I came into town — the boarded-up buildings and the bums and the hookers — now blended into the scenery, just like my old friend Camryn Manheim said they would. Within an hour of checking into my hotel, I was on the phone lining up some fun for that night.

Talk about pulling on an old pair of jeans; it took me all of one night on the town to fall right back in with my old theatre and club crowd and not even one night to fall back into my bad habits. As it turned out, I'd been gone just long enough for people to miss me, but not long enough for anything to really change. Most of the people I'd met my first time in New York were still around, except for a few of the theatre people, like Camryn unfortunately, who'd left to work in L.A. or something. It was my first real "adult" vacation, and I felt that same sense of freedom I felt when I first got my car, and again when I came to New York the first time.

A few days after getting into town I decided to give my old pal Philip Glass a call. It was only polite anyway, after all the man had done for me. And, of course, it never hurts to keep in contact with "the most innovative and influential composer of the 20th century."

Philip was delighted to hear I was in town, and he wanted to know all about how my career was going back home and all the rest of it. He said he thought getting an agent and going on the tour were steps in the right direction.

"Listen, if you're available tomorrow, we're having some people over for dinner and it would be great if you could come," he said, catching me by surprise.

I hesitated for a second; I mean it would mean burning a perfectly good clubbing night to sit around Philip's house and make pleasant conversation with some high-brow artists or some damn thing. Then again, I thought, "most influential composer" and all.

"Sure, I've got no schedule to keep. I'd love to come," I answered finally.

"Great. Did you bring your violin?"

"I did," I said, then hesitated again. Oh great, I thought to myself, I'm going to get my dinner, but I'm going to have to earn it with a party piece.

"Well bring it," he said. "A few of the guests would love to hear you play."

"Of course they would," I thought, grinding my teeth. And that was it. I'd landed a gig all right, but I was going to be paid in baked zucchini. It was too late to back out now though.

I took a cab to Philip's place the next evening and arrived at about 7:00. Philip met me at the door and, grabbing me by the fiddle case, nearing pulled me off my feet into the house.

"Great, you brought it. That's great," he said, without even so much as looking at me.

"Hello. It's nice to see you too, Philip," I cracked as he whisked me down the hall to the room where the other guests were waiting. By the time we got to the room, I had just managed to get one arm out of my coat as Philip dragged me up in front of the first guest.

"Ashley MacIsaac, I'd like you to meet Paul Simon."

Now, I'd heard what Philip said, but I'd been concentrating too hard on getting my coat off to really look the person I was meeting in the eye. When I did look up, I discovered Philip wasn't joking. It was Paul

Simon all right, all five foot nothing of him, standing in front of me with his hand out: "Pleased to meet you Ashley. Philip's told me a lot about you."

The night took on a sort of "stoned" feeling from about then on, and I hadn't even indulged before I left the hotel, strangely enough. I sat and talked to Paul Simon, and his wife Edie Brickell, and they both seemed really interested in Cape Breton and how I got into fiddle music and everything. After dinner, we all moved into a large sitting room where Philip had a piano and did a lot of writing because the acoustics were great. Then Philip finally dropped the penny.

"Hey Paul, you've got to hear this guy play the fiddle," he said. "Get your fiddle out Ashley and play us some real Cape Breton music."

So that was it. Philip wanted me to bring my fiddle just so I could play for Paul Simon. "Well OK," I thought. "If I can play for the Pope, I can play for Paul Simon." And play I did, four or five tunes in all, and soon had everyone in the room clapping and tapping their feet.

Things started to wind down around 11:00 and, as nice as the evening was, all I could think of was heading straight out to a club as soon as I could get a cab. Then, just as he was leaving, Paul came over to me and sort of took me aside.

"Listen Ashley," he said. "I'm working on a recording right now that I think your fiddle would work perfectly on. If you're interested, I'd like to get you into the studio before you leave to try a few things."

Of course I said the only thing you can say when an absolutely huge musical icon like Paul Simon asks you to come and record with him: "Pardon me?"

We made plans for him to send a car over for me late the next morning and spend the afternoon in his studio laying down some tracks. It turned out it wasn't actually for his record; it was for Edie Brickell's record. I didn't give a shit what it was for though; I was working with *Paul Simon* for Christ's sake.

I called Sheri Jones back in Halifax as soon as I got back to the hotel that night to tell her the news. I got her out of bed for it, but she was more excited than I was.

Always the businesswoman, Sheri immediately started thinking about what it could mean for my music career. First thing the next morning she started milking the publicity cow. I mean, it's not every day a Cape Breton fiddler gets asked to record with Paul Simon, after all, and she made sure everybody in the East Coast press knew about it. Press releases went out, and within a couple of days, pretty much every newspaper and radio station in the Maritimes had said something about it.

All of a sudden, people in the East Coast entertainment media knew my name. I had made somewhat of a name for myself by then through my band gigs and through touring with Ron Hynes, but that invite to record with Paul Simon did in a few days what often takes some acts years of touring to accomplish. There was a buzz around me now, and no mistake. People in the press and in the music industry were saying to themselves, "If Paul Simon knows who this guy is, maybe I should too."

That afternoon laying down some tracks turned into two and a half days of recording, and I loved every minute of it. For the first time in my life, I got to see how a true professional in the music business operates in the studio. I tried to stay as cool as possible, but I was just a wide-eyed kid for the most part.

Luckily, Paul Simon turned out to be an incredibly down-to-earth, humble guy — but a down-to-earth, humble guy who is also unbelievably fuckin' talented. I think I must have pinched myself 50 times before I settled down that first day.

Actually, the most amazing thing about the whole experience was I wasn't even very good at doing what he wanted me to do. But he was patient, and took the time he needed to basically teach me what he wanted. He didn't play the fiddle really, but his knowledge of music was so comprehensive he could probably make a decent stab at playing any instrument.

It must have worked out OK in the end, because he ended up using my fiddle part on the record. That really didn't matter though as far as the impact on my career was concerned; all that mattered was, I worked with the guy who wrote "Bridge Over Troubled Water."

My New York working vacation came to an end and I said goodbye to my new/old friends and my new/old life once again. I expected it would feel different for me the second time around in New York, and it did, for the most part.

Actually, what was really strange about my second visit there was the way I felt when I left. When I had flown back to Nova Scotia the previous January, I'd felt like I was having a limb amputated. I mean, I had just spent four months working this cool job with a bunch of cool people and making lots of money doing it. Plus, I'd discovered my sexuality and, for the first time in my life, I'd found a lifestyle that made me happy and a community that accepted me unconditionally. Then the whole dream stopped, cold turkey. I was back in high school and back in the closet in an out-of-the-way town, on an out-of-the-way island, in an out-of-the-way province. No wonder I was depressed.

Now, less than one year later, I was back on a plane headed from New York to Halifax after another life-altering experience, but the feeling was much different.

The truth is, I was actually feeling pretty good. A lot had happened in my personal life as well as my career since I got back from New York the first time, and I had every reason to believe things were going to get even better. I had an agent now, and I was working toward a record deal. I was finally off the endless round of weddings and square dances and on to real professional gigs with my own band. On the personal front, I'd found that the gay lifestyle I'd discovered in New York did exist, if not on the same scale, in places closer to home. New York may still have been my first choice, but now I knew that if I couldn't live there full-time at the moment, that didn't mean my life had to stay frozen in time in Creignish.

Just how much things had changed hit home as soon as I got back to Halifax. My little jam session with Paul Simon in New York had just the effect Sheri Jones was looking for: the East Coast entertainment press was all over me. There were requests for interviews from every newspaper, TV station and radio station in Nova Scotia and some from the other Maritime provinces as well. CBC Halifax wanted to interview me.

On top of all of that, Sheri told me she'd got a call from the organizers of the East Coast Music Awards and they wanted me to come and play at that event in three weeks in St. John's, Newfoundland. This would be my chance, she said, to get my music in front of every music industry big-wig on the East Coast, not to mention lots more from Toronto.

"This is it!" I remember her screaming. "'Fresh from his recording sessions with Paul Simon in New York City ...' You couldn't have a better introduction than that."

Needless to say, I was pumped when I got on the plane to fly to St. John's the day before the ECMAs. I was something else too: itchy. A few days before, I had started to feel itchy on my chest, and then the itch sort of migrated to the point where my whole body was feeling itchy. I'd been rubbing hand cream on myself for a couple of days, and it worked at first, but now the itch was taking over. Pot seemed to be the only thing that could control it, so I kept smoking pretty steady.

I showed up the next day for rehearsal lathered in cream and stoned. The show was taking place in a huge ballroom in the biggest hotel in St. John's. It was going to be broadcast nationwide by the CBC, so the place was crawling with technicians moving TV lights and cameras. It was a big deal, for sure.

I met the producers and we agreed that I would play a four-song medley made up of two Cape Breton fiddle tunes and a rock tune, the last song would be a sort of rocked-out Celtic version of "Staying Alive." They wanted me to run backstage before "Staying Alive" to change into bell-bottom pants, platform shoes and a big coloured Afro wig. It sounded like a good idea to me, seeing as I was just back from New York and still in full RuPaul mode.

The backing band was made up of a mish-mash of the best session musicians on the East Coast and they already had the tunes down. I was just supposed to come out and jam over top of them.

"Just do what you do best," the head producer told me. "You dance and play whatever you want to play. The guys in the band will keep up with you."

"No problem," I said. Poor bastards, they didn't know what they were in for.

By the time I got back to my hotel to rest up for the show, all hell was breaking loose, outside and in. First of all, a huge nor'easter was blowing in off the Atlantic and all of Newfoundland was battening down the hatches for a wild one. That was good on one count, because it meant more people would likely stay in and watch the show.

On the other hand though, while the weather was raging outside, my body was raging inside. I can remember standing in front of the bathroom mirror with my shirt off, and I was just covered from top to bottom in a fierce-looking red rash.

Sheri got a nurse in to look at me and it took her all of two seconds to pinpoint the problem. "Scabies," she said. "Full-blown case of scabies."

Now, anyone who's ever been a vagrant living on the street will be quite familiar with scabies. Scabies is a skin condition caused by a tiny little insect called an itch mite, or a chigger. The chigger gets in between the folds in your skin and lays its eggs. About four weeks later, the eggs hatch and you're basically infested with baby chiggers that proceed to shit all over you, and that's what makes you itch.

"Well where the hell would I pick up something like that?" I wondered out loud.

The nurse went on to tell me scabies is most commonly found among people who live in crowded, unsanitary conditions, where it's passed from one person to the next through body contact. "It usually starts between the fingers or in the genitals," she said.

Genitals, eh, I thought. Well that explained it. It was New York. I had been back to my old clubbing tricks again during my recent visit, and I must have gone home one night with the wrong guy. Well, it was too late to do anything about it at that point. The nurse said the condition was easily fixed with a certain special lotion, but that was going to be a little hard to come by at 7:00 on a Saturday night in St. John's with a fuckin' gale blowing outside. I'd have to tough it out for the show, which was just about an hour away, and try going to the hospital right after for treatment.

Sheri and the nurse left me alone in my hotel room to get ready for the show and try to calm down. I went back in the bathroom and lit a joint, hoping that might give me some relief to get through the show. No such luck though. This time, the pot seemed to have the exact opposite effect from what it had before, such that my nerves became ten times as sensitive as they were before. I was just wild with the itch; I felt like one of those moose you see running through the woods trying to get away from the flies. I swear to God, if I had had a potato peeler, I would have peeled off the top two or three layers of my skin right then and there. I just stared into the bathroom mirror and thought to myself, "Fresh from his recording sessions with Paul Simon in New York City ... Scabie Man!"

By the time the phone rang to tell me to come down for the show, the itch was so intense I was like a madman. When I got down to the hall, the intensity level went up a few more notches. There were people running around backstage and the TV lights were beating down and making it feel like it was about 500 degrees, which made me sweat and itch even more.

Between being hot, and itchy, and nervous, and excited, and stoned, I stood in the wings with my head just swimming. I could hear Sheri Jones' voice in my head saying, "This is it!" over and over again. For some reason, I started to think about the stories we'd heard in school about the Vikings coming across the ocean from Greenland. They'd be at sea for weeks, going through storms, getting trapped in fog, making wrong turns, starving and dying of thirst. Then, after going through all that crap, they finally saw the coast of Newfoundland. That must have been an amazing feeling, I thought, and it must have been a lot like the way I was feeling right at that moment. I mean, I'd gone through a lot of crap to get to that point, playing every little gig I could get, selling CDs out of my car, and now the key to all my dreams was sitting out in that audience. It was just my luck I wanted to tear my skin off.

Then I heard the magic words: "Now, just back from recording with Paul Simon in New York, from Creignish, Cape Breton Island, Nova Scotia, Ashley MacIsaac."

Now I don't know if it was the itching, or the nerves, or the excitement, or a combination of the three, but I went out and gave the most energetic, hard-stompin', smack-happy performance I'd ever given in my life. I was so intense, people told me afterwards, that there were a few moments when I was so "in your face" it was almost scary.

The band, as good as they were, did their best to keep up with me, but I still managed to lose them a few times. At one point, at the end of one of the traditional Cape Breton pieces, the band stopped playing but I just kept right on going, doing some crazy solo thing right off the top of my head. The other guys just sort of stared at me as I danced wildly around the stage; I guess they were trying to figure out whether they should try to join in or just let me do my thing.

What they didn't know was that I *couldn't* stop playing or dancing around. If I had stopped, even for a moment, I would have put down my fiddle and started scratching myself like a monkey in the zoo. Eventually, I just started playing the next song in the sequence and the band had a chance to jump back in.

While my wild playing may have given the band a few confusing moments, the audience just ate it up. I don't know if they were picking up on my energy or tapping into the power of the storm raging outside the hall, but the crowd was just electric. Everybody was on their feet, clapping and dancing and whooping at the top of their lungs. By the time we reached the end of the set, three thousand voices were singing in unison, "Ah, ah, ah, ah, staying alive, staying alive. Ah, ah, ah, ah, staying aliiiiiiiiiiiiive!"

That night at the East Coast Music Awards in 1994 was one of those rare nights you sometimes get as a performer when everyone in the place puts as much effort into making the performance go as you do. We brought the house down, no doubt about it.

After I walked off the stage that night, I walked into a scene that I can only describe as a "frenzy." There were media people and fans and other performers and record company people coming at me from everywhere. Everybody was talking at once: "Ashley, I'd like you to meet …," "Ashley can I ask you a few questions?" "Ashley, I represent …," "Ashley, could you sign this for my mother?" Ashley, Ashley, Ashley.

I had arrived, obviously, but instead of basking in the glow of it all, all I wanted to do was get out of there and get my hands on some "chigger" lotion. Luckily, the nurse who had looked at me earlier had made some calls and had managed to get her hands on a tube of the stuff. Within 45 minutes of walking off the stage, I was sitting in my hotel room covered head to toe in bug lotion and smoking a big fat joint.

In the days that followed my ECMA performance, I was offered record deals by every major label in Canada and a few from the States. Looking back on that time now, I remember I thought my life couldn't get any better. I soon found out that it could, and it did. It would get a lot worse too, in time.

~ 5 ~

Rich and Famous

Not long after my big night at the East Coast Music Awards, Sheri and I sat down in her office to figure out where we were and where we were going to go next. We knew I had the band and we had the music figured out, mostly, so we were ready to make a record. Now, thanks to the ECMAs, I had every record company in Canada offering me money to make a record. All we had to do was pick one.

Sheri was worried that I would fall into the trap of being dazzled by the money and the lure of the "big" record deal and want to snap up what might seem to be the juiciest offer.

"Don't think it gets easier from here," she warned me. "Making a record with a big label costs a lot of money and they expect results. You can't just take their money and think you're gonna sit back and enjoy it."

Sheri needn't have worried; now that I actually had the opportunity I'd been waiting for in my hands, I was more eager to work than ever.

"Listen, Sheri," I told her, "I've worked really hard to get to this point, and I think I'll be able to keep working hard. Besides, I don't think I'll *ever* have anything harder than the experience I just had."

She had to agree there. If I could give the performance of my life with my private parts alive with chiggers, then I could make a record. Anyway, I'd already made an independent record basically on my own. If anything, making a truly "professional" recording should be easier.

Eventually, we whittled the offers down to two companies. One was EMI. They were especially eager to work with us because they already knew Sheri really well, having done Ron Hynes' last record, and of course I'd toured with Ron in support of it. For some reason though, I got a weird vibe from EMI that turned me off a bit. I think I felt that because I was so young, they were going to try to really control the project. Anyway, we ended up not going that way.

The other company we liked was A&M, because they took pains to assure me they wanted to work on the record at my pace. That was really important to me, because I felt I now had a golden opportunity to take my Cape Breton fiddle music to a level I only dreamed was possible before, but only if I did it right. I wasn't interested in just getting something out there to take advantage of my new "celebrity" status.

Warner Brothers were in the mix too, at the end, but the closer we got to making the deal, the more the really huge companies scared me. Warner made it clear right off the bat that they weren't interested in working at my pace; they had a pace of their own, and they didn't make any exceptions. Maybe if I had gone that way I might have got bigger, faster. But, in retrospect, I think things got plenty big enough for me at my own pace anyway.

In the end we settled on A&M. The deal was signed, I got my advance, and at last I was an official "recording artist." Well, I had the recording contract anyway; now all I needed to do was make the record, and I would spend the better part of the next year doing that.

That wasn't all I did of course. In between writing, rehearsing and recording music for my first "big" record, I toured and toured and toured. I also did interviews every chance I got, including a few with my old pal Peter Gzowski, who was the first national journalist to really seek me out. I hadn't exactly "broke it" yet, but the momentum was building for sure, and the record was going to put me over the top.

By the time 1995 rolled around, I was feeling pretty good about how things were going. My relationship with Sheri was going great and A&M was being really supportive. The band we put together to tour the music for the record was sounding better than ever. We were getting top-level gigs now and making good money off of that. I settled on which music I wanted to record and I'd already laid down several tracks in Halifax.

Best of all though, especially from the perspective of my social life, the record company suggested that I move to Toronto to finish recording. So, at 20 years old, I had a new home in a big new city, new friends, a new record on the way and plenty of money in my pocket. I was on top of the world.

Then, just when I thought things couldn't get any better, my mom phoned to tell me someone had called me from New York. It could have been any one of a hundred people, but it turned out to be my old friend JoAnne Akalaitis, the woman who had seen me play at a square dance two and a half years before and ended up inviting me to be in the show in New York in the fall of '92. I got back to her as quick as I could; I was hoping she had another play for me or something else that could get me back to New York for another few months. It turned out to be even better.

JoAnne asked me if I wanted to come down to New York for a couple of days to play in a benefit concert for Tibet at Carnegie Hall. She said it was being put together by my old buddies Philip Glass and Paul Simon, and it was going to be a big celebrity shindig. There was this long list of musicians who were going to perform, she said, like David Byrne of the Talking Heads and Natalie Merchant from 10,000 Maniacs, and Richard Gere and Christie Brinkley and all kinds of movie stars were going to be there.

She started to go on about the benefit, and the Dalai Lama, and what they were going to do with the money but I didn't hear a word she said. In fact, I don't think I heard anything she said after, "come down to New York for a few days…," except maybe "*blah, blah, blah* Carnegie Hall … *blah, blah* Paul Simon—"

I cut her off mid-sentence: "Great. When do you want me?"

A few days later, I had a plane ticket to New York in my hand.

The folks at A&M were almost as excited as I was about the benefit, because they knew the publicity I would get off it would help set up my record release a few months down the road. I was excited about playing in Carnegie Hall, obviously, but I was just as excited about the prospect of hitting some of the Manhattan clubs and renewing acquaintances with my New York friends.

The schedule in New York was simple: I got into town on the Wednesday and checked into my hotel (JoAnne had left my music for me at the desk — I would be playing some of the tunes I recorded with Paul Simon for Edie Brickell the year before). I was supposed to show up for rehearsal for a couple of hours on Thursday and Friday, then a sound check at Carnegie on Saturday afternoon and the concert that night; then back to Toronto on Sunday.

That left me plenty of time to party and get into trouble, and that's exactly what I did of course.

You'd think playing the actual benefit concert would've been the highlight of that weekend, and it was, but it wasn't as earth-shattering an experience as it would've been if I hadn't spent any time in New York before. Playing Carnegie Hall was obviously very cool, and a crowning achievement for any musician, but by early 1995 I was already a veteran performer. I may have been young, but I wasn't a babe in the woods anymore. I'd played in a big theatre in New York before, and I'd played to bigger crowds when I was on tour with Ron Hynes, so I wasn't nervous about the performance part.

In fact, the scariest thing about the evening for me was being around really big celebrities, other than Philip and Paul, for the first time. After a couple of fat joints though, I didn't have any trouble blending in backstage.

Philip took me around a bit and introduced me to some of the other artists on the show. I met David Byrne and he told me how he'd seen me perform in Cape Breton when he was up there a year or two before on a vacation with his family. Then Philip led me over to this older man with big glasses and a bald head and a big black and grey beard and said, "Ashley MacIsaac, I'd like you to meet Allen Ginsberg."

Well, I'd heard the name Allen Ginsberg before, and Philip had said to me, "He's the guy who wrote the poem 'Howl,'" so I nodded like I knew. To be honest though, "Howl" didn't mean anything to me; I grew up in a part of Canada where they don't study poems like that because of the swear words.

Anyway, Allen was very pleasant and asked me to sit down and talk to him for a while, which I did, and throughout the conversation I was completely unaware of how amazing the situation was: Here I was, a 20-year-old Cape Breton fiddle player sitting backstage in Carnegie Hall having a conversation with an American literary giant.

Maybe it was the pot, but I wasn't intimidated at all talking with this respected, poetic "genius" who, I found out later, was one of the leaders of the whole "beatnik" movement that probably kicked off the '60s. In fact, after a few minutes I just picked up the vibe that I was talking to an old gay guy. He wanted to know all about my music and my background and what I planned to do with my career. He was especially interested to learn that I was gay, and he encouraged me to be an open "out" guy and live my life the way I wanted. The conversation was very pleasant, but it did have a few bizarre moments.

At one point he put his hand on my leg and said, "My gosh, you're a cute young fella."

I just played along with him, "Oh really, ya think so?" I said. "Well, you're a cute old fella yourself — nice glasses."

It went back and forth like that for a while, and he started getting quite friendly. I didn't think anything about it though; in fact, I thought it was hilarious. He touched me on the thigh again, this time a little higher.

"You know, I think you're going to really go someplace with your fiddle young man," he said. "You've got a real cute little look to you, a cute young Scottish boy."

I know he was only half-serious, but I was loving it anyway. In fact, I'd have to say my first encounter with Allen Ginsberg was probably the highlight of my first performance at Carnegie Hall. I ended up playing at other Tibet benefits in New York with him, and at a show in Halifax years later, and I always had a great time talking with him and found him to be an amazing individual and artist. And since he died, it's really come home to me just how rare and special those encounters were.

✻ ✻ ✻

By the time the ECMA thing happened, I'd already been touring for a year and a half. I signed my record deal with A&M within a couple of months of that, and then I toured for another year while I was working on the first record with the label before it actually came out in the early summer of 1995. As soon as *hi™ how are you today?* started getting press of course, I toured almost constantly for probably the next three years.

Mostly I was touring in Canada, but I did get opportunities to tour with different people during that time in the U.S. and Europe. I went out on the road with John McDermott on his tour, and then that led to an invitation to tour for a bit with the Chieftains. They were touring all across North America and even got down into Mexico. I never got down there with them, but they did take me across a lot of the States and all across Canada. After *hi™ how are you today?* came out, I even hooked up with them for a few shows in Italy.

Obviously, touring with other big music acts was cool and interesting, but that was really just a kind of one-off solo thing for me. Also during that time, between signing with A&M and the record coming out, I was also touring with the band that we'd put together to record, touring the music we were recording and writing. Stuart Cameron was the guitar player — he is the son of the great East Coast music legend John Allan Cameron, so there's your bloodlines covered right there. I went through a couple of different drummers, but the main drummer I had while we were recording was a guy named Adam Dowling. Other guys came and went, depending on where we were going or depending on the venue.

So between touring with my band and the solo things I was doing, I was really starting to get my name out there, but the pace was deadly. From the time I hooked up with Sheri Jones for about the next three or four years, I wouldn't be surprised if I did 300 shows a year. Now that's not necessarily 300 days a year, because some days I'd do two and three shows. Many's the time when I did more shows than there were days in a week.

And then, of course, there was the travel. Now, living on the road, you can imagine, can be pretty cool when you're young and single and have never had much experience with travelling or seeing the world. As a kid I'd got to places like Halifax and Toronto and Detroit, and then New York, of course, later on. But touring as an entertainer, or a professional athlete I guess, that's real travelling. You just put everything you need in a suitcase and go for months on end, never in the same place for more than two or three days at a stretch.

As I say, for me at that age — from 18 to 20 — being on the road was fun. You don't feel the pressure at that age. If someone had asked me back then if I enjoyed living out of a suitcase and working almost non-stop, I would have said, "Well, hell yes." I mean, what's not to like?

Having total freedom to do whatever the hell you want? Most other people that age are either away at university or living at home with their parents and working part-time at the grocery store or something.

I don't think you can live that kind of life if you're not single though. That's why so many entertainers and actors and professional athletes can't seem to keep a relationship together. I was in relationships at various times when I was touring and it was just way more of a hassle than finding sex or companionship or whatever on the road. When you're not travelling with the person you're in the relationship with, you're constantly calling and missing them and freaking out. And you start asking yourself, "Do I really want to be living in this hotel or do I want to be back with this person?" The problem is, if you want to make money and be successful in the entertainment business, you can't be asking yourself those questions. You just have to be single-minded and do what you've got to do. A relationship is just added pressure you don't need.

If my tour schedule was intense before the record came out, it got a lot worse after that. In the year leading up to my record deal, touring was new and fun and I felt like my career was going somewhere. Then, during the year or so that we were touring and working on the record, I was all excited about the prospect of having my CD in record stores across the country and all that. But I had never felt the pressure that comes when you're actually out touring a successful record.

Still, when *hi™ how are you today?* did finally come out, all the touring I'd done in the two and a half years leading up to it paid off in spades. Basically, you tour so people will get to know your name, and I guess that's just how it worked out for me. The record was pretty big right off the bat; I think it sold 50,000 copies in the first two or three weeks. Obviously, I was just ecstatic. I finally had the feeling I'd "arrived."

Although I was an old hand at touring by the time the record came out, afterward things were different. I'd travelled all over every inch of the East Coast before I even signed a record deal, and I'd made a few journeys into Ontario and Quebec when I was recording *hi™ how are you today?* so I figured I knew what it was all about pretty much. But once the record was in the stores, and I started to get some airplay and cause some major media buzz on a national scale, I found out just how different it is to tour as a "name" act. The truth was, I didn't have any idea just how big the world was or just how big I could get.

That feeling really hit me in the fall of '95, just about the time I came out to my parents and just before I came out publicly. *hi™ how are you today?* had been out in Canada for a few months by then and I was really starting to get some major media attention wherever I happened to be playing. In fact, it was mostly because of that increase in media attention that I was forced to tell my parents about my sexuality at that time. I was on my way out west to open for the Barenaked Ladies on the western leg of their Canadian tour, as well as to headline a bunch of gigs myself at smaller venues, and I knew the media back in Nova Scotia would be following my every move. I didn't want my parents to get any surprises when they opened the paper back home. Rumours are one thing; seeing it in black and white is another.

I got the chance to open for the Barenaked Ladies after meeting them a few months before when I was in the studio in Toronto finishing off *hi™ how are you today?* with the same producer they were working with at the time.

Anyway, I remember that western tour swing in particular because it was the first time I really toured far from home and people knew who I was before I got there. Without knowing it, I had crossed the invisible line every artist hopes to cross between professional entertainer and celebrity. I was no longer "Ashley MacIsaac, some guy from Cape Breton who plays the fiddle"; I was "Ashley MacIsaac, the fiddle player." People knew my name, they knew what I did, and some had already bought my record — and this was Western Canada.

I spent most of that western tour just tripping on the fact that everybody out West seemed to know who I was — the fans, the media, the radio stations, the local record company people. Everyone was treating me like I was a big deal, and I guess I was. I remember one night in particular, in Vancouver, when I was opening for the Ladies at this big theatre in the city. They were already really big in Canada by then and were just starting to catch on in the U.S., so there was a lot of energy surrounding both acts because we were like the "next wave" of Canadian talent.

The limousine picked me up at my hotel to take me to the theatre before the show, and I remember it was raining like crazy that night, like it often does in Vancouver. When we got to the theatre, there were thousands of people milling around outside, trying to see the band or to buy tickets or just wanting to be around the energy of the show.

Anyway, the driver figured it was too crowded to try and get into the place right then, so he decided to park the car down the street a bit and wait a few minutes while the crowd went inside. That was fine with me, because it gave me a chance to smoke a joint and just relax before the show.

So we parked the car, and I lit up a joint and just sat there watching all these people walking past in the rain. As I sat there, I started to think about where I was and where I'd come from, and how much my life had changed in just the two short years since I finished high school. The Pacific rain streamed down the window and I looked at the mountains off in the distance and thought to myself, "You're a long way from Creignish now, Ashley boy."

The more I thought about the situation, the more amazing it was to me that I was there at all. I mean, I was about to open a show for one of the top pop acts in Canada for Christ's sake; these were the guys who did the "Million Dollar" song. Who the fuck was I? Just a Cape Breton fiddler. I asked myself: "Jesus, am I really gettin' to go out and perform Cape Breton fiddle music for thousands of people in Vancouver?" It didn't seem real to me at all, but there it was.

As the great Okanagan Valley pot I was smoking started to take effect, I began to think more and more about what I was doing actually meant in a cultural sense. I had been so busy up to that point making my record and playing gigs and doing publicity for the record that I never really took the time to stand still for a minute and think about what I was doing. I now felt I'd taken the music I'd grown up with and played all my life to a place where it'd never been taken before, as far as I knew. I mean, I never heard of Don Messer opening up for the Monkees or any other pop act back in his day. Even Anne Murray, as great and popular and successful as she is, was never what you would call "hip." Well, I was a traditional musician and I was hip as hell, and I was performing on the same bill with a very hip pop band. I was in uncharted territory for sure, but it was cool as hell.

I think I smoked another joint then and got even higher and even more wound up. By the time we got in to the theatre and I went out for my set, I was probably more stoned and more excited than I actually wanted to be up on stage in front of maybe 3,000 people. Anyway, I got through it; I stomped around the stage and flipped my kilt up and got the whole place clapping and stomping their feet. All the while, I was thinking to myself, "This is just fuckin' great. I'm high. I'm playing the music I learned to love as a kid and I'm getting paid a ton of money to do it. And all these people from Vancouver who don't know a damn thing about Cape Breton Scottish music are just loving it."

After the show I went back to my hotel room and smoked some more and sat around with the guys from the band just basking in the post-show glow. It's not common practice for any 20-year-old to think very far ahead, especially one as reckless as I was at the time, but I remember thinking to myself that night, "Man, I can really handle this life: playing my fiddle and people loving it, smoking my dope, ordering room service, travelling around the world. Now if I can do all that, and be openly gay, and people will still pay me, then that's all I'll ever need."

As exciting as that first night opening for the Ladies was, the next night may have been even better. I stayed over in Vancouver for an extra day to play a gig at a small club in town called the Starfish Room. There was a real buzz around the second show because I was coming off the Ladies' show the night before and the club was absolutely packed to the rafters. Now the Ladies' show was a great experience, but because I was opening I only had to play for about 30 minutes. The next night though, I was the headliner, so I got to really show my range and leave people thinking, "Wow, now that guy is a great musician."

So, in the course of two days in Vancouver, I'd proven that I could keep a huge pop rock audience entertained one night and then pull off a virtuoso performance in an intimate venue the next night. The Ladies were impressed I guess, because I did the rest of their Western dates on that tour, then, over the course of the next couple of years, toured a bit in the States and did some other Canadian dates with them.

Anyway, those gigs in Western Canada with the Barenaked Ladies in late 1995 were really the beginning of what would become an insane touring schedule. From that time on for about the next three years, as *hi™ how are you today?* really took off and "Sleepy Maggie" started getting tons of radio play in the States as well as Canada, there were usually more days in a given week when I was playing than days when I wasn't. My success opening for the Barenaked Ladies led to U.S. tours with the Chieftains and the Crash Test Dummies and I toured the States as a headliner myself a couple of times. I remember stretches of 45 days without a day off. I once did 115 shows in four months, plus travel. It was just constant movement.

* * *

They always have the same classic scene in every movie ever made about a music personality: it's the one where the struggling artist finally hears his song on the radio for the first time after years of trying to get a break, and he just sits there stunned, listening to himself. Well, as hokey as those scenes are, I found out they're absolutely true.

In my case, I first heard my music on the radio at home in Nova Scotia, which was pretty cool, but I didn't have that big "stunned" moment until I heard myself for the first time on the radio in the States.

I happened to be in Los Angeles at the time and I was riding in a taxi along Sunset Boulevard. It was a beautiful sunny day, as usual, and I was just sitting in the back seat admiring the palm trees and thinking I was so cool because I was in L.A. We stopped at a light and this low-rider full of Mexican teenagers pulled up beside my cab with some kind of Spanish rap music playing and the bass thump, thump, thumping. It was so loud that the cab driver put up the automatic windows to block it out and that's when I noticed the radio in the cab for the first time. I leaned forward and listened … Sure as shit, that was me coming out of that cab radio on Sunset Boulevard in L.A., playing "Sleepy Maggie."

Well, you could've knocked me down with a stiff gust of wind right then. "Holy shit," I thought to myself. "Here I am in Los Angeles, surrounded by Mexicans, and I'm listening to a Canadian kid play a Cape Breton fiddle tune while a girl sings along in Gaelic." It was unreal.

I'm here to tell ya, if you ever want to know how a recording artist knows they've arrived, hearing yourself play on a car radio in another country is a pretty good indication. And that's one thing you never do get tired of hearing. I got a kick out of it again when my manager told me the song was at the top of the charts in Spain. I remember it got to number one on some radio stations in France. The whole thing was all just so freaking cool.

What made it even more amazing that "Sleepy Maggie" did so well was the fact that the singing was all in Gaelic, which meant hardly anyone could understand the words or sing along. "Sleepy Maggie" is actually a traditional Cape Breton fiddle tune that I've played for years just as an instrumental. For the CD, we had come up with English lyrics that we were going to have well-known Celtic singer Mary Jane Lamond sing. But Mary Jane sings lots of her own music in Gaelic and someone suggested it would be cool if she tried a Gaelic version of "Sleepy Maggie." We had the English lyrics translated then and we recorded the Gaelic version first. But once we got it down, we knew that that was the only way to go.

So, like most hits, it was just a last-minute, fluky idea that ended up giving the song that certain something that makes it a hit. And as a Cape Bretoner who is very proud of his culture and history, I've always been really pleased that we were able to put a traditional fiddle tune together with the ancient language of my ancestors and create a song that is appealing to people all over the world.

In fact, being part of the whole worldwide Celtic thing that was going on in the mid 1990s was really cool for me, especially coming from Cape Breton. Obviously I was already well connected to my Celtic heritage through the people I grew up around, and that feeling extended to the other people of the Maritimes I met when I started to tour outside of Nova Scotia. Eventually, when my career really took off in 1996, I got the chance to visit Scotland and Ireland and that was an amazing experience. It's hard to describe the feeling, but I guess it was kind of like the way you feel when you look at a really old picture of your great-grandparents and you see the family resemblance; it's as though you're looking at an ancient version of everything you know now. That's what Scotland and Ireland felt like to me: Cape Breton a hundred years ago.

I actually got a chance to teach step dancing in Scotland, believe it or not. I got out to the Isle of Skye and to a place called Egg, where my ancestors came from. (I always thought that was funny as hell, my ancestors coming from Egg; I mean, doesn't everybody come from egg?)

Obviously when I went to Scotland, I was returning to my ancestral homeland. But I can't really call it "going back" because I wasn't born there and neither were my parents, for that matter. But in a weird way it did kind of feel like I was going back. I guess I would have felt more that way if I had relatives there I knew and that I could have visited, but my gang left way too long ago. I suppose I could've looked into my genealogical roots before I went and tried to track down some of my long-lost relatives. But at the time, with my dyed fire engine–red hair and army boots, I doubt they'd have wanted anything to do with me.

As I travelled around Scotland, one of the things that really struck me was how harsh the landscape was. It's very mountainous and rocky, and from a distance the landscape has a kind of a deep, dark brown colour that reminds you of a tweed coat. It made me wonder why so many Scottish people settled in Cape Breton, because the landscape there is much more gentle and green, not like home at all for them. Cape Breton is what I'd call "pretty." But Scotland, while it's not ugly, is too old and weathered and harsh to be pretty. It's that Wuthering Heights kind of beauty. Ireland, on the other hand, is very lush and green; it's no wonder they call it the Emerald Isle. It was easy to see how people from Ireland might be attracted to Cape Breton.

To tell you the truth, Scotland made me think about what it must've been like living in the Dark Ages, in some cold, dark, damp castle. No wonder so much of the old Scottish music is so sad, I thought, being out on those mountains in a kilt freezing your ass off in the rain would hardly make ya feel like dancin' a jig. And after standing out there for a while, you could see how having sex with a sheep might not seem like such a bad idea. It would be a welcome change in your day I think.

Going "home" to Scotland also gave me a deeper understanding of Cape Breton fiddle music. I remember when I was just learning to play the fiddle, my teacher gave me these old music books with really old Scottish tunes in them to learn. At the beginning of many of the tunes there'd be a notation that instructed you to play the tune "solemnly" or "stoically" or "mournfully." It wasn't until I actually went to Scotland and saw that wind-swept landscape that I understood what the composers of those tunes were talking about; all they had to do was look out the window some days and they'd be melancholy as hell.

I mean, how is a kid who grew up in a little town on Cape Breton Island, eating Popsicles and pizza and watching WWF, ever gonna understand what "stately" means unless they've seen the source of that notation? But when you see those ancient places, you understand then that the tune was actually written to be played during some ceremony or procession through the halls of some great castle in the Scottish highlands. Then, if you keep that picture in your mind, it's possible to play in a "stately" manner. So, now all I have to do when I play one of those old tunes is think of the Isle of Skye on a cloudy day and I bet I hit the notes just right.

Now don't get me wrong, Scotland is not by any means the most depressing place on Earth — far from it. I mean, the landscape is harsh, and combined with a dark, rainy day it makes for a great set for a horror movie. The people of Scotland are anything but depressing though. The kids I taught to step dance were wonderful and alive, so you could also see where the joy in some Scottish dance music comes from.

It was all there for me to discover in Scotland, both sides, the happy and the sad, of the music I'd spent my life learning to play. I guess that was the role of the town fiddle player one hundred or two hundred years ago — to express the various feelings of the people in the music, whether it was at a funeral or a wedding. I believe that's what separates the great fiddle players from the good ones: a good fiddle player can play the notes right, but a great fiddle player can bring out the emotion behind the notes. I believe that's what going to Scotland did for me.

So I came back from my trip to Scotland and Ireland with a deeper knowledge of the music I thought I knew already. And after seeing my family's "ancestral homeland" for the first time, I also came home with an even deeper appreciation for my culture and history. I was just psyched then about being part of the whole "Celtic wave" of musicians coming out of the East Coast, and I wanted more than ever to take my music to as many people as I could. That gave me an enthusiasm for playing and touring that kept me going, along with the drugs, at an incredible pace for years.

✻ ✻ ✻

I had plenty of fantastic opportunities to meet, play and tour with major artists after *hi™ how are you today?* took off, but I have to say there was one in particular that outshone them all. It's hard for someone who isn't from Nova Scotia to really understand what this means, but one of the greatest thrills of my life was getting to play on the same bill with Anne Murray.

Obviously, Anne Murray is beloved right across Canada, but for Maritimers, and Nova Scotians in particular, she's even more special. Anne Murray was the first superstar to ever come out of that part of Canada, and she was just such a classy and elegant ambassador for her province and for Eastern Canada that the people there see her as a kind of mythic figure, like royalty. She was actually born just five hours down the road from my hometown, but on the mainland of Nova Scotia.

I've actually had about three or four really nice occasions to run into Anne Murray in my career. Mostly it was because of the friendship I've developed over the years with John Allan Cameron, an East Coast music legend in his own right for sure. John Allan, of course, has known Anne Murray from the very beginning, before she was a star. The two of them got to know each other as young artists playing around Nova Scotia in the 1960s at dances and festivals, just like I did before I hit it big. Both of them hit the national stage around the same time, appearing on TV on *Don Messer's Jubilee* and *The Tommy Hunter Show*.

The first time I ever met Anne Murray I can honestly say it was more exciting than the time I played for the Pope as a kid and more exciting than when I met the Queen in Victoria as an adult. It was in 1996, after *hi™ how are you today?* had made me a name, in Canada at least, and both Anne and I happened to be guests at the Governor General's Awards banquet in Ottawa. I was just a guest, but I think she was actually receiving an award.

Anyway, I happened to be sitting at the same table as Anne Murray's son, who I sort of knew about already because he had gone to school with Stuart Cameron, John Allan's son, who has played guitar on and off with me for years. So me and Anne's son struck up a conversation during dinner and became great friends talking back and forth.

Then, suddenly, right in the middle of this conversation, who should appear over this guy's shoulder but Anne Murray herself. Now I knew that I was talking to Anne Murray's son, and I knew that Anne Murray was somewhere in that banquet hall that night, but it still shocked the shit out of me when she was actually standing right there beside me.

We were introduced and she smiled that big, warm smile of hers and stuck out her hand and said, "Oh, hello Ashley. Of course I know who you are; I think everyone knows you now don't they?"

It was true: by mid-1996 I had a hit single and a hit record and I'd played with quite a few big stars in the music business, so you could say I was a bona fide celebrity by then in my own right. But I sure didn't feel like one. Sitting there staring up at Anne Murray, I was just in awe. In the part of the world I'm from, Anne Murray is an artist and a celebrity on a par with Elvis. In other words, Anne Murray is as big as it gets, and I'm sure I was just shivering with excitement.

It was like I was in a dream, looking up into her face just three feet away from mine. Then, after a good few seconds of dead air I'm sure, I suddenly realized she was talking to me. I scrambled to recover, but it was already too late. Both she and her son and the rest of the people at the table were all looking at me strange by then.

I let loose a 30-second sentence about how completely wonderful she was and how much I loved her, and my parents loved her, and my family loved her.

"Anne, you're just the biggest, best, most wonderful thing," I gushed, "and I can't believe I'm sitting here talking to you. I can't wait to tell my mother that I met you. She just thinks you're fabulous. And I think you're fabulous too. And the fact you're right here, I'm stunned. And I don't know what to say. And *blah, blah, blah…*" I think I must have said "Oh my God" about 25 times as well.

As soon as I stopped talking, she saw her chance and quickly shook my hand again and took off for her own table. I guess she didn't want me to get going again in case she missed out on dessert. Anyway, I was totally buzzing on that encounter for the rest of the night, and for most of the next day. I bet she didn't stop thinking about it right away either.

Since that first meeting, I've run into Anne Murray a few more times, but it was always in a sort of "working" environment. Once I was one of the opening acts at the opening night of a new theatre in Toronto where she was the big star attraction. I was on about an hour before her, so she actually arrived at the theatre while I was on stage. By the time I came off and the next act went on, she was in her dressing room, which was next to mine. She was getting ready to go on, so I couldn't exactly talk to her then. But I did get to sit in my dressing room and listen to her warming up next door.

She sang her new hit with Bryan Adams at the time, "What Does It Take To Make You Love Me," then she sang another big hit, "Could I Have This Dance," which I actually recorded an instrumental version of a couple of years later in tribute. She sounded just like an angel: pitch — perfect, tone — perfect, every note — perfect. Meanwhile, here's me standing in the next room with my ear against the wall thinking, "This is just too surreal. I'm listening to Anne Murray rehearse in her dressing room and I'm the only one who can hear her."

I closed my eyes and just listened. The sound of her voice reminded me of when I would sit at the kitchen table as a kid in Creignish doing my homework while my mom listened to Anne Murray on the record player in the living room.

I stuck around and watched most of her performance from the wings of the theatre until I had to leave to get ready to travel to a show the next day. Her performance on stage was as flawless as her singing in the dressing room, and that made a real impression on me. "Now that's a true artist," I thought to myself as I watched her. "The quality is there even when she thinks no one is listening."

Come to think of it, I haven't met a whole lot of really big Canadian stars in the music business — internationally known stars I mean. There's Anne Murray for sure, and I met her. But there's Celine Dion, who I haven't met. And Shania Twain and Joni Mitchell and k.d. lang, who I haven't met. And I haven't met a lot of the newer Canadian artists, like Nelly Furtado, Alanis Morrisette and Avril Lavigne and bands like Nickelback, because I just haven't been out on the road for the last couple of years, and that's where you tend to meet people.

One other internationally known Canadian artist I did get the chance to meet is Bryan Adams. It was back in early '96, again, and *hi™ how are you today?* was climbing the charts. Bryan Adams was doing a concert at Maple Leaf Gardens — this was before the Air Canada Centre opened, so Maple Leaf Gardens was still the big concert venue in the city. I happened to be signed to the Canadian subsidiary of Universal Entertainment, which was Bryan's international label at the time, so I was invited to the concert by the record company. It was gonna be a total "industry" schmooze-fest, complete with backstage passes and the whole bit. So what the hell, I went.

I arrived at the stage door of the Gardens with this guy I was dating at the time and got whisked right inside to the "hospitality" area set up backstage by the record company for VIPs. The room was full of beautiful people, milling around with free hors d'oeuvres and free drinks in their hands; it was definitely the "scene" that night, and me and my boyfriend fit right in. My career was still just getting off the ground in a big way then, so the whole "rock star" world was new and exciting to me and I was "lovin' every minute of it," as Bryan says. I almost didn't want to leave to go watch the show.

After the show, all the VIPs converged again in the hospitality room for another round of free booze and food. Most of the people there were either drunk or stoned, so the atmosphere was up and everybody was in a party mood. Then the man himself walked in, still towelling off from the show and sipping a bottle of water. Bryan sat down on one of the big armchairs and started to shake hands with people as they were introduced to him by the record company people, like a reception line at a wedding.

Eventually my turn came, and someone from my record company brought me and my boyfriend up to Bryan and introduced us. Although my record was doing very well and getting some airplay, I really didn't think a guy as big as Bryan Adams would've heard of me. But, to my surprise, he had.

"Ashley MacIsaac, sure," he said. "How'ya doing Ashley? It's really cool to see ya here, thanks for comin'."

I thanked him and thought that would be the end of it, but he started asking me all kinds of questions about how my career was going and complimenting me on my record.

Then he did something that I thought was really cool: he turned to my partner and started including him in the conversation. Now when you think about it, it's only polite to include anyone that's standing right in front of you in your conversation, rather that just pretend they're not there. But in the rock star world, it's more common to see famous people speaking only to people they either want to talk to or need to talk to. In my experience, and I've been guilty of it as well, famous people can be rude as hell. But not Bryan Adams; he made me and my partner feel very comfortable in his company.

I've always respected Bryan Adams as both an artist and a person since that night. I mean, to meet an artist of that calibre, someone who's recorded songs with the likes of Anne Murray and Tina Turner and Sting, and find them to be really down-to-earth had a big effect on me. Now I know I never got as famous as Bryan Adams, but I always tried to keep that down-to-earth perspective when I did get as famous as I got. I didn't always succeed, but I tried most of the time to be polite and friendly with everyone I met after that, regardless of who they were.

Although I've never performed with Anne Murray, I actually got to play on stage once with Bryan Adams. It was a few years after I met him at that show at Maple Leaf Gardens, and he was in Toronto to appear on MuchMusic in a live "Intimate and Interactive" session. Once again, one of the record company people I was working with from Universal asked me if I was interested in going down to CityTV as a special guest to see the show and I said I was. He didn't exactly say, "You can sit in with Bryan," but he did say I could bring my fiddle if I felt like it, that it would be cool if I could join him onstage.

I could see what Universal was thinking: using one of their hugely popular artists to shine a bit of light on another one of their artists who needed a bit of a positive press.

Anyway, I got there and the show started and Bryan was playing his tunes and talking to the host of the show. Then at one point the host said to Bryan between songs, "Well Bryan, we understand there's another Canadian artist here tonight who you've met before. Maybe we can get him to come up and join you for a few minutes. Let's hear it for Ashley MacIsaac..."

So, up I went, fiddle in hand, and shook hands with Bryan and exchanged pleasantries. Then, sure enough, he asked if I'd like to sit in for one song and I said, "OK," naturally, and away we went.

The song was a hit he had out back around that time and I just improvised on the fringes of the tune and tried not to screw up Bryan and the band. I did a little solo in the middle of it and the whole thing went over great.

After that one song, I was out of there, but shit, I was happy. How could I complain? I had managed to weasel in to playing with one of the biggest artists in Canada. I'd do it again if I ever got the chance.

I have to admit, that's by far one of the coolest things about being famous — getting the chance to perform with other big artists. It's not that I think I'm a big artist, but you have to have some kind of name and reputation before a really big name is going to let you up on stage beside them. After all, they're not going to put their own reputation at risk just to boost your career. But once you've been around for a while and you've proved you have the ability to perform at a professional level consistently, and you have enough fans of your own that the big star figures they can benefit from joining forces with you, you start to get the odd offer.

Once my own career took off, I started to get opportunities to open for all kinds of famous acts. I opened for the Canadian acts like Crash Test Dummies and the Tragically Hip and the Rankin Family and for U.S. or "foreign" acts like Sheryl Crow, Melissa Etheridge, the Chieftains and Los Lobos, among many others.

I remember Melissa Etheridge in particular was really nice to me, probably because of the whole "gay" thing. She complimented me on what I was doing and encouraged me to keep it going, and it was great to hear that from someone who was a real pro and who had to deal with shit related to her personal life in the media as well.

Sheryl Crow always stuck in my head too, but not because she was particularly kind to me, although she was nice. The reason I remember Sheryl Crow is because she was the only headliner I ever really stuck around to watch after I finished my set. She was such a great musician and a great, ballsy, hard-core blues singer and I had so much fun listening to her every day. I'd listen to part of the Tragically Hip show on most nights, and maybe watched the whole thing right through once. But for Sheryl Crow, I could sit around every night and listen to her sing every one of her songs frontwards and backwards twice. Her band cooked and she is just a smoking talent.

As for "hangin'" with the big artists, there was a bit of that, but not as much as you might think. Mostly when people are on tour they just go back to their hotel room after the show, have something to eat, maybe smoke a joint, and go to bed. I did get to party with the Tragically Hip once though. In a break from the tour I was on with the band, Gord Downie invited me up to this place he has in Eastern Ontario where they have a recording studio. We had a huge corn boil and I brought a bunch of Cape Breton lobsters up with me. The guys from the Tragically Hip are all smart and talented and rich and famous, but they're as nice as anyone you'd care to meet.

While opening for other famous acts was always cool, I really loved it when I got the chance to actually play with the person or the band I was opening for. As a musician, when you play with another really gifted musician you get to see what that person is all about and what makes them great at what they do. You can just hear the experience there. You can play off each other, and spar, and pass the tune back and forth and it's a revelation for anyone who loves to play music. It's like you're communicating and learning about one another without talking. I have to pinch myself when I think that I got to do that with people like Paul Simon and David Byrne.

Playing with another top-notch musician is a challenge too, for sure. It's like when I first played with Philip Glass as a 17-year-old; there's no better way to become more skilled as a musician than to play with truly gifted, professional musicians. Also, it gives you a lot of confidence, because you have to assume you must be a pretty good musician yourself if these people are willing to play with you. And if I'm that good, I must be giving the other artist the same great vibe that I get when I play with them.

It's a cool feeling that you can't really understand, I guess, unless you do something in close concert with someone else that requires real feel and timing. It's like rowing a boat in the Olympics, or sometimes you hear about hockey players who play together really "clicking."

Another cool thing I found out about music when I started really travelling is that it truly is a totally universal language. I've played in many different countries with musicians from all over the world — in the U.S., in Scotland, in Ireland, in Italy, in Japan — and that feeling of being "tight" with another musician or group of musicians is always the same. When you're playing together with other good musicians and you're in the groove and the tune is really rockin', you can just feel it come over you; it's like a continuous orgasm that lasts the whole song. If you're really in the groove, the feeling could last the whole gig.

Probably the coolest, and weirdest, thing you often get to do when you're famous, I found out, is appear in the odd movie or TV show. Directors love to grab famous musicians or politicians or anyone who's hot at that particular moment and stick them in a show — kind of like tossing a sprig of parsley on a dinner plate to give it some garnish.

My "cameos" allowed me to meet some pretty neat people and to travel to the other side of the world. If going to New York from Creignish at 17 was a shock to my system, going from North America to the Orient was just as big a shock. People from North America may see images of the Orient on their TV, but until you actually go there and see how the people live it's impossible to get the full effect.

I was lucky enough to get the chance to visit Japan first in 1997 for a gig in Tokyo, and then again in the fall of 1998 to appear in a Japanese movie called *Nabbie's Love*. The director of the film, a guy named Yuji Nakae, saw me play the gig in Tokyo and asked me if I'd come back to do the film. I played a bit part of an Irish guy who goes to the island of Okinawa in search of this Japanese opera singer he loves.

It was a totally bizarre experience: I learned to speak my Japanese lines phonetically, so I was going around saying shit and I didn't have a clue what I was saying. One of my lines translated to, "Congratulations, I'm sorry." To be fair though, Japanese is a hard goddamn language to speak, especially with a Cape Breton accent, let alone understand. I mean I can say *"Konechiwa"* right enough, but I'm still not sure if it means "Hello" or "Good evening" or "How ya doin'?" or what. I do know *"Domo arigato"* means "Thank you very much," I learned that much anyway.

For the movie, I had to say *"Domo arigato,"* four or five times in different scenes (did I mention the Japanese are really polite?); *"Watasi Ashley-san,"* or "My name is Ashley"; and I had to squeeze a girl's hand really tight and say, *"Goma n'sei,"* which meant "I'm sorry." So learning to say *"Goma n'sei"* has come in pretty handy for me 'cause I say "I'm sorry" quite a bit, and saying it in Japanese gives it a little variety.

The movie played in Japan and showed up at a few film festivals in North America. (It wasn't my first film role, though: when I was nine I step-danced in a CBC television movie about Cape Breton called *Island Love Song*.) I also recorded a half-dozen fiddle tunes for *Nabbie's Love*, one with a Japanese opera singer, another few with some traditional Okinawan singers, and some with a sort of Japanese party band. The soundtrack was released in Japan.

Japan for me was amazing because it was just so incredibly packed with people. I mean, I grew up in a tiny village on a remote section of coast on a remote island at the ass end of a vast country, so I know a thing or two about isolation. Well, Japan was the exact opposite of that.

There are probably lots of remote areas in Japan, but you sure don't get that feeling in the cities. I swear they must sleep three-to-a-bed in Tokyo, there's so fuckin' many of them. As soon as I got off the plane in Tokyo, it seemed like I was surrounded by millions of smiling Japanese people.

Now I'm not exactly Michael Jordan, but the Japanese made even me look like a basketball star. But they're polite as hell and they certainly have no shortcomings in terms of their culture, which is something I really admire because I have such a rich cultural heritage myself. The Japanese have great respect for their traditional music and art, and I enjoyed getting into all of that when I was there. They showed real interest in learning about my Cape Breton Scottish culture as well, which I really appreciated.

The food, of course, is fantastic; I think I ate enough sushi to fill Marineland when I was there, and even now I prefer rice as a side dish over potatoes.

Aside from the people and the culture, what tends to strike you in Japan is the architecture, because they have lots of unique, beautiful buildings, and the fact that the place is spotlessly clean. I know Toronto gets a lot of good press about being a clean city, and by North American standards it is, but Japanese clean and North American clean are two different things. The people wear white gloves and surgical masks on the subway, for Christ's sake, so they don't pick up any germs. With the way I looked — spiked hair, kilt, Doc Martens, leather jacket — I'm sure they must have thought I was just teeming with bacteria.

The toilets are incredible as well — the cleanest toilets in the world I'd say. They play nice music while you're crapping and they spray perfume as soon as you get up. I remember smoking a joint while I sat on a hotel toilet in Japan with the music just blasting and having one of the best times in my life. I'm tellin' ya, gettin' music out of a toilet and water that squirts up and cleans your ass — that's as good as it gets some days.

✱ ✱ ✱

I'll admit, being a famous musician does have its perks: travelling, meeting famous people, getting to be in movies and on TV, playing with great musicians. But I found out pretty soon after my first "big" record came out that the downside is just about as big or bigger.

The thing is, when an artist finally has that breakthrough record or hit song on the radio, the pressure to capitalize on it comes down like a ton of bricks. You've got to get the hell out there and get in front of as many people as possible so you can sell as many records as you can while people are still interested in you. And you have to stay out there as long as the record still has "legs," because, obviously, a point comes when all the people that are going to buy your record when it's new have bought it. Then it's time to start coming up with something new, and the record company doesn't waste any time letting you know when that time has come.

Of course, the real downside of the whole experience of "making it" and having a hit record and making a lot of money was that I had the opportunity to do a lot more drugs. Once again, I was on the road all the time, living in hotels, lonely quite a lot. The difference after *hi*™ *how are you today?* came out, though, was that I had the money not just to smoke as much pot as I wanted, but to start experimenting with "rock star" drugs. *hi*™ *how are you today?* came out in 1995 and I spent essentially the next three years doing nothing but touring that record. Based on the number of shows I did over that time and the number of records we sold, you couldn't really call that record anything but a success, but it was all a blur to me.

I sat down with a calculator recently and tried to figure out just how many dates I did play, starting when I went on tour with Ron Hynes when I was 18, and the numbers always leave me shaking my head. Even if I only played 200 dates a year between the ages of 18 and 25 — and I know that's on the light side — then that would be 1,600 dates right there. I'd say, without a doubt, by the time I turned 25 in February 2000, after touring for eight years, I'd played at least 2,000 shows. And that's not counting things like benefit concerts, and awards shows, and T.V. shows, and interviews, and all the shit you do for free just to get your face out there.

But I did have a hell of a lot of fun. I mean, how many people get to sit in a $1,000-a-night room at the King George IV Hotel in Paris, snorting cocaine and eating foie gras? Not many. How many Cape Breton fiddle players do you think ever got to do that? I'll tell ya: one.

You wouldn't think a person could get sick of fancy hotels, good food and lots of partying, and that's true — you never get sick of it. It's just that a point comes when the decadence of it blocks out your common sense, like it did with me, and you end up being overwhelmed by it all. Either that or the money runs out and you just can't afford it anymore, which happened to me too.

When it was all kind of over and I finally stood back and did a real accounting of it all, I realized that I probably didn't really make that much money at all from touring because I paid out so much money. That's not to say that wasn't mostly my fault; I liked to have a lot of cash in my pocket on the road, I liked to party, I liked to have my bag of dope every week, and the money for all that came right out of the cash flow generated by the shows. Plus, like any self-respecting professional musician with a hit record, I was staying in nice hotels and living basically off room service.

So I could do all these things, and I was definitely "living the life," but I wasn't really making any money on the road. The main money I was making in those years was coming from record sales. When there was any excess money on the road, I would always find a way to spend it. Say I was out on the road touring and the tour manager I had was maybe a little more lenient than others, I might be able to grab $3,000 from cash flow in a given week. Then I'd take that and buy a bag of cocaine or whatever, or fly some friends to where I was at and have a big party. It was easy come, easy go. But shit, I was only 20 when it all started, and I thought that was going to be my life forever.

In the first few years, the money was looked after by an accounting firm that Sheri Jones hooked me up with. Of course, I ended up going bankrupt at the end of it all, but I don't blame that on the accountants. They were always right on top of everything, and would call me up and very nicely tell me from time to time, "If you don't do something, you're going to run out of money." Of course, if people decide not to listen, then there's nothing the accountant can do about that. And that's what went on; I did it, and other people involved with me did the same thing.

You hear about rock bands that sell all kinds of records and make millions of dollars and then end up with nothing to show for it. I read about the Bay City Rollers back in the '70s, and they were the same as me; they looked up finally after years of touring only to find there was no money left.

In my case, the only wrongdoing was probably overspending. The road was expensive. We had a lot of musicians to pay, and a lot of greedy hands in the pot. If I did 300 dates a year at $10,000 a show for two years hard on, that's quite a bit of cash. But we went through it just the same. I mean, I never saw it. If I averaged, on a fair estimate, just 200 shows a year for the three years following the release of *hi™ how are you today?*, at $10,000 a show, that's $2,000,000 right there. And you do that for three years — that's a minimum of about $6,000,000 I took just from gate receipts.

On top of that, you factor in record sales of about 400,000 copies, from which I was supposed to be getting about $7 or $8 a record — that's another $3,000,000 or so. So everything combined, close to $10,000,000 went through my company in the three years following the release of my first big studio recording. I didn't see it go through, because I was too young or too naïve or too stoned to pay attention, but it went through.

And just like you can sit down with a pencil and figure out approximately how much you made, you can just as easily sit down and figure out where it all went. For starters, you've got 20 percent coming right off the top for management; that's $2,000,000. Then there's another 10 percent for your agent, that's another fuckin' million. Then there's musicians and roadies — say I had seven or eight musicians and roadies on the road with me doing at least 200 dates a year at an average of $3,000 a week. That's about $20,000 a week for 50 weeks a year, then you do that for three years straight. That's another fuckin' million. Then, of course, we haven't even talked about the taxman. He's going to take 50 percent of what you started with in the first place. So, just like that — there goes all your money.

You might've noticed I didn't count myself in there. Well, I didn't, but I did, because I was sort of part of the cost of running the whole thing in the first place. See, the way I got paid was I had to go to the tour manager and say, "Can I please have $2,000 of this cash flow now? I've just done 200 dates and I'd like to buy a bag of dope if you don't mind. Thank you very much. I mean, OK, I know I spend $300 a week on pot, but didn't I just make three million fuckin' dollars?"

Well, actually, no, I didn't. Everybody who worked with me did well but they had to pay their taxes the same as me and they did the work so I have no problem with that. But that doesn't mean it doesn't break my heart just to think about it. In the end, after selling close to half a million records and touring for three years incessantly, I really had nothing at all to show for it. What I got was a chance to live in fancy hotels for three years, and eat out all the time, and consume all kinds of drugs, and throw big parties for my friends all over North America and not have to think about money at all while I was doing it. That kind of personal freedom doesn't come cheap.

Actually, I'm telling a lie. There was one tangible thing that did come out of all that work and all those record sales following *hi*™ *how are you today?*. I managed to scrape together $150,000 and took out a mortgage for another $150,000 and built a house for myself and my family and friends to use up in Belle Cote back on Cape Breton. When I went to see my accountant to get the money to build the house, that was all that was left. I went there thinking I had something like $800,000 in the bank.

Jesus, I just shake my head now when I think about the money that was made and spent just as fast. One perfect example: I remember once in Toronto in 1997, when my career was riding really high, I played three big shows in one day. First off, at 10:00 in the morning, I was playing at some huge political party convention for $10,000. On top of that, I was booked to play that night at the Regal Constellation Hotel near the airport for Steven Spielberg and George Lucas and all the Hollywood crowd that were up in Toronto for the Film Festival for another $15,000. So I was all set for a pretty good day when, just a couple of nights before, my Toronto promoter called me at my hotel.

"Want to play a gig on Saturday afternoon for $15,000?" he asked.

"Sure," says I, without giving it a moment's thought. What the hell, I needed to kill some time between the other two gigs. It turned out Frank Stronach, who owns the big auto parts company Magna International, was having his annual company picnic at his estate just outside of Toronto that day and he invited me up to play in the afternoon. So, with that, I was in line for a $40,000 day, as much money as most people in Cape Breton wished they made in a year.

Well, I set out that Saturday morning with a bunch of rolled joints in my pocket and before I knew what hit me, it was all over. It was just a blur of music and pot and limo rides and shaking hands with people. The promoter who booked it all was waiting for me at the Regal Constellation after the last gig and he handed me $2,000 cash. As for the rest of the money, that went to my agent so he could pay for the band and transportation and commissions and whatever the hell else there was, but I wasn't thinking about that at the time. All I knew was I had just done three shows in one day and now I had money in my pocket so I could to go to my dealer and get a bag of magic mushrooms and another half of pot.

When I finally got back to my hotel with some of the guys from the band, I was feeling pretty damn good. I had this incredible day behind me. I had my bags of dope. I hadn't stopped to eat all day, so I picked up a bunch of Kentucky Fried Chicken for everybody. So I sat there on the couch just eating my chicken, smoking a joint and watching TV.

Then I started thinking.

"I must have made $25,000 today," I thought, mentally doing the math. "I mean, the band didn't get paid any more than $15,000, and then commissions. There should still be $25,000 left over from today I figure." I decided to look into it the next day.

A couple hours after I woke up and my head cleared a bit from the night before, I called my manager at the time to talk about the money. Looking back on the conversation now, I realize just how out to fuckin' lunch I was about everything.

"Listen," I said to my manager as I sparked up my first joint of the day. "Why don't we take the $25,000 and do something to promote the record in the States, because the record company isn't doing it. We could buy a billboard on Sunset in L.A. or something."

"No way," he said. "You don't have enough money to do something like that. Besides, you need that money so you can keep promoting the record in Canada."

Well, that didn't make any sense to me. By that point, the record had been out for two years and we'd toured it upside-down in Canada as far as I knew. I mean, Christ almighty, I thought, I'd sold a ton of records and played something like 700 dates in the three years previous and made a ton of money. But it always seemed I had nothing to show for it. I did have my house in Belle Cote, but that had a mortgage on it. And now, after all I'd accomplished, my manager was telling me I needed to work even harder because I still didn't have any money.

"To hell with this," I said, slamming down the phone.

It was about then that I started to get just a little bit contentious about the way my career was going. Unfortunately, my reaction to the situation only did more damage to my career and to me personally. But then again, I was still young, and young men do tend to fly off the handle when things don't work out the way they want. After I hung that phone up on my manager, I went on a tear. I took what was left of my $2,000 and spent the next week partying in Toronto.

"OK you bastards," I figured. "I'm just another expense here. I work three gigs in one day and all you give me is $2,000 to shut me up. Well, I'll show ya how I can spend $2,000."

I went downtown and checked into a cheap hotel and went straight out and bought myself some crack cocaine. Then I went back to that hotel and commenced smoking every bit of that crack myself.

After the $2,000 was gone, I came back down to earth a little bit, because I had to go back to work so I could get more money out of my manager and my record company. But that was to be the pattern for the next year and a half: work, get some money, get high. After a while I was happy to stop worrying about my finances. As long as I had enough money for dope I could stay in my fantasy world.

The joke of it was, while I was smoking crack almost every day, I continued to tour and perform at the "high-octane" level that everybody expected of me. I had the whole wild "punk" fiddle player image working for me, but people didn't necessarily link that with drugs like they probably would have if I was a rock guitar player who performed the same way, like Slash from Guns N' Roses or Jimi Hendrix or something. And the fact that I wasn't that kind of musician allowed me to continue to appear on nice things like *The CBC Presents: A National Tribute to Rick Hansen.*

It was nuts when you think about it — here I was standing onstage in Vancouver next to Rick Hansen, an idol to millions of people in Canada and around the world for all he's done for the disabled, and he's congratulating me on my career and telling me how innovative I am and how I've changed traditional music and the whole bit. Meanwhile, I'm just standing there thinking how I couldn't wait to get on the plane after the show and get back to Toronto so I could do some more cocaine.

It didn't matter where I was or what kind of show I was doing, I can remember always planning ahead and making sure I had enough money to get high. I might be on stage doing a show even, and between tunes I'd be thinking, "OK, I've got $100 in my pocket and that'll buy a bag of dope. Then I can go back to my hotel room and get high and just fuckin' hate everybody and it isn't going to matter because nobody's gonna fuckin' bug me."

Now I'm not blaming anybody for the position I got myself in with the drugs, but it is kind of disturbing when you think how smoothly my life and career went while I was really whacked out on drugs. The gigs were scheduled, the plane tickets got bought, the cars were always there to pick me up and take me to my hotel. And, most important, I always had enough money for my dope; because if Ashley ever didn't have enough money for his dope, that's when he started to act up.

So everything got done, everybody that needed to get paid got paid, and I got to get high. In truth, I was just breaking even, providing work for a whole bunch of people around me that I needed there so I could continue to get high and not worry about anything else.

As the drugs started taking over, I began to lose hope, I guess, of ever having control over my life and my career. I had control over whether or not I got high, and that seemed like all I could control. That made me pretty cynical about my career and the music industry after a while, and that feeling started to come out more and more as I sank deeper into the addiction.

The result was I came on like a total fuckin' prima donna. I guess I'd lost the hunger I had early on for success, and I didn't feel thankful at all for all the success I had enjoyed to that point. It was like I was on autopilot. I remember someone calling me up to offer me a gig, and my attitude was just, "OK, I'll show up. Have my money ready when I get there and I'll do one set. But don't expect anything else."

The most amazing thing for me about being addicted to cocaine was that, although I may have been thinking about doing drugs all the time, I was still able to play the fiddle good and function on stage and do lots of other things.

And I managed to do a lot more than play the fiddle during my whole "addict" phase. I even got invited to appear as myself in a TV show about a pro hockey team — I came out and played the national anthem on the fiddle before a hockey game in Hamilton. Gordon Pinsent played one of the coaches in the show and he step-danced while I played the fiddle in another scene. I even managed a few talk show appearances, although I tried to avoid them because it was just too hard to keep it together when I was just whacked on the drugs.

Eventually, even the drugs weren't enough. As time passed and my career became more and more like a treadmill where I kept running at top speed and never getting anywhere, depression started to set in. *hi*™ *how are you today?* hit it big when I was just 20 years old, then I toured that record for about three years without stopping. Then the record company put out my second record, *fine*® *thank you very much* — which was just a collection of traditional tunes recorded during the *hi*™ *how are you today?* sessions — because they were sick of waiting for me to record something new. Then it was more touring in support of that, but I was into the crack by then.

Shit, by the time I looked up from all that, I was 24, addicted to cocaine and with about the same amount of money in my bank account as I would have had if I'd had a paper route for that four or five years. That was after selling more than 400,000 records and playing over a thousand dates, making literally fuckin' millions of dollars. And all I had to show for it was a 1972 Olds Cutlass convertible that I was still paying for and a house I couldn't afford to pay the mortgage on.

- 6 -

DRUGS

I went to live in Toronto for the first time in the fall of 1994. I had been touring all across Canada since signing my recording contract with A&M earlier that year and living in my manager's house in Halifax when I was in town. I started recording tracks for what would eventually become *hi™ how are you today?* in Cape Breton that summer, but it was eventually decided by the record company that it would be better for me to record the rest of the record in Toronto. So off I went to T.O. and moved in to a little rented house at Gerrard and Sumach with another musician I was working with at the time.

When I wasn't off doing a gig someplace, I spent most of my days in Toronto either rehearsing music for the record or actually recording it in the studio. That left my nights free to prowl around the city and see what kind of trouble I could get into.

That was a really easy time for me; I had plenty of money, but I wasn't really famous yet so I still had lots of personal freedom and no pressure to be anyone or do anything, just play my fiddle. And when I wasn't playing my fiddle, I just smoked a lot of pot and hung out at the dance clubs around Church and Wellesley.

It was also a very exciting, creative time for me. I was working on my first record with a big label, and I was constantly surrounded by excellent musicians and producers and recording engineers. I was really excited by the energy surrounding all these people and the record, and I was eager to stretch myself as a musician and try new things. I was doing just that one afternoon at a friend's house at Dundas and Sherbourne, just sitting in the living room working out some chords for a tune on my fiddle. Ironically, that corner in downtown Toronto would become a very bad one for me a couple of years later, but that particular day is only full of pleasant memories

My friend was a musician as well, and we had been smoking pot and playing music for a couple of hours when he went into the bedroom and came back out with a little box. He put the box on the coffee table and took out two pink rectangular pieces of paper, about the size of a postage stamp. "Want to really expand your mind?" he asked me. "Try a hit of this."

What he was offering me was acid. I was a veteran pot smoker by that time, of course, but I'd never experimented with any kind of hard drug, not even on any of my many visits to New York. I'd seen it all of course, but so far I'd resisted the temptation. But, given the sort of creative frame of mind I was in at that particular time, I jumped at the chance to try something new and maybe gain a different perspective on my music. So I did it.

The high came over me almost right away, not creeping like pot did, and within about 20 minutes after popping the tab in my mouth I was really fucked up. I was fucked up, but not in the mellow way pot fucks you up; it was more of a "wired" feeling, like I'd just finished drinking 25 cups of coffee. I suddenly got the urge to move, so I decided to walk back to my place, which was just a few blocks away. I put my coat on, said goodbye to my friend and walked out into the clear afternoon.

I should have started walking north on Sherbourne to get to Gerrard, but instead I headed west along Dundas toward Yonge St., the very heart of all the action in Toronto. As I walked along the sidewalk I began to notice the not-so-subtle differences between the marijuana high, which I knew really well, and the acid trip I was on.

First of all, a pot high is more of a personal high, and by that I mean that you know you're high, but you're also aware that people around you are not high and the rest of the world outside your head is exactly the same as it always is. Acid it totally different: on acid your high kind of projects outside your head and starts fuckin' with everything around you as well. It changes the shapes and colours of things, turns people into animals and changes their voices. So with pot, you're different, but with acid, *everything* is different.

I got to Yonge and cruised slowly north toward Gerrard. On the way I just enjoyed the passing scenery of bright colours and beautiful people and animals that were flying by me on the street and in the air — it was like I was in a scene from the Beatles' *Yellow Submarine* movie.

I would've been delighted with the way the day turned out just based on that experience, but I would end up getting even more out of that hit of acid. When I finally got home, probably a good hour or more after leaving my friend's place, I immediately got my fiddle out and started playing around on it. I had all these melodies banging around in my head, so I just started to link them together. Then I took out a pen and a notebook and started to jot down words to go with the notes in the melodies. In an hour I had most of a song written, and what I started that day on my first acid trip ended up being the bonus track on *hi™ how are you today?*

I did acid pretty regularly after that, but it's not the kind of drug you can really do every day and still function normally. I could see why people like the Beatles talked about how acid helped them to write music and create songs. It really does open your mind up to imagining all kinds of things you probably couldn't imagine when you're not on it. To me, acid was like a key that unlocked hidden places in my brain, allowing me to create and conceptualize my music on a different level.

At the same time though, because acid sort of takes you to a different place, you can't really use it unless you're in a situation where you don't have to be "present" and "aware." I have taken acid at times when I probably shouldn't have, like before shows, and I've been criticized for acting "spaced out" or "remote." Well, I was there all right; it's just that to me the stage was probably floating on the Caribbean Sea and I was busy trying to deal with that and perform at the same time.

Cocaine was another proposition altogether. While acid was a different kind of high from the one I'd get from pot, the high I got from cocaine, especially crack cocaine, was 10 times more intense than both. I started using cocaine in 1996, after *hi™ how are you today?* had made me rich and famous and after the *Maclean's* scandal had made me a pariah in Canada. I wasn't depressed or anything when I tried cocaine, and

I wasn't all freaked out about the pressures of stardom and the media. Like pot and acid, I started doing cocaine as just something to pass the time between gigs — on "the days in between" as Blue Rodeo says.

In 1997, I was really getting into hip-hop music and culture and getting to know hip-hop artists and DJs, so I had been around crack in clubs and when I was touring. Also, I'd been buying dope for a long time by 1997, so I had been around crack dealers and met a lot of people who smoked it, but I'd still managed to stick mostly to my marijuana up to that point, with some powder cocaine and other goodies thrown in every now and then.

I can remember the day I smoked crack for the first time like it was yesterday. Once again, I was at a friend's house; I can't say who and I can't even say where it was in Canada, because that person may still like to smoke crack and I wouldn't want to cause any problems for them. I also don't blame anybody for introducing me to crack, because I believe I introduced myself to it. I was at this house with a few people, smoking pot as usual, when somebody pulled out a crack pipe and offered it to me — pretty much the same way I started smoking pot come to think of it. Never one to pass up an invitation, I took a drag off that pipe and that was pretty much me for the next two and a half years.

As soon as I took the pipe away from my lips and inhaled the smoke back into my brain, I blacked out and sort of crumpled to my knees. After a second or two, I lifted my head up and opened my eyes and I knew right away: I was fucked. There was no build up, no creeping high, just instant, complete annihilation.

Crack made me really intensely high, so high I didn't want to walk down the street or even get up off the couch. I immediately started talking a mile a minute to the people that were with me, telling them all about my various sexual experiences and anything else that came into my head. I felt instantly like I was so high I had no control whatsoever over what I said. I just started talking and talking and talking so fast I couldn't form the words properly and it all just ran together like verbal puke out of my mouth.

The other people in the room just looked at me like I'd suddenly grown another head on one shoulder, and the look on their faces made me stop. After a few seconds of really intense silence, I took a long, deep breath and said, "*Wheeeeeeeeeeew,* that's quite a buzz."

I absolutely loved the buzz I got off crack. I loved it so much at one point, I literally had to have it every day — that's what's so fuckin' dangerous about crack. It's like a little kid with Smarties: they love the taste so much, they'd just keep eating them and eating them until they threw up if they could, then they'd start again. The only way you can stop is after you've had so much of it that no amount satisfies you anymore, all it does is make you sick.

I was like that with crack. I didn't stop enjoying crack until I had got really screwed up physically in my lungs, and lost all my money, and almost lost my career and all my friends and family. It took all that shit happening to get me off it; I had to get almost to the very bottom before smoking crack was no longer enjoyable to me.

Until I reached that point though, crack was like this wonderful thing that brought nothing but happiness into my life. For a good couple of years there, I was convinced that when I smoked crack I was doing myself some kind of favour. Whenever the real world started crowding in on me — when my record company was on me for more product, when the press was on me about my personal life, when the government was after me for taxes — I just checked in with my old buddy Rock and everything went away.

At least, I thought I was escaping the real world, but of course all I was doing was making my real problems 10 times worse.

It started out with me just wanting to smoke some cocaine to have fun or kill time in my hotel room. But it quickly escalated to the point where I wanted to have that escape every day, then to the point where I *needed* that escape every day. Eventually, I needed it so bad, it was the first thing I thought about when I woke up in the morning.

The trouble was, the more I smoked, the more I needed to get as far away from my problems as I wanted to get. Crack gets so far inside you, you start to have conversations with yourself about it: "If I can just get more, I can get higher. Then if I smoke even more, I'll get even higher." It's like you're in a running race, and no matter how fast you run the finish line just keeps jumping back and back and back whenever you get close to it.

To my credit, I always tried to keep my crack and my music separate. I don't think I ever smoked crack right before playing a gig, although I might have when I was at my worst. Usually I waited until after a show, or until the next day, when I could just sit in my hotel room and get as fucked up as I wanted and didn't have to deal with anybody — not my manager, not the press, not the record company, not the fans, not even my family.

Unlike acid, and pot to some extent, crack doesn't "open your mind" and enhance your creativity; if anything, crack just deadens your brain completely, to the point where your mind really does go completely blank. I know people use that expression all the time, but until you've smoked crack, you don't really know what it means. When you smoke a joint or even drink too much beer, you can't think straight, but when you smoke crack, you are literally so stoned you can't think at all. And that state of mind isn't conducive to making music, obviously.

Although crack didn't do anything to make me a better musician, my love for crack and the whole crack culture did inspire me to start experimenting with hip-hop and rap. In 1998 I got together with some hip-hop artists and put together some hybrid tunes that incorporated my fiddle, and we toured a bit. I even added a hip-hop DJ to my regular band — which included a drummer, a keyboard player, a piper, a guitar player and a backup singer — and changed the name from the Kitchen Devils, in honour of the tune "Devil in the Kitchen" that was on *hi™ how are you today?* to the Nyanza Monster Bingo Players.

We were doing real good things, I thought, merging traditional Scottish tunes with R&B rhythms and hip-hop beats. But that caused a real rift with a lot of the fans who had been with me since the beginning and knew me as a traditional fiddle player and then continued to follow me when I went sort of "Celtic contemporary." It was about that time that people started walking out of shows because I guess they weren't hearing what they came to hear from me.

It was also about that time that my onstage behaviour started to go from energetic and in-your-face to downright rude. In one crazy five-day stretch in the summer of '98, I got in a fight with my road manager on the Thursday; split with my manager of five years on Friday; had several hundred people walk out of a show in Port Hawkesbury on Saturday because I told the crowd to "stick it up yer ass"; then didn't get paid for playing the Festival of Lights in Charlottetown on Monday because the promoter said I used profanity. The crack might've had something to do with all that, ya think?

When some reporter told me later how mad people were about the things I said at the Port Hawkesbury show, I showed no remorse at all.

"Excellent," I said. "Was it because I told 'em to fuck off? That's part of my show now."

And of course, they printed that in the paper and people got even more pissed off at me.

Then when another reporter told me the promoter from the Charlottetown show didn't want to pay me because I was rude at a "family show," I shot back, "It wasn't meant to be a family show; it was an Ashley MacIsaac show."

That about summed it up I guess. Before crack came into my life, an Ashley MacIsaac show meant fun and energy and emotion and skilful musicianship. After crack became a part of it though, an Ashley MacIsaac show meant all those things, plus vulgarity and sex and lewd gestures and anything else that came into my head, as far as I was concerned. So crack added another layer to an already intense experience, and a lot of people didn't think it was such a good layer. As long as I had my rock though, I didn't care; if they didn't like it, they could all fuck off — and a lot of people did just that.

It took me another year and a half of crack use, and a hell of a lot more bullshit, before I began to realize the circle of people around me and the number of fans who were sticking with me were getting smaller and smaller by the day. It was only then that I realized that crack wasn't something I was doing for fun anymore, it had become a need that was slowly but surely taking over my life.

It had started out as something I'd do maybe once a week at a party or after a big show. Then the one-off sessions turned into two-day affairs, and then that progressed to two or three days in a row in a given week, but that was about the worst I got. The next step, of course, would've been lying in a crack house smoking every day and only leaving to get money to buy more crack. I never got to that point. Luckily, I managed to pull out of my nosedive in time.

Looking back now, I'm amazed at how easy it was for me to become really addicted to crack specifically, instead of some other drug, because I tried 'em all. I did cocaine before I ever did crack and I probably enjoyed it more. Plus, although cocaine is a terrible addiction, it's a way less violent and dirty addiction than crack. On the other hand, cocaine is a hell of a lot more expensive than crack; that's why it was such a status symbol to do coke in the '80s. You want your coke pure, and you're willing to pay top dollar to get the best, purest cocaine.

When you're addicted to crack though, you don't care how shitty it is sometimes. You can go out on the streets of any city in the world probably — I've done it in most cities in North America — and buy a rock for as little as $10. If you're really desperate, you might get a rock the size of the head of a match for $2.

In fact, one of the reasons it took me so long to kick both my coke and crack habits, I think, was the fact that I had the money at that time to make being an addict fun. Most coke and crack addicts who don't have any money spend most of their time living in shitty places trying to scrape together just enough for a hit. In my case, I could, and did, jump on a plane and fly to Amsterdam for the weekend and find a quarter-ounce of coke and just sit in my hotel room looking out the window and getting high. One time I flew to Italy to get high and ended up having sex with some guy I picked up in Vatican City (he was really impressed that I'd met the Pope). Another time I went to Sao Paulo, Brazil. I did coke on the beach in Mexico.

In fact, I remember shooting the video for "Sleepy Maggie" in Mexico in 1996 and doing lots of cocaine. I remember I was staying in the "El Presidente" suite at this posh hotel in Mexico City. I was paying for the film crew to be there; I was paying for my management to be there; and I was paying for a bunch of friends to be there just to party. It was just amazing. And what more could I do, I figured, to make it even more of a party but to snort a bunch of cocaine. I remember sitting back on this huge waterbed, stoned as hell on cocaine, staring at myself in the mirror and thinking, "Boy, you sure got 'er good."

So I was in these exotic places, I was a recording star, I was snorting this very expensive narcotic; I felt just like some kind of Marlon Brando/Brian Wilson figure — a big, fat, rich, addicted pig. It was nothing for me to jump in a cab at the airport back then and say to the driver, "There's a couple of hundred dollars American here for ya if ya can find me some cocaine."

So cocaine was a whole scene for me. It was about money, and pleasure, and excess, and having no restrictions on what you could do at all. I always think of that scene in *Scarface* when Al Pacino is sitting in his mansion with his whole face buried in a huge bowl of cocaine; that's what I felt like when I was doing cocaine, oblivious to the truth.

Crack, on the other hand, was a different thing altogether. Crack wasn't about money, because it wasn't nearly as expensive as cocaine. And crack wasn't about pleasure either, because the pain of needing more and more of it cancelled out the brief pleasure I got from smoking it. Crack isn't a "partyin'" drug, like pot or cocaine, or even acid, can be; it's a "getting stoned" drug. Basically, crack was simply about needing to have it every day, just like food and water. Most people, unless they're obese and have an addiction to food, don't wake up every day absolutely out of their mind for want of a Big Mac and a milkshake. Eating and drinking is just something everybody has to do every day to stay alive. Well, that's how an addict eventually starts to think about crack. When you don't have any, you'll go around your place on your hands and knees picking up any little white thing stuck in the carpet in case it's a little piece of rock you might've dropped there the night before.

It wasn't exactly a secret that I was using cocaine and smoking crack, at least not among my friends and family and my manager and the various industry people around me. But like my sexuality, fans in general didn't know anything about it for sure until I came right out and said that I had a problem with it in late 1999. People might have suspected, just like lots of people suspected I was gay in 1995 and 1996 when I first became really famous, but everything's a rumour until the person confirms it themselves. Of course, I wasn't stupid about it either; I didn't go around asking everybody I met in the music industry if they could get me cocaine. I tried to keep it as private as possible, until I got over it that is.

And it wasn't like all these people around me who knew I was smoking crack and using cocaine didn't voice their concerns to me about it. My family were definitely on my case about it, but they were back in Cape Breton, so they couldn't do much over the phone.

The people who were working for me in one capacity or another tried to tell me I shouldn't be doing shit like that, but they couldn't be too intense about it, because I was paying their wages after all. My first manager, Sheri Jones, told me a thousand times in a thousand different ways: "Ashley, what are ya doin'? You'll kill yourself taking that stuff." "Ashley, that stuff is no good for you." "Ashley, don't throw your career away over that stuff." She even tried to get me to talk with people she knew in the music industry who had had bad cocaine habits back in the '80s and had got themselves out of it. I didn't listen though — I was young; I was rich; I was famous; I was invincible.

Eventually, of course, I found out I wasn't invincible. All addicts do, sooner or later, unless they end up dead first. My first taste of rock bottom came when I found myself sitting in my hotel room in Toronto at about 3:00 in the morning with no crack and no money at all — that I could get at — to buy it. I'd made five separate trips to buy crack that day alone, and all my ready cash was gone, and it was way too late to call my manager. At that specific moment I wasn't worried about selling records or making records or playing gigs; the only problem I had in the world was getting just enough money to buy another rock.

I started looking around the room for something I could sell or trade. My first thought was the TV, but the fuckin' thing was nailed down. Anyway, I thought, how the fuck would I get it down to the car? Then I spotted the clock radio; I could get $5 or $10 for that I figured. Then, as I was about to walk out, my eyes settled on my fiddle. Picking it up, I thought to myself, "You know what Ashley, the music business just hasn't worked out as well as you thought."

Twenty minutes later I was cruising the drug corners in my Olds with my fiddle and the clock radio lying in the passenger seat and just out of my mind for want of a fix. The crack dealers all knew me well by then; hell, they'd been seeing me for months and months, on and off, by then, and every day pretty much for about the last three weeks. I was the funny little "Scottish" guy in the nice Cutlass that was always looking for the cheapest crack, the $5 and $10 rocks. I spotted two guys I knew lurking in a doorway and pulled over.

"Hey, I want to trade this radio. What'll ya give me for it?" I called.

These two big black guys sauntered over to the car and leaned down to look in the window.

"No, no, man. I'm not interested in that," one of them said. "How about this car though; I'll give you $50 for this car."

Now I was desperate for some crack, but that little voice of reason inside me was still just strong enough to realize that $50 for a mint-condition classic muscle car was insane. "Come on guys, I can't do that," I said. "Come on, please, how about $10 worth for the radio?"

"No way man," the guy said, and the two of them started to move off down the street.

"Wait, how about $5 worth," I called after them as I moved the car along the curb beside them as they walked. They tried to ignore me, but the faster they walked, the faster I went, yelling out the window all the while. You could see they were starting to get a little pissed off with me now because I was drawing attention to them.

But the more they ignored me, the more desperate I got. Finally I chucked down the radio and held up my fiddle. "How about this fiddle," I yelled. "Give me $50 for this; you can sell it for a couple hundred. Come on guys, please."

I'd followed the dealers about 50 yards down the road by this time and they were just about ready to kill me. Suddenly they both turned and came quickly over to the car window. "Look man, you better get the fuck out of here," the biggest one said.

"OK, how about $25. Give me $25 worth for the fiddle. Come on, please," I said. I was really begging him now, and I was so frustrated that I was starting to cry.

At that point, this huge muscular black drug dealer sort of looked into my eyes and hesitated. Now this guy, I'm sure, had no idea who Ashley MacIsaac was, but he could probably tell that there was obviously something very fucked up about the situation. I mean, here was a young white guy driving around in a very nice car in the middle of the night trying to sell a very expensive instrument to get $25 worth of crack cocaine. He'd had enough of the whole thing then.

"Man, you're fucked. Get outta here now," he said, in a tone that meant I'd better do what he said. Then, as he walked away, he looked over his shoulder and added, "and don't come around here any fuckin' more."

After that, I went back to my hotel and just balled my eyes out. The saddest part of the whole thing was that I didn't cry because my career hadn't gone the way I'd expected, and it wasn't out of guilt because I'd tried to sell my fiddle. I cried because I couldn't get even 25 bucks for my fiddle to get some crack cocaine. Now that's rock bottom: when you're greatest asset isn't even worth the price of your next hit.

You'd think that night would've smartened me up, made me see the error of my ways and got me back on track. Well, It didn't. I cried myself to sleep that night, and as soon as I woke up, I was right on the phone to my manager to get some spending money so I could go right back out and buy some more crack cocaine.

I did feel different about though; where I used to be excited about buying crack and getting high, now I was more pissed off about it, like it wasn't as fun anymore. So while the experience of trying to sell my fiddle didn't get me off the cocaine, it did make me stop and think a bit about the place I'd come to in my life.

Obviously I hadn't decided to stop being an addict yet, but I knew I sure as hell didn't want to find myself without drugs and without money ever again. For no reason other than that, I decided I needed to wake the fuck up and get more control over my career. "You've been fucked around," I thought to myself. "OK, maybe you're fuckin' yourself up with the drugs right now, but you'll either decide to get off that or you won't. The rest of it though, the money, you left that to other people and now there's nothing left. Goddamn Ashley, wake up and do something about it."

Eventually I did manage to get off the crack. Most addicts only manage to get off really addictive drugs like cocaine by going into some residential rehab program or maybe by getting thrown in jail for a while. They need to get locked up in some place where they can't get at the drug until the craving for it dies down. In my case, my body just started rejecting the crack, and that made kicking it a lot easier.

First off, my lungs were full of crap all the time because I smoked a lot more when I was using, and it made me feel like I was always fighting the flu. That made me weird out onstage when I was playing my fiddle really hard because I just couldn't breathe. On top of that, mentally I felt like I was getting screwed up and I seemed to be crying all the time about everything. Any enjoyment that was ever in it was just gone.

The beginning of the end of my crack addition didn't come until a couple of days before my 26th birthday in February of 2001. I was living in a small apartment in Toronto. I had some money again, finally, because I had been playing some weird little gigs in clubs; it was a step back in my career, but considering everything that had gone on in the two years or so leading up to that point, I wasn't in any position to complain. I had bought some crack and I stayed up all night, just smoking and crying and thinking about how shitty everything had become.

"This is insane," I thought. "Here I am again, trying to dig myself out of a fuckin' hole. I've got a little bit of money now, so at least I'm paying the mortgage on my house for the moment, but I'm alone, as usual, smoking drugs. My friends and family are all mad at me. And it's my fuckin' birthday."

The next day I got what money I needed and I went to Pearson airport just to get the fuck away from it all. I didn't even know where I was going. I just got there and looked up at the board showing the flights going out and saw one for Mexico. That was it, I was going to Mexico. Of course, it wasn't a complete fluke I picked Mexico, because I had happy memories of shooting the video there in 1996 and I was pretty confident I could buy drugs fairly easily when I got there. I bought a ticket for cash and a couple of hours later I was on my way.

I still don't know what possessed me to get on that plane, except that I think I knew something weird would happen when I got to wherever I was going. The truth is, the last thing I intended to do in Mexico was quit dope. I just went there so I could get away from all the people who were on my case about the drugs and do my drugs and enjoy it. It was guilt, is what it was, good old Catholic guilt, which, of course, I know a good bit about. At the same time too, I was running away from the business, and the image, and the pressure, the whole fuckin' thing.

When I got off the plane in Mexico, it was about 110 degrees in the shade, or about an 80-degree change from Toronto. I had to take a bus through the mountains with a bunch of Mexicans for what seemed like five hours before I finally got to my hotel in Acapulco and I was just about ready to tear my eyes out for want of a joint. After I checked in, the first thing I did was ask — who else? — a cab driver where I could buy some pot, because once you find pot, it's easy to find anything else you may be after. He took me straight to a dealer, and before I knew it, I was back in my hotel room with a great big bag of pot and a bag of the purest pink Peruvian cocaine that I'd ever seen. The stuff had been shipped to Mexico, I'm sure, in a tank of gas, because you could smell it and it had that pink petroleum colour on it.

"Wonderful," I said to myself. "Things just got one heck of a lot better."

I did cocaine all that night. Then all the next day and night. I was whacked out of my mind in that little hotel room in Acapulco, just snorting, snorting, smoking, smoking, snorting, snorting, smoking .... Eventually, around dawn of the third day, when I was down to my last little roach of cocaine, the last little hit, for some reason I took that roach and threw it off my 16th floor balcony and watched it fall into the garden below.

I stood there on the balcony for a good 20 minutes staring down at the ground. I kept repeating to myself, "What the fuck are you doin'? What the fuck are you doin'?" It was obvious as hell that I couldn't go on like this. But even then, when you think you've reached the bottom of it, when you finally admit you're out of control and you have to find some way out of this mess one way or another, the addiction keeps fighting and fighting to get more drugs.

Some people pick the suicide route when they reach that point. Me? I went right out and got in the elevator and went down the 16 floors and out to the front of the hotel and started to grope around in the garden looking for that roach of cocaine — in my boxers, in 75 degrees of heat, in Acapulco, with the sun just coming up over the mountains. Now that's jonesin'.

Jesus, when I think about it now, I don't know how I didn't die on that trip to Mexico. Aside from the sheer amount of cocaine I did, I also left the hotel a couple of times over the course of the few days I was there to buy more drugs. I went out sometimes in the middle of the night and just wandered the strip in Acapulco looking for drugs, stoned as hell and looking like a fool; it's a wonder nobody knifed me and took all my money. You have to be nice to the tourists though; Cape Bretoners know all about that.

I don't know how much cocaine I snorted — four, five, six, seven, eight grams of hard, hard cocaine. I was high, sure, but then I would come down just as fast because when you jones like that you can't do enough to stay as high as you want to stay. I'm sure if I had had a pound of cocaine, I would have snorted it all. But that kind of jonesing was nothing new for me. Those 10-, 11-, 12-hour binges were the same thing I was doing in my apartment in Toronto, and had been doing for months and months.

Looking back on it now, it's easy to see how I got sucked into the whole scene. As my career picked up steam and the money got excessive, my cocaine use got more excessive. Unfortunately, I just wasn't making enough money to support this huge career and pay all these people that were around me and have this daily cocaine habit. I mean, I'm a Cape Breton fiddler for fuck's sake, not P. Diddy. It wasn't like I was selling 500,000 records every year and selling out 15,000-seat auditoriums. For the first couple of years after *hi™ how are you today?*, I was excessive because I could afford to be. I thought there was no way a couple thousand dollars a year on cocaine was going to screw me up. But by the time 1999 rolled around, of course, the money just wasn't there for it, and that ultimately took the fun out of it.

Finally, and as always, it was the lack of money that tripped me up. That's when I finally stopped. I didn't go out to look for more cocaine in Mexico because I had no money to buy any more cocaine. And, by that point, I really didn't want any more. I guess there's a point you reach when no amount of the stuff will get you high. Either that or you O.D. For me, that was Mexico. I went home to Toronto and never did cocaine again; quit, cold turkey.

A lot of people don't believe it when I tell them I kicked crack cocaine cold turkey, especially people who've been addicted to some substance themselves. People who've been through programs like Alcoholics Anonymous or Betty Ford or whatever just don't believe that it's possible to get off any addiction without a lot of help and support. And even if I did get off cocaine like I say I did, they don't believe I'll stay off it unless I get some help.

Well, nobody has to believe me, but only I know what I've done and what I'm doing, and I'm the only one who's going to keep me off cocaine or anything else I decide to do. Lots of people have tried to get me in programs over the years, but I've never been to one once, not even for a day or two to give it a try.

What I have been in is detox, a couple of times, but that's not exactly the same thing and anybody who's had the pleasure will know what I'm talking about. Detox is really just a kind of lock-up you get tossed into when the cops or your doctor or somebody who really "cares" about you decides you're so fucked up you might hurt yourself or somebody else. All they want to do in detox is dry you out if you're drunk or let you come down if you're high, then it's right back out on the street. They don't bother sitting in a circle with a bunch of other addicts talking about why you got so drunk or high in the first place.

I've never been in an anti-addiction program and I never would go in one, and I've turned on more than a few people who've suggested it to me over the years. Come to think of it, one of the first things Loggerhead Records did when they were trying to sign me to a record deal in 1999 was ask me to go into a program. As soon as I heard that I just said, "Thanks for your interest. Bye," and walked out of the meeting.

After that I went right out and started talking to another label, even though they didn't interest me as much as Loggerhead at the time. But I didn't care. I'd had enough of managers and record company people telling me how to live by that point. It worked out good in the end though: Loggerhead called me back a few days later and offered me more money and said they didn't care if I went in a program or not as long as I kept my drug use "under control."

Their big problem, apparently, was that the people behind the company were big Catholics and didn't want the company associated with drugs. Well, a fuckin' blind man could've seen that that relationship wasn't gonna work out, but of course I was in no position to walk away at the time. It was either sign with a company that already didn't like the way I lived or decide not to pay my tax bill that year. I guess I could've got a job a McDonalds or some place, but they probably would've had a problem with the drugs too.

At the time, all the fuss over my drug use was just a lot of bullshit as far as I was concerned. I mean, so what if I smoked a little pot and liked to do cocaine now and again; at least I wasn't a threat to other people. Christ almighty, I thought, what about guys like Suge Knight, and Tupac Shakur and Biggie Smalls and all these rap artists in the States making tons of money for record labels and running around shooting one another. Down there, record companies don't seem to be worried about being associated with violence. Look at Snoop Dogg — his record company doesn't care how violent his image is, or how disrespectful he is toward women, because all it does is sell more CDs. Shit, I saw him on TV a little while ago hosting the "Pimp of the Year" convention. And they say *I'm* a bad guy?

Not in Canada though. In Canada nobody does drugs, so a record company can't be associated with an artist who does drugs — at least not openly. Actually, all those record executives and promoters and managers and agents should thank their lucky stars that it was me they were dealing with for all those years while I was touring endlessly in my drug haze. Lord knows how many times it crossed my mind to kill one of them during that time. But I didn't. If one of those rap artists had to deal with the same shit I was dealing with all those years, they would've shot somebody for sure. Imagine some manager telling Snoop Dogg he couldn't have any money to buy dope after a show.

Maybe I did snap a couple of times, but considering all the touring I did and all the dates I played from the age of 17 until now, and all the financial pressure I was under, it's a wonder I didn't snap more often. I can't say why I didn't, but I think pot had something to do with it.

See, I'm not a nasty stone. Some people turn into violent jerks when they're drinking or using, but I'm the opposite. If anything, pot has a kind of blunting effect on me (pardon the pun). When all my problems get too much for me, I like to be numbed, and marijuana is a great number. Most people know how that feels, when they want to escape their problems in some kind of drug-induced or booze-induced haze. For other people it's sex or gambling, anything to get your shit out of your mind. Pink Floyd even wrote a song about it: "Comfortably Numb." That's how pot makes me feel.

As for cocaine, that usually gets people wound up to the point where they just have to go, go, go. But I was kind of a weird cocaine addict, because I could go to sleep on it. Either I would do it for days and get totally wound up on it and just want more and more or I would do one line and go in the corner and fall asleep.

There were only a few days during those four or five years when I was touring really hard that I didn't have any pot or cocaine. Well, at times like that, you didn't want to be around me on the second day, that's for sure. By the second day I was coming down, and that's a bad thing. Aside from being grumpy as hell because I have no dope, the worst thing about me coming down is that I can't shut my mouth. And it's when I can't shut my mouth that I get in trouble.

I can't blame anybody for the fact that I became addicted to crack cocaine. I had my own fucked-up reasons for starting to smoke it in the first place, be it the pressures of fame and the music business or Catholic self-loathing over my sexuality or the media or whatever, but nobody ever came up to me and said, "Here Ashley, you've got to smoke this rock of crack now."

So now that I'm off it, it's not like I can pick out one or two people to blame for all the problems crack created for me and spend the rest of my life hating them for it. But that doesn't mean I'm not full of anger and hatred and just horrible violent resentment about what I went through.

* * *

I don't think that I've ever pushed my pot use in anybody's face. I might not live the way people think I should. I've obviously screwed up a few live gigs and cancelled some others, and people who don't like me like to put that down to drugs. But I think it really bothers people that I've successfully done hundreds of live shows while I was high. And the shows went well and everybody had a good time and nobody cared.

When I performed on the Juno Awards and the elite of the Canadian music industry applauded me for being so spectacular … I was high.

When I played on *Morningside* for my old pal Peter Gzowski and everybody said, "Oh what a polite young boy, and isn't his kilt cute," … I was high.

When I played for the Queen of England, and the Queen came up and shook my hand and said, "Oh, what a wonderful performance," … I was high.

It's clear to me, even if my many critics don't like to hear it, that marijuana has, at times, had a positive effect on my career.

I got over my crack addiction, and I don't use cocaine anymore either, not even once in a while for fun. But even though I'm happy to be off that shit and proud as hell of myself for having the strength to kick it, I would never set myself up now as some kind of "born again" anti-drug crusader. I'm still a committed pot smoker for one thing, which kind of hurts the credibility.

At the same time though, I don't deny that marijuana probably served as a gateway drug for me to become addicted to harder drugs like cocaine. And, unlike with marijuana, I don't suggest for a minute that my experiences with cocaine have been anything but negative. Being addicted is a horrible thing; it's awful, there's no other way to describe it. The fact that I had good experiences with pot gave me the incentive to say "OK, I'll try something harder." But, of course, I didn't know that once you go down that road, it's hard to turn around and go back.

But now I am back, back to the point I was at when pot was the only drug I was interested in, and it's wonderful. Wonderful, for me, that is. I don't advise smoking pot to anyone who doesn't think they can get a positive experience out of it. I was a person who didn't think I needed it, but after the first time I smoked it, I knew it was something that could add something to my music and my life.

Anyway, Lord knows I'm not the only performer who thinks that about pot. I won't name names, although I could easily, but I would say a majority, if not a vast majority, of people working in the music industry are frequent marijuana users — and that includes some of the most respected artists around. For instance, I don't believe for a minute that a guy like Paul McCartney, who was a leader of the "drug" generation in the '60s and got busted for possession later on, doesn't still spark up the odd joint when he's relaxing at home — and he's over 60. But pot is just not a big deal for most artists and musicians. It's as common in that world as alcohol.

There are all kinds of drugs out there and they can give you all kinds of different experiences, as I can attest. And it's not hard to find one experience that you like so much you want to do it again and again, regardless of what gives you that experience, be it pot, hash, cocaine, crack, speed, acid, bennies, mushrooms, ecstasy, mescaline or whatever. You could put sex and gambling in there too if you wanted, and there are probably more than a few bored housewives out there who swear by a couple of Tylenol 3's and a few shots of Jack Daniels. So I'm not gonna stand on a soap box and try to tell people who know better that taking drugs is never, ever, ever a fun experience. If it wasn't fun, at the beginning at least, nobody would ever become an addict.

I liked the experience I got from crack cocaine so much that I became addicted to it. It was a lot of fun at the beginning, then it got scary as hell near the end. That's as much preaching on the subject of drug use as I'm willing to do. I think if people find their drug of choice, and for the vast majority of people that drug is alcohol, and they can enjoy that drug for pleasure only, without having it take over their lives, then who's to say that's a bad thing. As long as you don't give in to the drug, and as long as no one else gets hurt by it, I think anything is OK.

My message, I guess, if I have one at all, to people thinking about trying drugs of any kind would be: proceed if you really want to, but proceed with extreme caution. Because if you're going to be what I would call a "sensible" drug user, the kind that knows how to experience the fun that can come with drug use without letting the drugs harm you or anybody else, you have to be cautious all the time. That's the biggest lesson I've learned. You've got to remember too that the whole world of drugs does have a very seedy side to it, even if you just smoke marijuana. It's all illegal in North America, for starters, so the people that are involved in the "business" of manufacturing and selling drugs are criminals, and I don't care if you're buying your dope off of your next-door neighbour.

For me, being a "cautious, sensible" drug user means even more than that. It means never trying to kid myself into thinking that I could ever use cocaine again in any form, even once. Because if I did, it would be just like an alcoholic taking that first drink again after being on the wagon for years. I mean, I've quit smoking tobacco five or six times in the last couple of years. I can go maybe two or three months without a cigarette and then I'll have one at a club or at a party and I'm back smoking again until the next time I've got the strength to quit. I couldn't take that risk with a real hard drug though.

Anyway, if you want to talk about gateway drugs, how about alcohol? Show me any teenager smoking pot today and I'll bet you a million dollars that kid started out drinking beer or liquor at parties. That's one thing that amazes people about me, that I can have such an addictive personality when it comes to some things but never had any interest in booze.

Liquor, of course, is the drug of choice where I come from. We had liquor in the house, but it was mostly for visitors. My dad would maybe have one drink a year, at Christmas, and my mom would have one every two years. So, I'm sorry to inform the head-shrinkers, I didn't have any negative role models for substance abuse in my house growing up — and I know how hard that must be for some of you to believe.

I think the biggest factor in my becoming a "tea-totaller" was that I was around alcohol so much as a young teenager, much more so than regular kids. When I was just 13, I started to play a lot of bars and clubs. Obviously, I wasn't old enough to drink legally, and I was always there with my dad, but I could see first hand the effect drink could have on an individual. I think I've seen more fights brought on by too much drink than I've ever seen brought on by smoking pot. And I'm sure more than a few people have staggered out of my shows over the years and jumped in their cars to drive home.

Now, I'm not against alcohol by any means; I have alcohol in my house for friends to have a drink if they want one when they come over. But as an addictive substance, alcohol has always struck me as being particularly nasty, just like hard drugs. Pot makes you hungry, and too much food will make you fat, and cigarettes can give you cancer, but alcohol and hard drugs, they cause as many problems for the people around you as they do for you.

I've been hearing for years from all kinds of different people, my family and friends and others, that pot is just a crutch, that I don't need pot to get along in life or to be successful. That's absolutely true. I know pot is a crutch for me. Maybe I don't need it, but maybe I like to have a crutch.

Besides, I believe everyone has lots of crutches in their lives, and a crutch doesn't necessarily need to be drugs or alcohol. A psychological crutch can be anything that a person leans on for comfort and support during the bad times in their lives, and when that turns out to be drugs or alcohol, it can obviously be a very bad thing. But a crutch can also just be something that is a constant source of positive feelings, something that helps you to block out negative thoughts and feel good about yourself. For me, pot does that, but I guess a dog could do the same thing too.

If you look at it that way, my fiddle is a crutch for me just as much as pot is. My fiddle is the one thing that I've kept beside me since the age of nine. It gives me pleasure just through the pure joy of playing it, plus it makes it possible for me to earn the money I need to keep a roof over my head and to purchase my other crutches. Could I get along without my fiddle? Well, I don't suppose I'd keel over dead if I couldn't play anymore, but I'm in no hurry to find out what life would be like without my fiddle. So no, I don't believe that I'm so insane that my very existence depends on a hunk of wood with strings across it. But, like a one-legged man and his crutch, that hunk of wood sure makes life easier for me.

Actually, ever since drugs came into my life my fiddle has been less of a crutch for me. Now instead of picking up my fiddle every day, the way I once did, to get that shot of pleasure and to push negative thoughts out of my head, I can smoke a joint. In fact, smoking a joint often gives me the boost I sometimes need now to play my fiddle.

On any given day, if someone sticks a fiddle in my face and says "Play it," I just don't want to do it. I will if I'm forced to, like when I had to play some really terrible gigs in order to get some money in my pocket, but there's no pleasure in it for me. When you're playing night after night, it's like too much of anything — you get sick of it. So, in my case, a joint makes it easier for me to get in the frame of mind I need to be in to perform — one crutch leaning on the other.

It can get the better of you, of course, and I ran into that problem a few times. If you become too psychologically dependent on your little booster — or if you fall into the trap of using really hard, really addictive drugs — you can convince yourself that you literally can't perform without it. That's crap, obviously, but it's not crap to you when you're in it. You panic, and say to yourself, "OK, if I don't get some pot, I'm not showing up." That's happened to me about five times out of the maybe 2,000 times I've performed since I started smoking pot. Not too bad. At least I did perform 99 percent of the time, even when I was hooked on hard drugs. Some addict-artists get to the point where they're so messed up they can't perform at all, drugs or no drugs.

I'm not addicted to marijuana the way I was addicted to cocaine though, because marijuana just isn't that kind of thing. But that doesn't mean I would want to stop smoking any time soon. In fact, I can't imagine not smoking pot now, just like I can't imagine not playing music. That's playing music for pleasure, as opposed to being a professional artist. I can imagine what life would be like if I wasn't a professional artist: I could just sit at home and smoke my pot and play my fiddle for fun just for myself and for anybody who wanted to hear me. I don't think I could ever not play for people; I've been doing it for too long.

Actually, pot's become so much a part of my routine now that I build time to smoke into my schedule. I'm always aware of how much pot I have at any given time and how much I'm going to need over the course of the next few days, depending on what I'm doing. If I have to travel, I have to take into consideration where I'm going and whether or not I can bring my dope with me. If I can't, I have to make arrangements to make sure I can get some dope easily when I get to where I'm going if I'm going to be there for any length of time, say more than a day. If I can't bring pot to the place I'm suppose to go, or I can't buy any when I get there, well then I guess I'm not goin'.

Pot has also become a part of my "performance day" ritual. That's especially true when I'm in a situation where I don't have any choice in the matter — when I must do the show whether I want to or not because I need to pay my bills. It's also especially true when I'm playing a gig where I know I'm not getting enough money to make it worth my while. In these cases, I still play the show, but I must be high. If I don't have dope and it comes time for me to go onstage, there's a very real possibility people are going to be pissed off that I did go onstage. I'll go out and I'll do the show, but people are going to see I'm struggling.

That almost happened to me about two years ago in Nelson, British Columbia. I miscalculated my supply, so I had to call the promoter from my hotel room a couple of hours before the show and ask him to get me some more pot. He told me he wasn't a dope dealer and he didn't know the first thing about buying dope, which made me wonder just how long he'd been working with musicians.

"Look," I told him, "get me some pot before I do this show. I've done this thousands of times; I'm used to this now."

"There's only a couple of hours to go before the show," he argued. "Where the fuck am I supposed to get pot right this minute?"

I tried to keep my cool. "Look, it's not that big a deal; you can do this for me," I said slowly and quietly. "We're in Nelson, B.C., the home of B.C. pot for fuck's sake, so don't tell me you don't know anybody with dope. Now I'm gonna be at the theatre about 15 minutes before the show, and unless you want me to walk onstage and ask someone in the audience if they can get me some pot, please do your best to get me even one joint."

"How about for after the show?" he asked.

"No, no, I'm sorry," I said. "I haven't had the greatest day in the world, and I would really like to smoke a joint before the show, so could you please find me one. I really don't think it's a lot to ask. I mean, there's all kinds of booze in this hotel room for me that I don't even want. Surely you can find me one lousy joint."

Well, I arrived at the theatre on time and there was a nice fat joint of B.C. home-grown waiting for me. It was a good thing too, because in the hours between when I called the promoter and when I got my joint, absolute chaos ensued. I put my foot through things. People threatened to stop working with me. People said they'd never speak to me again because of some of the things I said. The things that came out of my mouth were scary. I was violent and rude. And that was all because I wanted to smoke a joint and I couldn't.

So I got my joint, and I smoked it all myself. Then I went onstage and did a great show. I was right into it that night and all the negative shit from the few hours before the show was forgotten. I was happy; the audience went home happy; and the promoter was happy, although he was a bit freaked out by the whole experience. So pot saved the day for everyone.

Pot's pretty much standard procedure before a show for me, but it's not exactly my drug of choice when it comes to performing. When I'm doing a gig I'm really psyched about, and I'm in a really happy mood, I still love to drop some acid before the show. In fact, I'd say some of the best shows I've ever done in my career, the ones where the audience left really happy and just ready to dance in the street, I did on acid. I haven't done it too much in the last couple of years because it's just easier to smoke pot. But I hope to get an opportunity to perform in public again in the future when I do have some acid, because I believe I perform better on that drug than I do when I'm not on it. I usually put on a good show in any case; it's just that the acid adds a whole other dimension, for me and for the audience.

So pot is my drug of choice now, the only drug I use with any kind of regularity anymore. I'm not exactly a 24-hour-a-day, crazy, Cheech and Chong–type pothead, but I do smoke regularly. It keeps me sane and gives me a good enough high that I don't crave other kinds of drugs that are a lot more addictive, not to mention expensive.

Also, I've found it's quite possible to live on a restricted income and still enjoy smoking a joint or two every day. I don't care how poor somebody is, the last thing they're willing to give up is their case of beer, or their bottle of booze, or their smokes for the week. Pot's just the same for me. With cocaine it was different though; then I was trying to pay for my cocaine as well as the things that were supposed to go with it —

the lobster and the foie gras and the nice hotel rooms. Now I can just roll a joint and order some KFC and I'm happy as a clam.

Anyway, I'm just beginning to crawl my way back out of my bankruptcy now, so I have to budget for everything, including my pot. I know that I like to smoke a certain amount every week, and that costs X dollars, so I know I have to earn at least that much times 52 just to cover my dope for a year. Then my rent and my food and my clothes and basic living expenses are on top of that. If I wanted to drive a nice car, I'd have to make sure I earned enough extra money to do that. And any vacations or other luxuries I wanted would go on top of that again. But the pot money can't be touched for anything else.

So I guess you could say I'm a dedicated pot smoker. I like what pot does for me; it reverts me back to my true inner self. It gets me relaxed enough to feel comfortable with who I am at that given point. Whenever I need to I can do that, when I'm not feeling so good about my life or myself. Pot allows me to forget about my problems and just think about the essentials. When I'm stoned, I can say to myself, "OK, you're a fiddle player. Nobody can take that away from you but you, and that's all that matters."

Of course, I don't need pot to be able to do that. I managed to be comfortable enough with myself, in spite of my inner turmoil over my sexuality, for years before I discovered pot. So I'll admit pot's a crutch, but it's a crutch I enjoy. And if I can afford that crutch to make my life more enjoyable, why shouldn't I use it? Besides, it's not like everyone who smokes pot is a bad person. I mean, anyone can probably find a whole bunch of people they know and respect who smoke pot.

But, of course, that doesn't mean my saying that I smoke pot on a daily basis won't be scandalous. Everybody knows that Ashley MacIsaac smokes pot and has had drug problems, but they're so caught up in reading negative stories about me that they can't help but be shocked by whatever they read, even if it's not really that shocking. I know some people will read this and say, "Wow, I had no idea he smoked that much dope. He's such a crazy nut." But those very people probably know somebody who smokes just as much dope as me.

Goddamnit, in the music business, if you didn't trust people who smoke dope to be professionals and do a good job, you wouldn't have anyone left to work with. I have to trust my new manager to work hard for me and make good business decisions regarding my career, and he smokes pot all the time. A good friend of mine who is a great songwriter and who wrote a tune I included on *hi™ how are you today?* is a daily pot smoker. I can't remember the number of good musicians and producers I've been around who smoke dope; they were all nice enough people and I can honestly say I've never had a real problem with a pot smoker in the music business. Drinkers, yes. Potheads, no.

Usually though, I'm not on edge on the day of a show like I was that day in B.C., and I'm not a prima donna by nature, even when I have pot. The reason that doesn't happen more often is because I've usually got my dope thing under control. It was rare for me to show up for a gig without any dope on me, especially back in the days when things were really riding high. Of course back then I didn't even have to think about it because there was always somebody — my manager, the promoter, my agent, someone from the record company — making sure "Ashley had his dope."

In the last couple of years though, since I went bankrupt and had my record company problems, there have been quite a few times when I showed up in towns to do gigs and I had no money getting there. Even worse, I often knew I'd have no money leaving either because the money I was getting for the gig was already spent on bills back home. In those situations I always tried to make sure I had a little spliff tucked away somewhere beforehand, because I knew I wasn't gonna be able to buy any dope when I got to the show. If I didn't have a joint, I'd have a little piece of hash I could eat. And if I didn't have that, I'd usually take some ephedrine, but that was as a last resort.

I'm older and wiser now for sure, but I don't think I could condemn any young person for experiencing something new, even if it's potentially dangerous for them. I think it's enough for me just to be honest about the many unnecessary mind warps I experienced when I was using hard drugs. But some people might like those mind warps, so who am I to say what's good and what's not good? I think the key is recognizing when *wanting* the experience turns into *needing* the experience. As a person who was never shy about going out into the world and trying new things, I can't tell people not to go out and experience anything they want to experience. All I can do is let them know about the scary experiences I had when I was addicted.

Christ, come to think of it, I should be the fuckin' Canadian poster boy for the perils of addiction. Most of the negative shit that has happened to me in my career, although it was mostly of my own doing, was related to my addiction to cocaine. I don't know if people know that, by and large, or if people just think I'm a prick, but it doesn't matter now because what's done is done. I did some stupid things and said some stupid things because of cocaine, and I'm sure I'll continue to do and say things some people think are stupid now that I'm off it. The important thing is, I know I'm not under the spell of the drug anymore.

I don't smoke tobacco anywhere near as much as I once did. Now it's just every once in a while when the mood strikes me. My attitude now is, "Well, one butt isn't gonna kill me, so why not?" Of course, the problem is, one butt usually leads to another, and another.

In reality though, I might smoke one pack of cigarettes now in a whole month, instead of in a day. Holy God, I smoke a hell of lot more pot now than I do tobacco; with pot I might smoke as much as an ounce every four or five days. But considering the number of unsafe sexual experiences I've had, I'd say the few cigarettes I smoke are probably the least of my worries. And anyway, I figure if I was to get HIV and die, I'd regret like hell on my deathbed that I never had that smoke once in a while when I felt like it. Can you imagine that: lying on your deathbed and thinking, "Thank God I never smoked cigarettes!"

Now I know there are going to be people out there in the media and elsewhere in Canada who read this and say, "Oh there goes that crazy bastard Ashley MacIsaac again, shooting his mouth off about how much he loves smoking pot. He should be locked up." But I don't have any respect for anyone who would criticize me for being a pot smoker if they haven't tried pot themselves. They're the losers as far as I'm concerned, because all they're doing is missing out on the possibility that they might end up agreeing with me.

I'm not saying that people who've never experienced something have no right to have an opinion about it, but they should only speak for themselves. Another person can't tell me smoking marijuana is a bad thing for me to do; I don't stand outside bars and tell people coming out that drinking alcohol is bad for them just because I don't do that.

Even the Canadian government is starting to catch on to that way of thinking now. Apparently the government is going to bring in a new law that'll make it OK to have up to 30 grams of pot in your possession. You'll still get a ticket for having it, but they may not throw you in jail anymore. Makes sense to me. They finally figured out that it doesn't make sense to try and chase down everyone in the country who smokes a little bit of pot once they found out that about one-third of Canadians do it at least once in a while. And why the fuck not? Pot is no worse for you than cigarettes or booze, and legally you can ingest as much of that shit as you want.

I was actually hit with a possession charge one time, but I appealed it and I was granted an absolute discharge. The government better decriminalize pot fast though, or the police'll be coming for me again soon. I don't know what good it'll do though, throwing a stoned fiddle player in jail for possessing marijuana. I'm not hurting anyone. I'm not causing a disturbance. I'm just smoking a little weed in my apartment. I could see why the cops would want to arrest me if I was standing on the corner of Yonge and Dundas smoking a joint, basically laughing at their authority. I could see it too if I was driving down the street with a joint in my mouth. But you can keep an open case of beer in the trunk of your car, so why not a little bag of pot?

Besides, how many times has somebody stoned on pot crashed their car into a schoolbus full of kids? I'm not saying it's never happened, but there's a hell of a bigger problem with drunks on the road than there is with potheads. That's why it makes sense to change the laws so recreational pot smokers aren't punished 10 times worse than drinkers.

Anyway, I don't see any reason at all why Canada shouldn't have the same attitude toward marijuana that they have in sensible countries like Holland and Denmark. We never will though as long as we keep looking south for direction. The United States is the wealthiest and most powerful country in the world, but it has got its head so far up its ass when it comes to things like drugs and sex that I don't know if it'll ever get it out. I know the actor Woody Harrelson, from *Cheers* and *Natural Born Killers,* has got a movement going in the States now to try and promote hemp products and legalize pot smoking, and I wish him luck. But I don't believe Woody'll get very far, because the U.S. is just so far behind Europe and Canada in terms of legislating morality. At the rate they're going, by the time the U.S government legalizes pot we'll all be flying around in spaceships I'm sure.

The problem, of course, is the fact that there are too many god-damn "born again Christians" in the government in the States. They talk a lot about the separation of church and state, but the fact is religion has a huge hand in running the government down there. They'll probably never legalize pot, and they're always trying to stop women having legal abortions. I've struggled with that issue as well because of my Catholic upbringing, but you can't let religious leaders make your laws for you. Look what that did for Afghanistan, for Christ's sake. But the Americans still had the gall to go over there and kick the Taliban out because their laws were too "fundamentalist." The Americans can't seem to see how stupid they look sometimes though: they'll let a celebrity get away with murder, but they don't want anybody to smoke a joint and capital punishment is accepted.

Canadians have more sense, thank God. Canadians have come a long way in terms of having tolerance for pot smokers, and I hope we continue to move in that direction. Of course, people don't want to hear me say that, especially not publicly. But I'm gonna tell people the truth about it if they ask me; that's something I've always done, whether it was drugs or sex or music or politics or whatever. If you don't want to hear the truth, don't ask.

We've already legalized pot use in Canada for medical purposes. In fact, I think the biggest grower of marijuana in the country is the federal government. Well, I consider myself a "medical" user of marijuana in a way. Cancer patients use pot to reduce the pain and nausea of chemotherapy; other people use pot to battle clinical depression and epilepsy; I use pot to help my body and mind recover from the ravages of cocaine addiction and musical performances.

Also, as a person with an admittedly addictive personality, I think marijuana has a positive effect on my life because I believe it helps to keep me off harder drugs. I can't say for sure, but I believe I'm better off smoking pot than I would be if I didn't. You've heard the old saying: "An apple a day keeps the doctor away"; well, in my case it's "A joint a day keeps the psychiatrist away." Pot, for me, is a positive high, and it helps me to maintain a positive outlook on life. That, in turn, allows me to make positive, happy music.

Actually, the decriminalization of pot may ultimately end up keeping me in Canada. I've often thought that I might be happier if I just packed my bags and moved to Amsterdam. Now, don't get me wrong, I love Canada — it's my home and we Canadians have all kinds of freedom to think and say and do pretty much what we want. Unfortunately for me though, we don't have the freedom — yet — to do something that I want to do, which is smoke pot. I don't enjoy feeling like a criminal when I buy my pot, and technically I am, and I don't like the fact that I can't sit outside at a café in Toronto on a summer's day and smoke a joint. It's like if you're a pot smoker in Canada, you still have to stay in the closet, and Lord knows, I hate being in the closet.

Anyway, we have a great tradition of pot smoking in this country that we shouldn't ignore. Just think back to that image of John Lennon and Yoko Ono sitting in their hotel bed in Montreal, smoking pot and talking about peace. Lennon was sending out a totally positive message about the way people should treat one another, and he picked Canada as the place to send that message because he admired our tolerant society so much. So John Lennon smoked pot, but that doesn't stop people from respecting and admiring him for being a great artist and a great humanitarian.

I can understand why people still gasp today when they hear that some movie star or rock star is hooked on cocaine or heroin or some other hard drug. But pot? Aren't we over pot yet? Jesus Christ, the Canadian senate just discovered that one-third of the entire population of Canada has tried pot at one time or another, and a large proportion of that group uses pot regularly. That means chances are if the person reading this book has never tried pot in their life, they sure as shit know somebody who has. Does anybody really think all those dope-smoking hippies who went to Woodstock back in the '60s suddenly stopped smoking the minute they got their first steady job? Well, they didn't, and now they're your lawyer, and your bank manager, and your kid's science teacher, and your Member of Parliament.

So Ashley MacIsaac smokes marijuana — big fuckin' deal. He smoked it before concerts, and the people who went to the concerts were entertained and they enjoyed themselves and went home happy. He smoked it in the recording studio and he still managed to make records that people bought and enjoyed. So I think if people can have respect for John Lennon the pot-smoker, for what he did as a musician, they can have a little bit of respect for me.

To tell ya the truth, if the day ever comes when Canadians embrace me again as an artist the way they did when I first burst on the scene in a big way in 1996, it'll be a real significant step forward for the entire country. Back then, Canadians loved me because I was this new young, exciting, energetic, talented fiddle player from a quaint little town on Cape Breton Island. Well, I'm still all those things, except now I'm also gay, a former crack addict, I've been bankrupt, and I'm a proud pot smoker. If Canadians can love me now, boy I tell ya — that's a tolerant society.

~ 7 ~

Media

To be honest, I think the *Maclean's* scandal came down to the simple fact that people were pissed off because they felt they'd been taken in by me somehow.

I came out almost a year before that article came out in November '96, so it wasn't like people didn't know I was gay. But I hadn't talked about my sexuality publicly much for my parents' sake, so lots of people may have thought it was just a rumour or didn't know at all. It didn't seem to be an issue either, because my record was huge, my performances were all sold-out, and I was getting tons of positive press wherever I went. People were excited about me and about what I was doing with Celtic music. I was just the bright new star on the music horizon. And, best of all, I was Canadian, and I was from the Maritimes, and I was a nice, friendly kid, and Canadians loved me for that.

So, as long as the Canadian public and the Canadian press didn't know too much about me, I had this great love affair going with the whole country that lasted about a year and a half — until the fall of '96. That's when everyone learned the "horrible truth": Ashley MacIsaac *is* really gay; and he sleeps with teenaged boys; and he's into kinky sex. Well, holy shit. Right away the whole country collectively said, "I knew he was too good to be true; that little fairy thought he had us all fooled, but there was always something funny about that kid."

Maclean's, of course, was especially pissed off, because the success I enjoyed that year basically forced them to put me on their honour roll of Canadians for 1996. I don't believe they ever wanted to include me though, and the fact that I spoke so candidly to *The Advocate* gave them the opportunity they needed to wiggle out of it.

It was lucky for them really — can you imagine how mortified *Maclean's* would've been if they didn't know anything about the *Advocate* interview until after their honour roll issue came out? My God, would the readers of *Maclean's* have ever forgiven them if they had a guy who had kinky sex with minors on their list of "Canadians who made a difference"?

Did I deserve to be on that honour roll of Canadians in 1996? You bet your fuckin' ass I did. That's why the editors at *Maclean's* put me on in the first place, because I deserved it. That's not the question. The question is, did I deserve to get bounced from the list at the last minute? I think I should've earned enough respect for the things that I accomplished in 1996 as an artist and a Canadian that it shouldn't have been wiped away because of my sexuality. The problem was, I was too much of an "uppity fruit" to be featured in a publication that was going to sit in dentists' offices in Winnipeg and Edmonton and Ottawa, and Creignish, Nova Scotia, for that matter.

Of course I was pissed off that *Maclean's* dropped me from their honour roll. Why the fuck shouldn't I have been? I don't know how many artists from Cape Breton, or even the East Coast of Canada, have played Carnegie Hall, but by the time I was 21 years old in 1996, I'd played Carnegie Hall three or four times, and with some of the biggest names in the music business. Then to have *Maclean's* more or less say that the fact I was gay and had a younger boyfriend disgraced me in the eyes of the country, you're damn right I was pissed off.

And speaking of piss, it's not like it was my idea that they publish in their magazine that I indulged in urination during sex. Their writer asked me about it because I told *The Advocate* about it, but *The Advocate* is a magazine written "by" the gay community "for" the gay community. The readers of *The Advocate* didn't get upset about what I said to that magazine because they don't consider sex between two young guys, however kinky it may be, abnormal. But I didn't figure my musings about my sex life had anything to do with my music or the fact that I deserved to be on *Maclean's* honour roll. I certainly didn't think *Maclean's* would print it.

To this day I can't figure out why *Maclean's* reacted the way they did back in 1996 and why the rest of the media and a good part of the public reacted the way they did. I know it was only a few years ago that it all happened, but all I can think of is that it was Canada and it was the time that it was. Sometimes I think that the scandal got as big as it did because I was from the Maritimes, a very old, very religious, very traditional region of the country; that maybe if I had been from Toronto the reaction might have been different.

I'm not so sure it would have been different though. In Canada, in 1996, it probably wouldn't have mattered where I was from after *Maclean's* printed what they did in the way they did.

If you ask me, I couldn't have been any more polite and forthcoming than I was to the writer who interviewed me for *Maclean's* in 1996. But the bottom line is, I didn't offer any information that the writer hadn't asked for. If all I was asked about was my music and growing up on Cape Breton, that's all I would've talked about. But that's not the way it went; I was asked very pointed questions about my personal life outside of my music and outside of my heritage and I made the mistake of being very candid in my answers.

Obviously, when the editors back at *Maclean's* heard the tape, they decided that candid answers about my personal life would sell a hell of a lot more magazines than candid answers about my music or my heritage. Of course, they were right — I just didn't know that *Maclean's* had suddenly turned into Canada's answer to the *National Enquirer*. Either that, or they were trying to get me to say something provocative just so they could dump me from their honour roll.

You have to remember too, in November of 1996 I was still just getting used to being famous. *hi™ how are you today?* had only been out a little over a year and "Sleepy Maggie" was just hitting the charts in the U.S., so I was still on my rock star "honeymoon" where you're the hot new thing and everybody likes you 'cause you haven't done anything to piss anybody off yet. Unfortunately, that's also the time when people start to look for ways to knock you down a peg, especially the press. So, I went in to that *Maclean's* interview like a deer in the headlights. I was so high on the success of my record and everyone being so nice to me and telling me how great I was that I guess I figured it didn't matter what I said or did, people were still going to like me. Wrong.

Before the *Maclean's* article, I was considered exciting, energetic, revolutionary, maybe a little wild, but basically a positive musician playing positive music. After the scandal though, my image took on a whole new "seedy" tone that obscured all the positive stuff. I was hurt by that whole *Maclean's* affair, primarily because it ended up turning me into some kind of criminal in the eyes of a lot of people, and that just wasn't the case.

Maclean's can deny it all they want, but if I had been a heterosexual 21-year-old musician talking about my teenage girlfriend, no way would their reaction have been the same. And I doubt they would have kicked me off their honour roll just for being a 21-year-old musician who liked to smoke pot; God knows there aren't many of those.

I guess I thought being a recording star was going to be just a never-ending love-in for me, but I lost my innocence pretty quick after the "scandal." And since I had the "freak" label hung around my neck, I figured I might as well act the part, right?

After the *Maclean's* thing, the press in general took on a whole new look for me. They weren't my friends anymore, certainly, and they weren't my enemies either because they were just doing their job. From that point on though, I looked on the press strictly as the most wonderful, available source of free publicity I could ever hope to find. I no longer spoke to the press just to speak to them; I had to have a reason, and that reason had to have something to do with me selling more CDs or selling tickets to a show.

The truth went right out the window in interviews as well; the truth came back and bit me in the ass once, so I wasn't going to let it bite me in the ass a second time. I lied, I was tongue-in-cheek, I spoke in tongues — whatever I needed to do to achieve my goal of attracting attention to my music, that's what I did. If I came off crazy afterwards, well so what. That's what people expected from Ashley MacIsaac, right? Onstage and off. And that's the way it's been, pretty much, since 1996.

I don't know why, to this day, some people in the media choose to dwell on what I do or don't do when it comes to my sex life, but lots do. Actually, most of the information that has been circulated about my sex life has been based on off-the-cuff, joking remarks I've made to reporters, rather than sober, thoughtful personal comments. The problem is, lots of people tend to take whatever scrap they can get and run with it — end of story. Obviously, I have said things in the past, publicly, about my sexuality that people have taken and maybe blown out of proportion. Some things I said were ill-advised, I know, but often in the past I was in no condition to really think about the ramifications of what I was saying or of a joke I tried to make.

People ask me if I was just trying to jerk the writer's chain when I said all those things to *Maclean's* about my personal life. Well, I wasn't; I was being completely candid with my answers because I thought it would be OK to be candid. I know I have a reputation now for jerking interviewers around sometimes, but that's been since the *Maclean's* thing when there's been times when members of the media misquoted me or lied to me when they said they'd keep some of my comments off the record and didn't. I've been burned by the media pretty good a number of times, so what I consider unethical publications shouldn't be surprised when I'm less than straight with them now. Would I yank the chain of a publication that has run nothing but negative stories about me and kicked me when I was down? Yeah, I might yank a few chains in that case if I got the chance.

Other than when it comes to my sex life, I don't think the media has portrayed me unfairly. By and large, I think they've got it right. There's only been a few things that have happened in my career, like my supposed nervous breakdown in Cleveland and my fight with my road manager in Fort Erie for instance, where I felt the way I was portrayed was overly negative and nasty and, from my perspective, inaccurate.

Unfortunately, it's those unfair, inaccurate, negative portrayals that cause people to have a negative attitude towards me, whether they've listened to my music or not. Obviously the only way people in Canada or anywhere else in the world are going to get to know me is through the media. And if that media is always slanted toward the negative side, it gets harder and harder to overcome that.

On the other hand, people generally react positively to my music when they take the time to listen to it. But if I want to expose more and more people to my music, I know I'm going to have to break down that negative barrier that's been built up over the years. I won't hold my breath, though, waiting for the media to help me with that.

Still, I know I'm ultimately responsible for things that were published about me and it was really up to me to judge what I wanted to share with the media. That was true even with the *Maclean's* story. But there were then, and still are, some things that I don't like to talk about, believe it or not. I talked, obviously, in the press about being gay, but I never talked about how difficult it was for my family to accept that and some of the terrible times we went through because of the media's obsession with that aspect of my life.

But even when you look back on all the negative press I've received, or provoked, over the years, everything I've done has been pretty harmless when you think about it. What have I said? I enjoy playin' the fiddle. I enjoy bein' a pothead. I enjoy havin' sex. Well holy shit, what a maniac.

I think the fact that I'm older now will help to break down some of the negativity surrounding my image. If my big break in the music business had come when I was 25, instead of when I was a teenager, nobody would've given a shit about what I did in my spare time. I mean, gay people in the music business is hardly anything new: Elton John is gay; k.d. lang is gay, the Indigo Girls, Melissa Etheridge; Boy George was gay as hell way back in the '80s. And people smoking pot and doing dope in the music business is sure as hell nothing new. So why all the fuss about me?

The truth is, people have more trouble with the sex part of my image than with anything else, even the drugs. Face it: before I came along, when Canadians thought of East Coast fiddle players they thought of Don Messer, and it's tough to think of Don Messer having sex at all, let alone gay sex. (Sorry Don, that image even bothers me.) But the fact is, everybody has sex, of one kind or another, and as far as I know, most people enjoy it. Canadians just don't want you standing up and *saying* you enjoy it. Maybe if I had said I had had gay sex but I didn't like it people would have reacted differently.

On the other hand, I can't deny that having that whole sex aspect attached to my image has helped to sell CDs. Sex sells, whether it's a flash of breast in a movie, some girls in bikinis in a beer commercial, or a promiscuous fiddle player. So, after *Maclean's* turned me into a dangerous sexual "deviant," I had no choice but to allow my sex life, if not my personal relationships, to become fair game in the media. And I was pretty good at playing the part too. I know sex isn't dinner conversation for most people, but I have no problem talking about sex over dinner, because I'm sure I've had sex on the dinner table a few times.

But that's the joke of the whole thing: lots of people have probably had sex on the dinner table once or twice in their lives, or maybe it was the breakfast table, or a pool table. And if they never did, they probably imagined doing it. So all I did, really, was talk openly about things most people are too uptight to talk about: their sexual preferences and desires.

Unfortunately, not only were people pissed off that I was talking about my sexual preferences and desires, they were pissed off that I did it so easily. Unlike most people, it was always easy to see that I don't have a lot of hang-ups, and that makes lots of people insecure and mad. But the way I looked at it, I spent years getting past my sexual demons, and once I was over them, I wasn't goin' back for anybody.

Actually, the way the press and society reacted to my open sexuality said a lot more about them than it said about me. First of all, after the *Maclean's* scandal the press couldn't ask me enough questions about my sex life. But when I answered them honestly, they got all pissed off. It was like people wanted to know, but then they didn't.

I realized then that when people were saying to me, "Shut your mouth Ashley, the whole world doesn't want to know what you do in your bedroom," what they were also saying was, "Geez, I've got a lot of weird sexual skeletons in my closet too, but no way would I have the guts to come out and talk about them. I better shut this guy up before someone asks me what turns me on."

Also, on top of the fact that I was just comfortable with the subject of sex, I always felt that I had a kind of obligation to be open when I was talking about sex, and that's something that is difficult to understand unless you're part of the gay community. Gay people just tend to be more open about sex generally than straight people, but that's because they have to be. After all, gay people know they can get killed if they aren't comfortable being open about sex. It's like this: if you can't talk openly about sex in terms of preferences and desires, how the fuck are you going to talk openly about things like STDs and AIDS?

Believe it or not, this country and the world has changed a lot, even since 1996, when it comes to accepting the homosexual lifestyle.

Remember it was back around that time that Ellen DeGeneres got her show cancelled because the American public just refused to embrace a gay lead character in a TV show. Today, *Will and Grace* is one of the most popular shows on TV, and that show has a couple of gay lead characters. Christ, I can turn on my TV at 10:00 at night now and watch two men fucking on *Queer As Folk*. There wasn't anything on TV like that in 1996 that I remember.

Actually, as a member of the gay community, I should probably be happy that shows like *Queer As Folk* are shown now on regular TV during primetime, but sometimes I'm torn about it. Of course, I enjoy watching it on one level because it's a show that reflects my reality. On another level though, all it does is piss me off. I see two guys having sex on my TV screen and I think of all the heterosexual people sitting at home watching it who told me back in 1996 how fuckin' awful I was for doing exactly that. For Christ's sake, two of the main characters in *Queer As Folk* are a guy who looks a lot older than 21 who is having a relationship, and lots of gay sex, with a high school kid. Why isn't *Maclean's* and all the rest of the press in Canada up in arms about that?

The characters in that show are living the young, rich, gay lifestyle: they all have good jobs; they all have money; they drive nice cars; they live in nice condos; they like to go to clubs and dance; and they like to have sex. That's all I was doing, but they hung me out to dry for it in every possible way — *Maclean's* did; the media did; the recording industry did; people who worked with me who I trusted did. And why? Because I am gay, no other reason.

Still, things are getting better I guess. At the highest levels of debate in this country, in Parliament, straight politicians are arguing now over whether or not gays should be allowed to get married. Whether or not they approve it, just the fact that they're having the debate is a huge step forward. Because by having that debate, the government is already admitting that homosexuality is here, and it's real, and there's nothing anybody can do about it. So, now that everybody accepts the fact that we're here, all that's left to decide is whether or not homosexuals are going to get the same respect as everybody else. Canada was a long way from reaching that point in 1996, as my experience with *Maclean's* demonstrated I think. And even today, we still have a long way to go.

I'd like to think the whole *Maclean's* thing is so far behind me now that it doesn't have any impact on the way people see me today, but that wouldn't be realistic. For lots of people out there, that scandal branded me for life in their mind and I'll never overcome it.

If you don't believe most of the negative stigma I've had to deal with dates back to that event, consider this: In March 2002, five and a half years after the *Maclean's* scandal broke, *The Globe and Mail* ran a story in its Entertainment section called "The Fame Index: The Canadian Top 100." It was a sort of tongue-in-cheek assessment of where various Canadian celebrities, from Peter Mansbridge to Mario Lemieux, stood on the fame scale. The *Globe* rated me a "three-star" Canadian celebrity at that time ("You've hit the celebrity jackpot in this country and perhaps even beyond. Your picture appears in the paper, and people approach you in restaurants on your way to the can.") but decided I was on my way down.

In summing up my career to that point, the *Globe* wrote just one line: "There are no more bodily fluids for us to see." I wonder what they meant by that?

❋ ❋ ❋

Artists are in a unique position in that they have the power to bring important issues before millions of people, and I think they have a duty to do that.

Now, I never set myself up as a poster boy for the homosexual community, but my mere presence on the international stage, as a young, gay artist, proud of my sexuality and not ashamed to talk about it, meant people were forced to deal with the fact that people like me exist.

Unfortunately, lots of people, especially in Canada, like to pretend unashamed gay people don't exist, so my outspoken personality made me a lightning rod for criticism. Just look at k.d. lang: she's as homosexual as I am, but nobody shits on her in the Canadian media because she basically stays in L.A. and doesn't push her sexuality in anybody's face.

But pushing my sexuality in everybody's face was exactly what I did on network TV in the States not long after the *Maclean's* scandal broke. It was in February '97, and the uproar over the whole *Maclean's* thing was still going strong. *Maclean's* shit on me in December, and for the next couple of months I had had to deal with a steady diet of questions from the press about my "teenage" boyfriend and what I got up to in bed with him. For a time I thought they all forgot I played the fiddle. Anyway, by February, when I was booked to appear on *Late Night with Conan O'Brien,* I was just about fed up with running from the press and dodging sex questions. I was right pissed off, in fact, and I had the attitude, "OK, all you bastards want is sex, I'll give ya sex."

I actually warned the producers and the camera people before I went on about what could potentially happen.

"You know I like to step dance while I play, right?" I asked one of the producers before the show.

"Yeah, that's great," he said.

"And you know my kilt tends to fly up when I get going really good?" I asked.

"Yeaaaah...," he said, curious now.

"Well, you know what Scottish people wear under their kilts, right? If you shoot too low when I'm dancin', you might see something you don't wanna see. That's all I'm sayin'."

He shook his head as if he understood. "Whatever, Ashley. You just do your thing out there and it'll be great."

So that's what I did. I went out and gave a thigh-slappin' (in more ways than one), foot-stompin' Ashley MacIsaac Cape Breton fiddle performance. And I step danced, of course, and my kilt flew up, as it usually does, and millions of Americans in their living rooms in places like Kansas City and Spokane got three or four really good flashes of my private parts.

When I finished the song — "Sleepy Maggie" — the crew sort of stood around thinking, "Should we do it over again?" Conan stepped in though and basically said it was great as it was. They ended up running the segment with some digital blurring over my you-know-what.

The *Conan O'Brien* people could've shot me from the waist up, just like Ed Sullivan did with Elvis, but they didn't. They let it all hang out, knowing full well it was hanging all out. By the next day, my "performance" was all anybody was talking about in the U.S. entertainment media. They showed it again and again, with my private parts obscured of course, on the news and all the entertainment shows that week. *Rolling Stone* even ran a freeze-frame from the performance in their issue that week — without the digital imaging over my willy, mind you.

Now, people have accused me of exposing myself on national TV in the States just to get publicity, and that's true, but it was about more than just selling CDs. I went on *Conan O'Brien* and showed my nuts for a reason. Here I was, on national television in the United States, in front of an audience of millions of people, and I was gay, and I was Canadian, and I was proud of it, and goddamnit, everybody was gonna know about it that night. I had just got my face slapped in Canada for being gay and outspoken and flamboyant, but damned if I was gonna crawl back inside my closet and cut my hair nice and stand still on stage and be the nice little Canadian boy playing a nice little fiddle tune for all the nice Americans. Fuck that, I thought, that's not what I'm about as a performer or a person. If anything, I'm about bringing out the passion, and the fire, and the uninhibited pyromaniac inside every little boy.

That's what was thrilling about that performance. That was me saying, "This is what I am. Now deal with it." I was saying it on U.S. TV, but I was saying it to Canada, and to the world, and to the press, and especially to *Maclean's* magazine.

To tell you the truth, although Canada prides itself on how tolerant and liberal it is compared to the U.S., Americans often deal with free spirits a lot better than Canadians do. You only have to look as far as Ozzy Osbourne. Ozzy has hung his whole career on a negative image: he's "The Prince of Darkness." He's had all kinds of drug and alcohol problems. He has actually bit the heads off live birds and been accused of causing kids to commit suicide with his music. But there he is now with one of the top-rated shows in the U.S., and all he does is swear his ass off in it. Still, people fuckin' love the guy; he even got to visit the President.

A Canadian couldn't get away with that shit. Can you imagine a reality show on CBC about my life with a camera crew wandering around my condo and me smoking my pot and arguing with my partner and saying "fuck" every second word? Then I'd go to 24 Sussex Drive and shake hands with Jean Chretien and Aline ... It'd never happen, not in this country.

But I tell ya, if it did, it'd be just the kind of shake-up Canada needs to get the thumb out of its ass.

Face it: Canada needs a guy like me.

People accuse Canada of not having any culture, but that's not true. Canada does have culture; it's just too fuckin' polite to stand up and tell anybody about it. Think about it: when you think of music and the United States what comes to mind? Elvis Presley — good lookin', slick, larger-than-life, patriotic, but still messed up enough to be dangerous. If you think of Britain, it's the same thing for the Beatles. But what do you think of when you think of the ultimate Canadian musical icon? It's Anne Murray, and every Canadian knows that's true.

Now I'm not knocking Anne Murray, God forbid. She's from Nova Scotia just like me and she's one of the greatest performers this country ever produced and I love her. I don't even mind that she's what people tend to think of when they think of Canadian music. I just think that there's more to Canadians than just being pleasant, and polite, and not making any waves. There's another side to us that we rarely let out; it's loud and opinionated and brash and energetic, and maybe even a little vulgar and dangerous at times too. That's the side that Canadians like me represent. Me and Don Cherry anyway.

Every society — and every person in that society for that matter — has to have that certain something in it that allows it to say what it stands for and to stand up for its beliefs. If a society can't or won't stand up and be counted, it'll either be ignored or pushed aside. Canadians are often so goddamn polite that our society is always in danger of being ignored or pushed aside, usually by our loudmouth neighbours to the south. That's why Canada needs its own strong voices and flamboyant personalities, to stand up and let the world know we're here if nothing else. Christ, if we couldn't play hockey, would anybody know Canada even exists?

So yeah, I can be a loudmouthed, foulmouthed, opinionated bastard, but so what? You can walk down University Avenue in Toronto on any day of the week and see people from all over the world — Israel, Palestine, Serbia, Somalia, Cuba — marching in front of the U.S. consulate voicing their opinions about shit that's not even happening in Canada and really has nothing to do with this country. No one complains about those people, but watch them complain about loudmouthed, opinionated Canadian bastards like myself.

I am the genuine article. I got up in the morning when I was a little kid and I watched *Mr. Dressup*; then I watched the CBC news at six o'clock; and on Saturday night I watched *Hockey Night in Canada.* So, as a Canadian, I figure I should be able to talk openly about my sexuality or about smoking pot without having the sky fall down. I mean that's what Canada is all about isn't it — tolerance.

I could never understand why Canadians are so willing to put up with people from other parts of the world standing on the soapbox and saying "Look at me," but hate it so much when one of their own does it. Anyway, I would've thought that the standard of living we enjoy here in Canada would be enough to make those people from other countries stop complaining about all the shit that goes on in the crappy places they couldn't wait to get out of.

I admit I've expressed strong opinions in my career, often with language that lots of people find offensive, but I've always felt that my opinion was as valid as anyone else's, unlike a lot of Canadians. And I admit sometimes my comments and opinions sounded like they came from a dark and dangerous mind. But people have to remember that there's been times in my career, when I was tormented about my sexuality or when I had drug problems or money problems, when I was in a very dark and dangerous place and that's what came out. Like any artist, my actions often reflected my emotions. If they didn't, I'd just be another plastic pop star, like Britney Spears or Justin Timberlake. But I'm not a pop star am I? I'm a Cape Breton fiddle player.

The truth is though, at my core I stand for a lot of nice things, like music, and art, and culture, and heritage, and love, and tolerance. My whole life has been devoted to playing happy tunes that allow people to dance and get the party going and to feel closer to their community; if I've done that once, I've done it a thousand times. I think deep down inside, I'm really a peaceful, happy-go-lucky person. If I wasn't, I could never play the fiddle the way I do, because the fiddle is an emotional instrument. In the hands of the right person, a fiddle, or violin if you prefer, can relay the innermost feelings of the musician and the composer almost better than any other instrument.

Anyway, the press loved all those good, fun qualities that made me such a popular entertainer in the beginning, and they couldn't say enough nice things about me and my music at first. But those qualities were still there even after the press turned on me. They had to be, or people wouldn't have continued to come to my shows for all these years.

I may have a negative image in the media, but I can honestly say I've only probably given a handful of what I would call "negative" performances in my life. I mean, I'm not exactly Marilyn Manson. And even then, I bet I've never put on a performance in my life where not even one person walked out happy — OK, maybe one. So, God almighty, maybe five negative performances and maybe another five cancellations out of what? Two thousand shows?

I can also say honestly that any negative vibe that does hang around my image is only there in Canada. When I go to the States or to Europe and do shows, it's just all about being fun and flamboyant and high energy and unashamedly Canadian. And, judging by the reaction I get from international audiences, I don't believe the fact I can be an in-your-face, outspoken performer leaves people from other countries with a negative impression of Canada. If anything, it makes them more interested in our country.

I believe that's true even in Canada. No matter where I perform, from Nova Scotia to Ontario to the Prairies to Vancouver, and even up in the territories where I have been a couple of times, people always tell me that hearing my music always makes them feel more Canadian. That seems to hold true no matter what their descent too; they can be Jews or Muslims or Catholics; they can be black or white, Asian or First Nations. When you go to an Ashley MacIsaac show, you're a Cape Bretoner for the night and you're gonna see an exciting, memorable show.

I've shook hands with the Queen of England and had a little conversation with her, and I've sat and had a conversation with a homeless crack addict on the streets of Toronto, but I'm proud to say I always try to treat everyone I meet the same. What the hell, the Queen's just a person at the end of the day just like the crack addict, why shouldn't I be able to have a conversation with whoever I meet? The same thing goes for my music: I've been paid to play at a party by Frank Stronach, one of the richest men in Canada, and I've played for free for elementary school kids in Cape Breton, but I'm pretty sure I didn't play any different for the rich people than I did for the kids. That's one of the greatest things about music: music doesn't care who you are, anyone can listen and anyone who wants to take the time to learn can play.

Another thing I'm proud of is the fact I've never judged people in the same way some people have tended to judge me. I mean, I grew up in a small town with regular people with not a lot of money, but I never tried to hide from that fact when I had lots of money myself. I've always been a proud Cape Bretoner, in spite of the fact I was forced to leave Cape Breton for business and personal reasons as an adult. I'm a proud Nova Scotian, and a proud Maritimer, and a proud Canadian, and I've never been shy about saying so, whether it was onstage on Parliament Hill on Canada Day or on the *Conan O'Brien* show on U.S. network television. You'd think I'd get some credit from the Canadian media for that at least.

I'm living proof that lots of Canadians have still got a lot to learn about standing up and being proud of who they are. With all the smart and talented people we have in our relatively small population of 30 million, we shouldn't be ashamed to set an example for other countries around the world. Instead of looking for ways to drag down strong people who aren't afraid to stand out on the world stage and say what they think — like that woman from the government who called George Bush a "moron" for one — Canadians should get behind their strong voices and strong personalities and celebrate them.

My God, just look at the music industry; we have such a rich assortment of great Canadian artists, some of the best in the world at what they do. Celine Dion is probably the most popular singer in the world today. Christ, she goes on holiday for a couple of years, then comes back and her new album enters the charts at number one all over the world. And who produced her record? Just the best producer in the world, David Foster, another Canadian. Those two together can make a hit record just by snapping their fingers. Anyway, if Celine Dion isn't the most popular singer in the world, then Shania Twain is, and she's Canadian too.

The talent comes from right across the country, too. There's all kinds of great artists from the East Coast, of course, and I think I'm one of 'em. Celine Dion's from Quebec. Shania Twain and Blue Rodeo and the Tragically Hip and the Barenaked Ladies are all from Ontario. Some great bands have come out of the Prairies in the last few years, like the Waltons and Crash Test Dummies, and k.d. lang, of course is from Alberta. British Columbia has Bryan Adams and Sarah McLachlan and 54-40, among others. Then you think of all the comedians and actors and athletes we produce — for a small country, it's really amazing.

So Canadians have got the talent, obviously, to be front-and-centre on the world stage. What I don't see enough of though, from Canadians in the public eye, is passion and fearlessness. It's almost like we're embarrassed to be famous and talented and be the people we are. We're so frigging polite, and it's drilled into us our whole lives not to offend anyone, that we're afraid to speak our minds, on any subject. I mean, I sure as hell don't have any problem at all with Celine Dion collecting her $100 million for singing her songs, but for Christ's sake, while she's got the world's attention, at least say something interesting. Make a wave damn it!

We've got the big stars here in Canada, but what we don't have is a Bono, or an Elton John — a big star who's willing to lay their thoughts and emotions bare even if it harms their career. Bono steps up, because he knows he's famous and people will listen to him, and tells the World Bank and the United States that they're all bastards for the things they do to developing countries.

Elton John meanwhile, a guy who for the first 10 years of his career was basically forced to conceal his homosexuality so as not to offend anybody who might want to buy one of his records, is now the "poster boy" gay rock star, and proud of it. He uses his fame to go out and raise millions for AIDS research. Elton John has probably been involved in some pretty wild gay sex in his life I would think, and he was a coke addict just like me. But while I got tossed off an honour roll of Canadians, Elton John was knighted by the Queen. Only in Canada you say? Fuckin' right it's a pity.

So what did I learn from the whole sordid *Maclean's* affair? It's simple: if you want to get on the *Maclean's* honour roll as a musician, all you have to do is have a top10 single; have your debut CD go double platinum in Canada; be a huge sensation in the U.S. and Europe; have all kinds of American TV shows and magazines falling over themselves to have you be a guest or to take your picture; and be a great ambassador for Canada to boot. Oh, and if you're already on the list and you want to get off, just be a homosexual who actually has sex and then tell someone about it.

I also learned that celebrity isn't really worth much in Canada. If I had been born an American or born in some European country, an artist as colourful as me would be rich 10 times over. But after I sell platinum records in Canada, I have just enough money left over to keep on touring so I can make more records. And then, after my record company made nothing but profit off me selling 400,000 copies of one record and 50,000 each of two more, they decide they aren't happy with me because I "attract too much negative publicity." What the fuck do I have to do, you have to ask yourself.

Maclean's has called me many times over the years since the big "honour roll" flap to do articles about one thing or another, usually something negative. And given that whole fuckin' mess, not many people would blame me if I just told them to fuck off, but I didn't, and I won't.

I remember I sat down with a writer from *Maclean's* one time a couple of years after the "scandal." The interview took place at the opening of the Air Canada Centre in Toronto. Of course, it was a great big deal, and I was attending a gala reception that was taking place in the new arena. They invited me, I suppose, because they wanted as many recognizable faces in the crowd as they could get just to add to the excitement, like a Hollywood opening or something. All the pro athletes and the mayor and all the big-wigs from the business community in Toronto were there; it was really a major deal.

This writer from *Maclean's* picked me out and introduced himself and asked if we could chat for a few minutes. Not being one to hold a grudge (*Oh yeah?* says you), I said, "Hi, how are you. Oh, you're with *Maclean's*. Yeah, sure. That's great; I *love Maclean's*."

That should have been a warning to him, but we went and sat down at a table off to the side anyway. The first thing the guy told me was that it was his first interview for the magazine.

"Lucky you," I said, smiling.

I then proceeded to give the rudest, most uncommunicative interview I think I ever gave in my life. I made it an utter waste of time for the poor writer guy on his first day, but at least it was all downhill for him after that one.

Anyway, *Maclean's* didn't use any of it. They didn't even acknowledge I was there that night, although they mentioned most of the other celebrity guests. They haven't bothered me much since.

~ 8 ~

Sex

Obviously, the first inklings that anyone has of whether they're gay or straight would have to go back to the first time they had an inkling that they were a sexual being.

For me, unlike many gay people I know, my first sexual inkling was not what I would call a homosexual one. My first sexual experiences definitely weren't with men. In fact, my first sexual desires weren't necessarily for men either. Even today, I don't think that my sexual triggers revolve exclusively around young, gay men. For me, physical attractiveness comes in many forms: in the morning, I might admire a young guy with a nice body jogging along the road; in the afternoon, I might admire a woman with a beautiful body in a tight dress; then that night, I might admire a good-looking older man in an expensive business suit.

People ask me all the time, "Are you gay?" Well, first of all, I hate labels, because people like to use labels to hold people back. I don't think I've ever described myself as being strictly "gay"; I only really describe myself as being gay to gay people.

I've been asked quite a few times, "Are you gay or bi?" I say gay if the person asking the question is gay, because I assume, from experience, that that's what they're looking for me to say in the context of that conversation. Likewise, if I was having the same conversation with someone who I expected was looking for someone who was bisexual or heterosexual as a partner, I would tell them what they needed to hear at that time. The fact is there are lots of heterosexuals and homosexuals who just aren't interested in being with someone who is willing to be with either sex.

While I was very curious and open about sex and vulgarity as a kid, I got punished enough times for it that I began to go the other way by the time I reached my teens. In a complete turn-around from my "wild-child" days before high school, when I loved to talk about sex and use foul language to talk about it, as a teenager I became really kind of introverted sexually. I didn't like to talk about it or joke about it, which obviously made it pretty hard for me to fit in with other adolescent boys. As a result, I ended up doing the whole "guy who hangs out with the girls" thing that so many gay men can relate to.

So, by the time I started to think a lot about sex and what it meant for me, I had really become quite a shy guy. While other kids my age were busy trying to "do it," I had my hands full trying to decide if I wanted to "do it" at all, and who with.

But being an introverted teen didn't bother me much because my music tended to isolate me from other kids my age anyway. Being a dancer, I was athletic and coordinated, but I didn't get involved in sports at all after about age 12. I started playing the fiddle at nine, and by twelve I had got quite serious about it, so by the time I was in high school I was completely immersed in my musical career. I just didn't have time for "normal" teenage stuff you could say, sex included.

That's not to say I wasn't inquisitive about sex in my teen years, because I was eager to learn about everything then. I mean, other than my schoolwork, I didn't really learn about anything other than music from age nine on. In a severely repressed Catholic community like the one I grew up in, you can imagine it was tough to get information about young guys and girls and their teenage sex lives. All you knew was what you heard whispered in the schoolyard. It's wasn't like today, when all a curious kid has to do is type a word in to the computer to get connected to all kinds of information and other teenagers asking the same kinds of questions. Hell, we didn't know anything. Our teachers didn't talk about anything. It was all about searching for answers by yourself. The Internet would have been a godsend for a shy, confused kid like me, but I had to figure it out the hard way.

Of course, I've gotten over my shyness in many ways since my early teens — especially with respect to sex and my personal life. In fact, I don't consider myself even as shy as the average person anymore. In fact — and *Maclean's* magazine will say "aye" to this — I could probably stand to be a little shyer today; it would have saved me a lot of trouble.

I'm pretty sure that by the time I was maybe 12, I'd already figured out that I wasn't exactly the same as all the other boys. Back then, of course, I really didn't have any idea what it meant to be "gay." For that matter, I didn't have any idea what it meant to be straight either; sex was this weird, dirty thing that adults did that us kids couldn't really figure out, except that we knew it involved taking your clothes off. One thing us Catholic kids did know about sex though, was that it was something a man and a woman did.

I know that there were a handful of gay people in my area when I was growing up, but they kept a really low profile. They kept such a low profile, in fact, that it took me years to figure out they were there at all. I know the gay community hates it when people try to stereotype gays as looking a certain way, or talking a certain way, or doing certain jobs, but sometimes stereotypes are absolutely essential. That's especially true in remote communities where homosexuality is a cardinal sin (unless of course the local priest is involved).

When you're a young person with no sexual experience and you think you might be gay but you're not sure, the only way you can even start to try to figure it out is by checking out the stereotypes and seeing if they make any sense to you. It sounds like a joke, but if you're in a small town and you want to know who even might be gay, you start at the hairdresser's and go from there. Eventually, you might get a hint.

In my case, I found out through the grapevine that one of the teachers at my school was gay, even though he led a heterosexual life on the surface. I never said anything to him, but once I knew somebody who was gay, that allowed me to continue to move forward with my own sexual discovery because I knew then that homosexuals weren't just some mythical creatures that only existed in my imagination.

The next step was to move from a sort of *National Geographic*–style quest to prove the actual existence of gay men to a real sexual appreciation of the male body. Like every other red-blooded male on Earth, my first real encounter with nudity and arousal was related to the *Playboy* and *Penthouse* magazines some kids would steal off their dads and bring to school. Then, like every other kid, you finally figure out what erections are for and you build a little teenie-bopper sex life for yourself related to masturbation and fantasy. The confusion kicked in for me about that time when the fantasies started to revolve around naked men as well as naked women.

As I grew and became a full-fledged adolescent, complete with working pubic hair, the slow realization that I wasn't really interested in looking at *Playboy* like the other guys my age started to freak me out a bit. I sort of knew what a gay person was by then, although the only one I'd ever seen for sure was probably Boy George, and I prayed every night that I wouldn't end up like him.

"What d'ya think of that guy?" I asked my older brother when we were looking at videos on TV one day.

"Who, Boy George? He's a big fairy," he scoffed.

"He's a pretty good singer though, isn't he," I said in Boy's defence.

"Maybe," sneered my brother, "but he's still a big fairy."

That might sound a bit harsh, but that was likely the consensus among folks in Creignish, Nova Scotia, in the late 1980s. Given that attitude, it's not hard to see why the thought that I might be gay was pretty terrifying for me as an adolescent. Other than black, gay was about the last thing you wanted to be if you came from my part of the world.

Everyone always talks about their first sexual experience in the context of having sex with another person, but, in reality, almost everybody's first sexual experience is with themselves. Most people discover masturbation as an adolescent, or I did anyway, and it's then that they start to develop a kind of fantasy sex life for themselves, long before they ever have a real live partner. Young boys usually dream about their teacher, or the 18-year-old girl next door who lies out in her bikini in the summer time. Girls, meanwhile, dream about the captain of the football team or the lifeguard at the beach. I knew I was probably in trouble when the lifeguard kept showing up in my fantasies and asking my teacher to leave.

So my first sex life, the one in my head, was gay, and that bothered the shit out of me. It didn't stop me masturbating though; I just felt guilty as hell about what I was thinking when I did it, which is exactly what the Catholic Church wants you to do. When I wasn't masturbating, I continued to hope that I'd become more interested in girls and eventually grow up and marry one, like every other guy from my town did.

Around the same time — say 12, 13 years old — I started to get into the juvenile "sex-play" that kids get into. You know: chasing girls around the schoolyard and grabbing their breasts, or grabbing their ass as they walk by in the hallway or them grabbing your crotch as they run by. I was always up for that type of thing because I was always "into" sex, even from a very young age. I don't know that I had the desire then to grab other guys in their privates, but that wasn't something you'd do in the schoolyard anyway at that age, not unless you wanted to get thumped. The roles were strictly defined, especially at my small-town Catholic school, and to even call somebody "gay" to their face was a real insult.

Eventually, a year or two later, the schoolyard sex-play progressed to the little "feel-up" in the bushes or out in the dunes. I had my experiences with that as well, but, as I say, it was more of an experimental thing than what I would call sex. By that time, naked men had become a permanent fixture of my fantasy sex life and my primary source of "arousal."

The main reason I experimented with girls was because I could; there may have been another guy my age in my area that would have liked to experiment with me in the same way, but good luck finding each other. The sort of ingrained condemnation of anything gay that exists in a small, very Catholic place like the west coast of Cape Breton island is enough to stop anyone from sending out any gay signals at all, let alone coming right out and asking some kid of the same sex if they're interested in playing doctor with you.

Groping in the bushes was good though, for a while. What I discovered through my early teenage experiments with girls was that that kind of sex, if you can call groping sex, was not the kind of sex I had in mind. I even had a couple of girlfriends for a while, but I knew in my heart that I was just biding my time until I could get a chance to really experiment with my sexuality. I wasn't sure exactly what that meant, but I was pretty sure it had something to do with all the naked men I was fantasizing about.

I was haunted by my homosexual fantasies mainly because it was drilled into us as Catholic school kids that sex between members of the same sex was "unnatural." Now unnatural to me, as a 13-, 14-, 15-year-old, meant something that had no place on this Earth, something that would not take place in nature because it didn't serve any purpose. That was a lot for a confused kid to comprehend, that I would have no place on this Earth if I ever actually acted on my fantasies.

I even asked the priest in confession once, "Father, can two people of the same sex ever be together?"

The priest told me straight, "Anyone who lives like that can never hope to live a normal life with normal people." He was right too, in Cape Breton anyway.

Then I saw something one day that changed my whole perspective on my problem. It was a summer's day and I was sitting on the front step of my parents' house looking at a magazine or something when I noticed the neighbour's dog come roaring across our front lawn. I looked up to see where he was going and saw he was making a bee-line for another dog about 50 yards down the road. I jumped up to watch them, because I thought to myself, "For sure, this is gonna be a fight."

There was no fight though. To my surprise, the neighbour's dog stopped beside the other dog, sniffed its ass a bit, then hopped up on it and started humping like there was no tomorrow. The other dog didn't fight or try to run away, it just stood there and took it. Then — surprise, surprise — as I looked a little closer, I realized that both dogs were male.

I thought about those two dogs for weeks after that. What the hell did it mean? Was my neighbour's dog just so stupid that he couldn't tell the other one was a male too? And why didn't the male getting humped move off? Did he like it? Were they both just so horny that they didn't care? Were they gay? I didn't know the answer to any of those questions, but I did know one thing: those dogs were just doing what came naturally to them, so I figured sex between two creatures of the same sex wasn't so "unnatural" after all.

From that point on, I relaxed about the whole subject of sex. I realized if I just did what came naturally to me, I could stop worrying about what I found sexually attractive and sexually stimulating. If I was going to find sexual pleasure and acceptance with a woman, I thought, then that was fine, but that wasn't necessarily the only place I could find sexual pleasure and acceptance. I found out later that people find sexual pleasure and acceptance with all kinds of partners — women, men, transgender, food, inanimate objects, even animals. Now, you can say that one choice is morally right or morally good and another isn't, but that's a "religious" or "legal" constraint, not a natural constraint. Nature doesn't dictate who or what gives a particular person sexual pleasure; nature just dictates how species reproduce, which is another topic altogether.

Coming to that realization allowed me to have my homosexual fantasies and enjoy my sex life in my head as a teenager. But it didn't give me enough confidence to come right out and admit that I was gay. I was still in Creignish, Nova Scotia, after all. I still had to go to school every day, and I still had to go to church on Sunday and listen to the priest try to make me feel insecure about myself. I knew though, by the time I was about 16, maybe a year before I went to New York the first time, that all the bullshit I'd been listening to from the Church about how "it's unnatural to be homosexual," and "homosexuality is an abomination," was nothing but that: bullshit.

So, by the time I was 16, I was finished praying to God to make me not be gay and I had pretty much given up forcing myself to be interested in girls. My fantasy sex life kept right on rolling though, and pretty soon I knew I was gonna bust if I didn't find myself a real-live male partner. The closest I got was when I got into wrestling matches at the beach a couple of times with male friends, and that turned me on but it never went anywhere. Luckily, I had my car by then, and it was relatively easy for me to line up a gig in Halifax about once a month, so I went on a mission to find myself a boyfriend.

I didn't know the first thing about cruising for gay men, but after several unsuccessful trips I finally did end up hooking up with a guy. He was a little older than me and he worked in a clothing store at a mall I went into one day. We ended up meeting after he got off work and making out in my car. I went back the next weekend and we hooked up in the car again and went a bit farther.

Eventually we fell into a pattern where I would show up in Halifax about once every couple of weeks and we'd have a heavy petting session in the back seat of my Parisienne. It wasn't a real relationship and it wasn't hard-core, but it was my first real gay encounter, and I knew then that there was no going back.

That arrangement faded away after a few months, and I was back to the fantasy world again. I'd had a taste, so to speak, of what I was after now though, and I was more willing to take chances to get it. That led me to do some stupid things, like hook up with complete strangers — the whole gay nightmare. I had lots of unpleasant experiences looking for sex that way, but it served a purpose, I figured, so I kept going back.

I was after sex, sure, at a minimum, but after a while I wanted to experience what it was like to have a real relationship with another guy, one where we could got out and do things together and have conversations and be affectionate, plus have some serious sex, the kind where you're not freezing your ass off in a car or in a park and you're not afraid someone will walk in on you.

It might sound weird, but I was really starved for male companionship when I was a teenager. When I started to experience homosexual fantasies as an adolescent, I began to consciously avoid other guys my age. I didn't try out for sports teams and I didn't hang around the ball park or the corner store with the other guys. I didn't want to talk about girls and sex, like they did, and I didn't want them asking me why I wasn't like them. I didn't have any "buddies" I hung around with; my friends in school were mostly girls. What I wanted was to be able to talk and interact with another guy just on a friendly level, and be sexual with him as well — a boyfriend, in other words. Then I went to New York.

By the time I went to New York I was really "ready" to be gay. Obviously, I knew I was attracted to men sexually long before I got there, and I had had some sexual experiences with men in Halifax, but I had never fully experienced the gay lifestyle. Mostly, I'd just been gay in my mind, and for brief moments away from home. I was like someone who'd been hitting balls on the driving range for years but had never actually played a game of golf. Before I went to New York, I'd say I'd had as many heterosexual experiences as homosexual experiences. So, I was ready, to put it mildly.

I really had no concept of just how many gay people there are in the world until I went to New York for the first time. And I certainly couldn't imagine ever being able to pick one out on the street; I guess I just assumed they'd all be invisible like they were at home. But once the gay people I met from the theatre showed me around, I quickly got the hang of picking out gay guys and introducing myself. Soon I was meeting 18- and 19-year-old guys at clubs, through ads in the newspaper, on the street and in restaurants and at coffeehouses late at night. Before I knew it, I had a whole "peer group" around me that had more in common with me than just my age, and that was more than enough to keep me busy.

Once I got comfortable in my new community and felt more sure of myself, I wasn't shy about indulging every fantasy I'd ever had when I was growing up back in Creignish. There were multiple partners and orgies. I had a couple of encounters with transvestites. In fact, I got into situations as an inexperienced 17-and-a-half-year-old that would be dangerous for a worldly 30-year-old.

I wasn't completely out of my mind though. My internal survival mechanism kept working in spite of me. There were some things I wouldn't do, and people I wouldn't do, and places I wouldn't go. I made sure never to be alone anywhere dark late at night, and I stuck pretty much to Manhattan — I don't think I made it above 125th Street the first time. If I ever felt nervous about a situation or a person, I just bailed out of it.

And I wasn't on drugs the first time I went to New York, so I had my wits about me a little more then, which was probably a good thing. It wasn't until I was much older and I got into the hard drugs that I was brazen enough to do things I would have considered insane before, things like walking around Harlem looking for crack and getting in the back of a cab with a crack dealer in Central Park — just crazy shit, the kind that gets you killed.

Going to New York gave me the opportunity not only to experience gay sex like never before, but also to actually "live" gay. Back home, it was only maybe every second weekend when I'd get down to Halifax and meet my "friend" or pick up a stranger and be "gay" for a couple of hours. After that, it was back to Creignish again, where I went back to being the weird, in-the-closet, fiddle player guy that nobody could figure out but wasn't "for sure" gay as far as anybody knew. I really longed to find out what it would be like to live my sexuality every day, and to be able to have sex every day if I wanted to, and for people around me to know I was gay and not give a shit. I finally got that chance in New York.

To be honest, when I actually got to New York, I can say without a doubt that I was probably more than gay. My desire to be gay had been bottled up for so long that it just burst like a shaken can of pop when my chance came. It wasn't enough for me to just be gay in New York, I had to be "over-the-top" gay. Before, I fantasized about meeting any good-looking guy and going home with him. But in New York I went looking specifically for actual gay porn stars to go home with. It was a quantum leap in just over a year, from dreaming of having gay sex while still fooling around with girls, to actually looking for gay sex, to having a little bit of gay sex in Halifax, then to having the craziest, most hard-core gay sex a porno director could ever imagine in New York.

I was only in New York for about three months that first time, so that didn't really lend itself to a long-term relationship. Mostly I had one-night stands with guys I met at clubs and around town. I hooked up with some partners several times while I was there, but there was nothing exclusive about it. I just made friends very easily, and within a few hours they were either in bed with me or I was making new friends the next day; I kept a strict revolving bedroom door policy.

I had a lot of club sex too, meaning actual sex in the clubs where I'd go to dance and party. That was a very common aspect of the club scene in New York at that time, which was kinda good from a safety stand-point. If you could get sex right in the club, it meant you didn't have to take a chance and go home with someone you just picked up.

Then, just a few weeks before I was supposed to go home, the worst possible thing happened: I fell in love. He was much older and very sex-ually experienced, and it was very intense, because we both knew that I didn't have a lot of time. I can honestly say, of all my "firsts" in New York, being in love for the first time was easily the most overwhelming.

In truth, that relationship only lasted probably a couple of weeks, so a lot of people wouldn't even consider it a serious relationship. But a couple of weeks was longer than anything I'd ever experienced before, and I know I felt differently than I had with all the other people I'd met in New York. It had to end, obviously, when I went home, but it went on in my mind for maybe a year after that. I wrote letters and called him a few times from home in the months that followed. My whole life was built around, "OK, maybe I'll get back to New York soon and we'll get back together," but it never happened. I never did see him again, although I've returned to New York many times since then.

By the time I got back to Creignish after my New York experience, I was well and truly "out" in my own mind. But my parents didn't know that, and neither did my brother and sister or anybody else in town. They might've suspected, but nobody could say for sure, because I never said one way or the other. Sure, I had dyed my hair blond in New York and I started to wear pretty freaky clothes by Creignish standards, but not having any other gay guys to compare me with, nobody could say definitively that I was. Plus, I've always been kind of "butch" as gay guys go, so it was easy for me to hide it. In fact, even a year and a half later, when I got my big break at the East Coast Music Awards in St. John's in 1994, most people who knew of me in the Maritimes didn't know me as some flaming queen.

When I came back from New York my sex life basically went from 100 miles per hour to a dead stop in 24 hours, and it stayed that way for several weeks, if not months. Eventually I got back into my old pattern of driving to Halifax as often as possible to meet partners. Things stayed like that until I met my first manager and moved in with her in Halifax, and started touring outside the Maritimes for the first time. That improved my sex life, but it didn't make it any easier to have a relationship. Then, a year or so later, I got my first record deal, and about a year after that, *hi*™ *how are you today?* came out and I hit the road for good for most of the next four years.

So for about seven years, from 1993 until 2000, my sex life consisted almost exclusively of one-night stands with strange men. And the one time I did get into a steady relationship, *Maclean's* magazine basically said I was a child molester and fucked that up for me. So it was easier for me to take my sex on the fly, in the shadows you might say, and a lot more dangerous as well.

Obviously, STDs and AIDS have got to be a major concern for anyone who has the kind of appetite for sex that I do and isn't in a monogamous relationship. Like everybody else, I first started hearing about STDs in school, back in the late '80s; it was the standard sex education class crap about things like gonorrhea and syphilis and crabs and scabies (which, of course, I would learn a lot more about first-hand later). You have to remember though, that this was a sex education class in a Catholic school on Cape Breton Island, so it probably didn't go into the kind of detail that kids in other places got. It was more like, "If you have sex before you're married, all these terrible things will happen to you."

As for gay sex, well there was just no such thing as gay sex and that was it. Besides, if you were to do something like that, it was understood, you had a lot worse things to worry about than crabs and scabies; you'd be lucky if you weren't struck dead by lightning right on the spot.

As for AIDS education, we didn't get any of that. AIDS only really came on the scene in the early 1980s — which is to say that it had about another 20 years to go before anyone would hear about it on Cape Breton. Besides, AIDS was a "gay" sex disease, so if you didn't have gay sex, AIDS shouldn't worry you anyway. That was the thinking — no shit.

It wasn't until I got to New York in 1992 that I started to learn about AIDS from people who'd already been dealing with it for 10 years. Aside from AIDS, I also learned about HIV in New York, which to me is a much scarier thing; I think something like 95 per cent of the people in the world who are infected with HIV don't even know it.

By the time I got to New York, the whole HIV/AIDS "epidemic" had come full circle in the gay community. In the late '70s, before AIDS really hit, I was told the gay community was just this bastion of sexual freedom that was creeping into the heterosexual world. By the early '80s though, gay men were dying and a sort of freeze came over everyone in the gay community, and the heterosexual community started backing away. Then by the late '80s, when straight people started to get it, the gay community was basically blamed for all the devastation AIDS was causing around the world.

But that had all passed when I got to New York in September 1992. The gay community knew by then that AIDS wasn't just a "gay" disease and that it was possible to live a semi-normal life if you took care of yourself. That's when they started to reclaim some of the sexual freedom they used to have back in the '70s, and I arrived just in time to take advantage of that.

The people that I met in the gay community in New York in the early 1990s had all been touched by AIDS somehow. They all knew someone who had died of it within the last 10 years. They had all been involved in ACT-UP and the early days of the AIDS education movement, trying to teach gay men about the risks and convince straight people that they weren't immune to it. So I learned about AIDS and HIV from people who had been dealing with it from day one, and you can't get a better education than that.

There was a lot of bitterness in the gay community about AIDS and HIV when I got there in 1992. The right-wing Christians, under Ronald Reagan and George Bush, had been in control in the U.S. since AIDS first hit the press in the early '80s, so the government had done hardly anything to stop it. And the sort of unspoken message from the top was that the gay community had caused the whole thing anyway.

The gay people that I met were fed up with being blamed. By that time, the scientists had figured out that the disease probably originated in Africa and that it could be transmitted by heterosexuals and homosexuals, men and women; AIDS had nothing to do with sexual orientation. In fact, gay men had really been like the canary in the coalmine, warning the heterosexual world that the disease was there and that they better start paying attention to it. Today, out of all the people in the world with HIV/AIDS, only about 10 per cent are gay. There is something like 40 million people in the world today who are infected with HIV/AIDS, and over half of them are women. Whose fuckin' fault is that?

Anyway, by 1992, the New York gay community was sick of being blamed for killing everyone, and sick of not having sex, and sick of worrying about it when they did have sex. So, "Fuck it," people started to say, and things sort of returned to the way it must have been back in the '70s. Obviously, people took care to protect themselves, but the scene opened right up again. Instead of being a little scared to admit being gay, people were right up front with their sexuality again and they refused to stop living.

I remember one older guy I met in New York at the time who had had a bunch of friends and lovers die on him, and he had what I thought was an amazing philosophy about the whole thing. He just said to me, "Kid, protect yourself as best as you can, but you're gonna get it or you're gonna get it, or you're gonna get it or you're gonna get it."

To me, his message was as clear as crystal: I was, for sure, gonna get AIDS if I had sex with homosexual men in New York if I thought for a minute that I wouldn't get AIDS if I had sex with homosexual men in New York. In other words, if I thought I could go around picking guys up in clubs and having unsafe casual sex with them like men did back in the '70s, it was guaranteed I would get AIDS. There were just so many infected men in that community by that time that the odds were stacked against not coming in contact with someone who had HIV. You had to know that before you got involved in that world. Once you knew that and accepted it as reality, you could make your own decision.

Well, I had that decision to make and I made it. "Well, that's it isn't it," I said to myself. "I'll do my best not to get it; but if I get it, I get it."

Fortunately, I'm happy to say, I haven't contracted HIV, and I don't know if that's because of the efforts I made to avoid it or just dumb luck. I tend to think it's more luck than anything, because I haven't always taken good care of myself. I've had lots of safe sex, for sure, but I've probably had more unsafe sex. It's no excuse, but obviously the kind of lifestyle that I've lived tends to lend itself to unsafe sexual practices: groupies, bath houses, people you're never going to see again and don't care about.

In fact, there's probably no group of people in the world who are more prone to having unsafe sex than professional musicians. I mean, if you really want to have sex and you don't really give a shit who you do it with, then it's much easier to do it with a groupie than with someone you might see again. For a musician, gay or straight, groupies provide a constant source of sex on the road if you want it. Think about it: if you do a show and there are two or three thousand people there and they all loved it, do you not think there isn't somebody in that two or three thousand who'll have sex with you?

Living the "rock star" lifestyle, I'm sure I've had sex with more people in my life than it's even necessary to say. I've changed my lifestyle considerably in the last couple of years, but early in my career, I took full advantage of every opportunity I had to have sex with just about anyone who'd offer. So you could say I was spinning the AIDS roulette wheel almost every day at one point. I've learned since then that my life is worth more than that. But back then every day didn't feel as important; like every stupid kid, I thought I could go on forever doing just what I was doing right then.

In fact, I found I almost couldn't be wild enough to satisfy my urges. There was all kinds of crazy unsafe sex in all kinds of crazy places. There were wild sexual situations involving multiple partners and what have you. There were orgies. I never got tired of it either; I could do it all day, if I had the time, and then go right back at it the next day if I got the chance.

The weird thing about it though was that I had no more sex, and a no more unusual sex life, than any other gay person that I knew that was around my age. And that held true not just in New York, but in Halifax and Toronto and any other place I lived or visited where there was a sizeable gay community. Now I'm not saying that there are no gay people in committed relationships; I'm in one myself right now and have been for a few years. But what I am saying is, most, if not all, young gay guys, just like young straight guys, have multiple sex partners and take sex anywhere they find it.

Heterosexuals like to think that they're not as promiscuous as homosexuals, but that's a load of crap. Are you trying to tell me that if some gorgeous woman walked up to a 20-year-old guy in a bar and said, "Hey, let's go out to my car and fool around," that that guy would say, "Oh sorry, I can't. I have a girlfriend"? Like shit he would.

Most of the musicians I toured with were heterosexual and many of them were just as bad as me when it came to sex and groupies. If we were on tour and hit four or five different towns in a week, it would be nothing for a few of my bandmates to score with four or five women, or maybe more, in that week. But they didn't have to be musicians; I've known roadies and just guys at home, mechanics or truck drivers, who had a knack for picking up girls at bars or dances. Those guys were doing something with somebody almost every night of the week.

From my perspective back in those days, I didn't think I was doing anything wrong or anything unusual. Why shouldn't I sleep around, I thought, if lots of the heterosexual people I knew did it? Because I was gay? Fuck that, I thought. So I searched out that type of lifestyle, and I soon found that there are lots of gay men who live that way and enjoy it immensely. That really pisses all these super-hetero Christians right off, because in the back of their minds, they'd love to be just as slutty but they're too hung up to admit it even to themselves.

Now I know that a life of serial unsafe sex with a different person every other night, and the odd multiple-partner experience, or even the odd orgy, isn't for everyone. But for me, as a young person just sowing his wild oats, so to speak, it was fun. I don't think I experienced anything really extraordinary. And I could argue that that was really the only lifestyle available to me at the time. I had sex with different partners mostly because I was travelling a lot and I couldn't have sex with the same person all the time. At that point in my life and career, a serious, monogamous relationship would have been out of the question.

That's probably the real reason I split with the boyfriend I had when the *Maclean's* thing hit. Besides, he didn't want to get any more caught up in the media crap that came from that article than he already was, and I got that; if you think it sucks trying to be in a relationship when you're famous, it's even worse to be in a relationship with a famous person. I like to think I'm still friends with that person, and I have nothing but wonderful memories of that relationship. I also learned enough from that experience that I'll never let my career get in the way of my life again.

The *Maclean's* experience changed my whole perspective on monogamous relationships. If *Maclean's* and the rest of Canada didn't like what I was doing in the open with my steady boyfriend, I thought, I'd have to go back to having sex with strangers. From then on, I made a conscious decision to take the Wilt Chamberlain approach.

✳ ✳ ✳

As is the case with most gays and lesbians, I think my family probably had a pretty good idea I was gay before I came out to them. Still, I waited till I was out of the house and on my own before I said it to them officially. But as long as I was living in my parents' house, in the town I grew up in, I didn't say anything about it and they didn't ask.

I don't think my family or anybody else in my town had any real reason to think I was gay until maybe I was as old as 17. I mean, I would take my copies of the *Village Voice* to school in grade 11 and it would get passed around among the kids my age as they all hung around the dug-out at the baseball diamond. They didn't know what it was, but they read it and I think a few of them maybe picked up a vibe that, by bringing in this paper and pointing out all the bizarre things in it, I was subconsciously saying that I was interested in an "alternative"

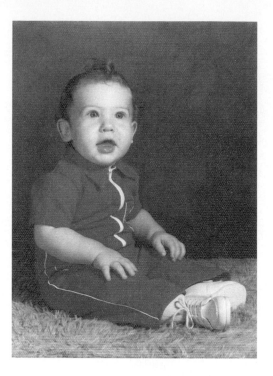

This is me at nine months and sixteen months.

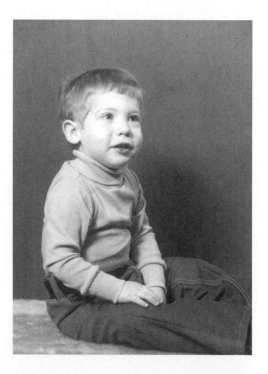

My childhood was normal and happy.
There was always lots of dances and parties.

Buddy MacMaster (*above*), one of Cape Breton's greatest fiddlers, was an early role model. A wonderful musician.

Here I am in 1993; quite a contrast to my later performing style (and attire).

Singer John McDermott was among the first musicians I toured with.

Working with Philip Glass (*left*) is one of the highlights of my life. It gave me a taste of a world outside Cape Breton.

Philip introduced me to Paul Simon, who I recorded with early in my career. Watching him work in the studio taught me a lot.

I met Allen Ginsberg (*right*) on several occasions, which was very special. Few people get an opportunity to meet and joke with a world-famous poet.

The Chieftains are the royal family of Celtic music. Touring with them was a terrific opportunity to work with the best.

The Best of The Chieftains

lifestyle myself. If I was, that was the only hint I ever gave anybody. On the surface, I was just like any one of those kids in the dug-out, experimenting with sex and relationships, partying and trying to make some money, getting my licence and experiencing freedom for the first time and trying to figure out what the hell I was going to do when I got out of school.

I had had a few girlfriends here and there right up until I was about 16, and I always had a lot of girls who were my friends, so my family at least saw me around girls. I wasn't into sports because all my time was taken up by my music, but I always came across, among straight people that is, as a guy's guy. I think I was like any other guy from Creignish; there was nothing ever effeminate or "fruity" about my behaviour that would cause people to automatically assume, "Oh yeah, he's a pole smoker."

When I turned 16 and I got my own car, I finally had the ability to get away from my hometown and make an attempt to find gay sex partners. But when I jumped in my car on the weekend to go to Halifax, I usually had a gig booked there anyway, so as far as anybody in Creignish knew, I was just doing what I had been doing for three or four years anyway. Of course, I didn't come back home to Creignish and go into school on Monday and tell all my school friends that I'd fooled around with a guy in the back seat of my car in a mall parking lot in Halifax the day before. So I guess my sexuality was a "deep, dark, secret," right up until long after I left Creignish for good.

I came out to myself at least when I visited New York for the first time when I was 17, going on 18. And I found such unconditional acceptance there that all the years of pent-up frustration, both sexual and emotional, exploded in three months of "super-sexual" behaviour. When I wrote home to my parents from New York, I obviously didn't tell them exactly what I was up to; they both would've dropped dead from heart attacks if I did. But I did talk about the people I was meeting from the theatre and about going dancing in clubs and about a special "friend" I made near the end of my visit. I think I even told my mother about how great it was to meet a transvestite for the first time. So my parents might have suspected then, but I didn't say it in so many words, so they didn't have to believe it if they didn't want to.

Of course when I got back from New York I just reverted to form, although that was painful as hell for me. New York had made its mark though: I dyed my hair and started to wear flamboyant clothes and people in town starting to notice just how "different" Ashley was. I think by then my family must have been wondering why I hadn't had a girlfriend in a couple of years. Or maybe they didn't, I don't know.

By the time I was finished high school at 18, I was also out of the house for good pretty much, so my parents no longer had any idea at all what I did with my time. When I wasn't on the road touring, I was living in Halifax, so I was free to be "gayer" than I'd ever been when I lived in Creignish. And although I was making a bit of a name for myself on the East Coast, I wasn't so important that people wanted to know who the hell I was sleeping with. That was probably one of the best times in my life, actually, from a sexual perspective, because I was able to have partners and have a boyfriend on the road and in Halifax and still not be "out" to my family, plus the media didn't give a shit about me yet. That all changed, of course, when I "made it."

After my big breakout performance at the East Coast Music Awards in 1994, the East Coast press started to take a real interest in me. That regional attention led to a couple of national interviews on CBC Radio with Peter Gzowski and eventually to an invitation to tour with the Chieftains. At that point, in late 1994, I moved from being a regional sensation to a bit of a national sensation. And when *hi™ how are you today?* came out in the summer of '95, that made me a bona fide "star." From about then on, my personal life was just as important to the press and the fans as my music.

At first I was naïve enough to think, "Oh yeah, I can be famous and sell lots of CDs and play big shows with top acts from around the world, and be gay, and nobody will say a word about it if I don't." I figured out pretty fast though that it wasn't like it was back in Rock Hudson's day, when the press basically looked the other way when it came to gay celebrities. Nope, I had to make a decision: either I could come out myself to my family and the world, or I could wait for someone in the press to "out" me. Both things kind of ended up happening at the same time.

I moved to Toronto in the fall of 1994 to start recording *hi™ how are you today?* and I was still living there a year later, although I was out on the road maybe 80 percent of the time. Anyway, there had been lots of rumours floating around in the press about my sexuality — "Is Ashley MacIsaac gay or not?" "Is Ashley MacIsaac bi?" — and I had been basically avoiding the question as much as I could. But I was kind of getting tired of hiding, and I started dropping a few subtle hints here and there in interviews around the country just to soften the blow when I did finally admit it. Then one day my manager called me up and told me that *Frank* magazine had some information and they were going to "out" me in their next issue.

That was it then, I didn't really have a choice anymore. As soon as I put down the phone to my manager, I picked it up again to phone home. My mom answered.

"Hi Mom, it's me, Ashley."

"Hi dear, how's everything goin'?"

"Great. Look Mom, I've got something to tell you."

"Oh yeah, what's that?"

"I'm gay…"

"OK—" *click!* Just like that, she hung up the phone. So, I hung up and dialled her number again. She picked it up on half a ring.

"What," she snapped.

"Well, are you gonna tell Dad?"

"Yes, when he comes in from work,"

"Do you think he'll be OK with it?"

"No, I think he'll take a heart attack. What am I supposed to do about that? Goodbye." *click!* She hung up again. So I phoned back again.

"*What!*" she snapped again.

"Mom, you're not gonna take a heart attack are ya?"

"I don't know; I might. But your dad'll take a heart attack for sure."

"Would it be better if I told him myself?"

"Whatever. Goodbye." *click!*

It went on like that for about 15 minutes. My mom told my dad about four hours later when he got home from work. He didn't take a heart attack, but my mom did say he went to bed early complaining of chest pains.

So I had finally come out to my family and nobody died, so I guess I'd have to say it went well. We probably only talked two or three times in the next six months, but, all things considered, it could've been a lot worse. My dad could've sat down at the kitchen table with the Saturday paper and got it full-on in the face.

As for my brother and sister, they took it a lot easier than my parents. My brother, of course, wasn't shocked at all. "I knew it all along," he said. "I saw the signs when you were a teenager."

"Oh yeah?" I smirked. "What signs were those? You were off working during the day when I was a teenager, and I was off playing the fiddle most nights."

"Don't worry," he said. "There were signs."

If he saw the signs, I guess everybody else in Creignish saw them too, although nobody ever said anything to me.

Unfortunately for my sister, she was still at home when all this happened, so she had to deal with Mom and Dad losing their minds over it. On top of that, she had to go on being a teenager herself in the same tiny, traditional community that I couldn't wait to get away from and I'm sure she had to put up with a lot of bullshit at school over it.

I came out officially in the media a few months later, in early 1996. I was 21; I had my first big record out; and, best of all, the secret I'd spent years hiding was finally out, and I was free to live the life I dreamed of living when I would read those stale copies of the *Village Voice* as a teenager. In less than a year though, I would find out the hard way that there's a limit to just how far you can come "out."

I've been out for a long time now, and once I was out I continued to be very open about my sexuality in spite of all the trouble it caused me. I struggled with my Catholic guilt for years, but I'm happy to say I feel very comfortable in my skin today. As far as my parents are concerned though, I don't think they'll ever be completely comfortable with my sexuality. I don't think it affects their day-to-day life now the way it did for a couple of years. Still, it's got to be hard when someone goes for almost 21 years thinking and hoping that the person they loved and raised was one thing, only to find out that that person is something completely different. I know it's gonna take them some time to adjust, if they ever do, and that's probably the normal course these things take.

The same thing goes for my hometown, and Cape Breton itself for that matter. Even today, that's still a very traditional, very Catholic corner of the world, and people are very closed-minded when it comes to practising homosexuals. But I still go home to see my family and I find

I haven't endured nearly as many rude comments and middle fingers in the last couple of years as I used to. I think people may not like my lifestyle but have come to accept it. And they still seem to like listening to me play, so they're willing to forget that I'm gay for at least an hour or so at a square dance.

Deep down inside though, I don't think the fact that I'm gay will change any attitudes in the place where I grew up. The neighbours in Creignish who didn't think it was an OK thing the first time they read it, still don't think it's OK. In fact, I bet there's more than a few who love to think that I fouled up and went bankrupt and put it down to the fact that I'm gay and smoke pot.

On top of that, I don't think the fact that I'm gay is going to inspire other gay kids from Cape Breton to stand up and say, "Hey, Ashley MacIsaac's from down the road and he's gay, and you know what? I'm gay too." They'll just grow up in the closet and leave for Halifax or Toronto or wherever as soon as they get the chance, just like I did. The Catholic Church has got its claws stuck in so deep in that part of the world there are still people complaining that they dropped the Latin mass.

And speaking of the Church, it always struck me as ironic as hell that the first really "big" show I ever played in was for the Pope. I was only nine, of course, and he must have just looked at me and said to himself, "Well, isn't that a nice little Catholic boy there playing his little heart out." If he only knew then what we all know now, he probably would've stuck me dead with a bolt of lightning right then and there; think of the trouble he would've saved everyone, me included.

Anyway, I still hold out hope that that performance had as much of an effect on the Pope as it had on me. Hopefully, he'll come to his senses soon and announce to the world finally that it's OK to be gay. If he'd just do that, he'd eliminate 90 percent of the problems he has with all these pedophile priests. See, the real problem is, most of these guys aren't pedophiles at all; they're really gay guys who need sex but are absolutely terrified to have it with anybody who might tell. That's why they focus on kids, because they think they can intimidate them into staying quiet. If they could just come out and be gay, they could start having sex with each other and leave the altar boys alone. The ones who don't leave the altar boys alone after that, they're your pedophiles.

If that doesn't suit the Pope, there's nothing saying that these priests can't be gay and celibate. You can be gay and celibate, straight and celibate, bisexual and celibate; whether or not you actually have sex has nothing to do with what kind of sex you prefer. But that's what the Church is having so much trouble getting its head around. If the Pope could just come out and say, "Sex is not evil. It's OK to have sex, and it's OK not to have sex, but the main thing is it's OK to be whatever you want to be," so many of these problems would disappear.

And if only he knew that that little, innocent, harmless boy from Cape Breton fiddling for him that day in Halifax in 1984 was gay, maybe he would change his mind.

Anyway, it really doesn't matter what the hell the Pope or the Catholic Church thinks about homosexuality, because the world is changing all around them. You can see that in the way the general public treats celebrities that are gay today. Back in the 1950s and '60s and earlier, you just couldn't be gay, that was it. Celebrities like Rock Hudson and Liberace were gay as hell, but they both stayed in the closet their whole lives. It was only when Rock Hudson was a walking skeleton that he admitted he had AIDS, and even then he didn't admit he was gay.

In the 1970s and '80s it was trendy to be gay, but people who were gay were still considered "abnormal" by most people. Then in the '90s we had Ellen DeGeneres, and she tried to make a homosexual person seem as normal as anybody else on her TV show, but she got cancelled anyway and nobody wanted her anymore. Now we have a huge TV and movie star, Rosie O'Donnell, coming out and admitting to the world that she's a lesbian. I mean we all knew she was a lesbian, but she finally had the guts to admit it to all the little housewives across America who watched her show. And you know what? I don't think it hurt her at all. She's still popular, and she has kids and is a regular person like everyone else. The born again Christians don't like it, but I don't see anyone in the regular media saying that Rosie is "abnormal," or "evil," or anything like that. I think the days of people turning on someone if they find out that person is gay may finally be on the wane.

Now I'm not stupid enough to think that prejudice against gays and lesbians is anything but alive and well. But I think the people who think like that are getting older every day, and there aren't as many young people who are willing to believe the same things their parents and grand-parents believed. You'll always have some prejudice, but I think it's fading in its intensity. Eventually we'll get to the point where mainstream heterosexual society is willing to accept everything but the most extreme aspects of the gay lifestyle — the drag queens and the fetishes and the transgender stuff. The fact that *Queer As Folk* comes on TV every week without everybody over 50 having a heart attack shows that people can handle seeing two young naked guys together having sex now.

That's my perspective as a gay person living in Canada. In Europe, of course, they were at this point long ago. The U.S has a little farther to go to catch up to us in Canada even, but I think that's the way it's going, in spite of what the born again Christians say.

Even today, when I'm living quite happily in a same-sex relationship, I'm not prepared to label myself as being strictly gay. I have had my fair share of sexual experiences with females in my life, and I valued those experiences and found them as pleasurable as any male relationship I've had. I'm not prepared to take the sexual experiences I've had with women and the relationships I've had with women and throw them away as useless to me. I think you have to take each experience in your life and examine it and decide if it was useful to you and if you would want to have an experience like that again. In my case, I don't believe that it's impossible for me to have a positive experience with a woman ever again.

Today, however, I can truthfully say that sex with women is not my premier choice of sex, and that has everything to do with the relationship I'm in right now. At this point in my life, I see gay sex as something that is simply a part of being with the person I care about the most, and that person happens to be male.

But that doesn't mean I've got it all figured out; I'm aware that my music has allowed me to pack more experiences into my life before the age of 30 than most people get in their whole lives. But all that does is allow me to have a wider range of choices when it comes to figuring out how I want to live the rest of my life. I'm still looking at my experiences, and weighing them, and asking myself, "What do I really want?" Do I want to be the way I am today for the rest of my life? Do I want a harem? Do I want the revolving-door club scene I used to have? Do I want a wife and family?

I don't know the answer to any one of those questions. But I do know I'm happy with my life and my sexuality the way they are right now, and I'll let the rest of that stuff take care of itself. One thing I do know for sure, though, after all the experiences I've had and the scrutiny I've had to endure, is that I would like to have the freedom to express my own desires sexually without hurting others and without anyone hurting me. That's it.

~ 9 ~

Happy Fuckin' New Year

I started to get into cocaine in late 1996, right around the time the *Maclean's* scandal broke.

In the beginning, I basically did cocaine whenever I got the chance, but it was never a daily ritual for me. Not like pot. For instance, I would never use cocaine when I was playing a particular gig or touring with a particular act where using hard drugs just wouldn't be appropriate. So I might do cocaine the day I was going to play at a pub in a university somewhere, but I wouldn't use it if I was going to play at some folk festival on a Saturday afternoon in the summer in front of a bunch of families. So I wasn't a total idiot about it anyway.

The dope kept me going most of the time, but occasionally even that couldn't get me in the frame of mind I needed to be in to be the Ashley MacIsaac everybody expected. That's exactly what happened one night in Cleveland in late March 1997, when all the pressure that'd been building up since the previous fall came to a head.

Actually, a couple of nights before that gig I had enjoyed one of the greatest nights of my professional life. I performed at the Junos and the performance went just fantastic. On top of that, I was up for a few awards for *hi™ how are you today?* and even won a couple, so you can imagine I was absolutely flying. That night was unlike any other in my life before or since. I had a hit record and the respect of my peers.

Unfortunately, the pressure of all the negative publicity I'd had to deal with since the *Maclean's* thing had me at the end of my rope. Plus, I'd been touring basically non-stop since the record was released. I was using heavily and headed for a fall. I ended up rescheduling a gig in Buffalo that I was supposed to play the night after the Junos because I came down with the flu.

About a week later, I was on my way to the Cleveland gig, but my heart was definitely not in it. I was just getting over my flu, and the Junos had been just such an incredible high, as I was crossing the border at Buffalo I was saying to myself, "Oh God, the Junos were so good, I just know this gig is gonna suck."

In fact, I was so burnt out by the time I got to Cleveland it didn't even matter to me whether I found good pot waiting for me there or not (I hadn't taken the chance of crossing the border with any). As it turned out, the promoter did find me some good pot, and by the time the gig came around I had my bag of dope and I'd been in my hotel room for a few hours so I should have been in a great mood. But I wasn't. I just plain didn't want to play that day.

Of course, my critics jumped all over me for it later, saying, "If Ashley was a professional, he should have been able to come off a great gig and play just as well a couple of nights later at a smaller gig." And yeah, that's true. In fact, I've done it hundreds and hundreds of times over the years. But think about it: I go from performing on a national awards show for the cream of the Canadian music industry, televised nationwide on the CBC and everybody loving me, to some shitty club in Cleveland. I didn't want to be there — is that so hard to fuckin' understand?

Anyway, I just couldn't face it and I had a meltdown in my hotel room about an hour before the show. I smashed an old spare violin I had and told the promoter I couldn't play because I tripped and fell on my good violin. The reaction, of course, was not good. Absolutely everybody involved, from my manager to the record company to the promoter, went ballistic.

"You got no choice," they all started telling me, "you've got to do this show."

Well that just pissed me right off. I'd just won two Juno Awards, which to me was just as good as winning a Grammy. I'd made fuckin' tons of money selling my music. Now these people were telling me I didn't have a choice about playing a shitty little gig in a club in Cleveland. I know I said I'd do it, but I was worn out from touring and I just didn't feel up to it. Anyway, I didn't think I owed anybody an excuse.

"Fuck, Sheri," I said to my manager when she called to try to talk me into it. "In my whole life, I bet I've only missed maybe six or seven shows that I was booked to play out of maybe a couple of thousand. Give me a fuckin' break."

Honestly, if you worked as a surgeon for 10 years and did 2,000 surgeries, you'd probably expect to lose at least six or seven patients in that time. Is six or seven out of 2,000 a reasonable success rate? Well I sure as hell think it is. And my record is even more amazing when you consider that I was stoned for a big proportion of those dates.

"You know what they're going to say don't you," Sheri warned. "'Ashley's all whacked out, and he's an idiot and he ought to be in detox.'"

"Well, that's fine. Fuck 'em," I said. "I've played for about 700,000 people in the last six months and they all loved it. So, sorry to the 200 people down in the club, but you lose tonight." Shit, all I wanted was a night off.

So I never played Cleveland that night, and everybody lived. I managed to make the next two gigs on the tour though, in Cincinnati the next night, then Indianapolis, and they both went fine. Finally the tour wrapped up the next week with a couple of gigs at Tramps in New York. All the press wanted to talk about though was the night I had my "nervous breakdown" in Cleveland.

As nervous breakdowns go, I guess mine was a pretty mild one. Within six weeks of the Cleveland gig, I was right back at it, playing three sold-out nights at the Orpheum Theatre in Vancouver with the Vancouver Symphony Orchestra. I followed that up by joining the Chieftains for some one-off gigs in Japan and China, then I stuck around with them for part of their U.S. tour. Unfortunately, that led me straight into another publicity land mine.

I've toured with the Chieftains a couple of times in my career and actually made a lot of money touring with them. On top of that, having the opportunity to play with such gifted musicians has made me a far better musician I think. So, out of respect, I never did cocaine when I was touring with the Chieftains. That didn't mean I didn't have my pot though.

Another great thing about touring with the Chieftains was that I never had any money problems when I was with them; I'd get paid cash, bang, right after each show. So I would get my cash and go out and buy my pot and go back to my hotel room and smoke. They probably knew I smoked pot, but they were cool with it as long as it didn't interfere with what I was doing on stage. Musicians are musicians I guess, regardless of where they're from, and they tend to be a little less judgemental than your average person.

Now there are exceptions to every rule, and I ran into one of those on that U.S. tour with the Chieftains in the fall of '97. There happened to be another artist on the same tour, a singer from Ireland named Brigid Boden. She was actually a writer of traditional Irish stories and poems who had sort of burst on to the scene out of the blue like a lot of other artists who rode that wave of Celtic fever that *Riverdance* started in the early '90s. I guess she was sitting under her shawl at home in Ireland one day when one of the modern Celtic tunes came on the radio and she decided she should put her poems to music. It worked for her I guess, because she became the "next big Irish thing" for a while.

Her big problem with me was not pot, actually, but cigarette smoke. Being a singer, she was always worried about her voice, so she didn't want anyone on the tour smoking cigarettes or anything else in her presence. Well, I could see where she was coming from with that, but then one night we were all having dinner in a big restaurant, in the smoking section I might add, and she told me to put my cigarette out. I told her, in probably not so nice a manner, where she could put out my cigarette, and that was it. She up and quit the tour that night.

Ironically, I've quit smoking a bunch of times since then, but I still don't think she was in the right. Some people, when they're trying to quit, don't want people around them who smoke because they say it makes it harder for them to quit. But I never asked someone to stop smoking around me then, and I won't do it now, even when I'm not smoking myself. I guess it's because I was one of those stupid smokers before and I suppose they have rights like anyone else. Second-hand smoke sucks, sure, but if you don't like it, move. It's just as easy for the non-smoker to move as it is for the smoker to move, but if the smoker is outside or in a smoking section why should they move?

Anyway, I figured if Brigid was a professional singer, then it was her job to protect her voice, not mine. Smoking may not be the smartest thing in the world to do, but I can think of a lot worse things, and I've done most of 'em. I haven't heard much of Brigid since. I guess that was my fault as well.

Of course, when it came out in the press about Brigid quitting the tour, the story was that I was a foul-mouthed, selfish idiot that she just found it impossible to work with or be around. So just when I thought I was starting to come out from under the cloud of negative publicity that'd been dogging me for almost a year by that point, something else happened that only ended up adding fuel to the whole madman image. There wasn't much I could do about it by then though. People were gonna believe what they wanted to believe. So I just did what I always did: keep on playing and to hell with all of 'em.

As 1997 turned into 1998, my "experimentation" with cocaine turned into a full-blown cocaine habit. Then, as I started to get more and more into rap and hip-hip music and the whole "gangsta" culture thing, crack became part of the ritual as well. Eventually, it started to influence every area of my life and career. I added a DJ to my regular touring band and I started playing a lot more hybrid tunes in my show while taking out more and more traditional fiddle music. As the months passed, I was just getting farther and farther out there. My manager wasn't happy about it; the record company wasn't happy about it; and, most important, my fans weren't happy about it.

From my drugged-out perspective at the time, all I could see was negative shit coming at me from all sides: the press was shitting on me every chance they got; I was getting crap for the music I was playing; I was getting crap because I wasn't working on a new record; people were walking out on shows, or worse, staying and shouting shit at me on the stage; and I wasn't making any money, so my financial situation was getting worse by the day.

On top of all that, my manager and my family and friends were on me constantly about my drug use, which, as far as I could see, was the only thing in my life that was giving me any pleasure. I was angry and frustrated. That's when I started to lash out onstage, cursing and making lewd comments and anything else I could think of to piss people off even more.

"Fuck 'em all," I thought. "As long as I can make enough money to buy my dope, I don't give a shit anymore."

The last straw for my long-time, long-suffering manager Sheri Jones came in July 1998. I was in Fort Erie, Ontario, at, of all things, the Friendship Festival. That's where I got into a knock-down, drag-out fist fight with Wayne O'Connor, my road manager and Sheri's husband.

I was probably at the height of my cocaine use by then, and I was getting more and more pissed off about always having to fight to get money out of Wayne so I could buy dope. In their way, I guess, they were trying to help me by making it harder for me to get high, but I sure didn't see it that way.

I finally blew my top when Wayne got mad at me for basically throwing a big party with about 25 people after the show in this little trailer they'd provided for me. I was high, of course, and everyone was drinking, including Wayne. I was lying on the bed, I remember, and someone pissed me off, so I screamed at them to get the fuck out of my trailer. Wayne told me to shut up or something, and I just flipped out.

"Fuck you," I yelled at him. "You're not going to treat me like a child anymore. Don't tell me what to do, because it's my career and I'm the guy who's done all the work and I've got no fuckin' money."

At that point, I guess he'd heard enough and finally did what he'd probably been dying to do for a long time: he jumped me. He came flying at me head first, and I automatically put my feet up to protect myself. When he landed on me he just started throwing punches and hitting me in the face.

It took me a second or two to react, but once I did, I just went berserk. You have to remember, I'd just come off doing a foot-stomping show for an hour on a few hits of acid, so my energy level was pretty fuckin' high. I kicked both my feet out into his chest and just about sent him through the wall of the trailer. Of course, there are a number of versions of what happened that night, but that's how I remember it.

Well, obviously, you can't do kung-fu on the management and expect them to take it with a grain of salt, so that was the end of the road for me and Sheri Jones. I talked to her after and tried to explain things, but Wayne said he couldn't work with me anymore, to which I answered, "Fuckin' right ya can't." The drugs, on my part, and the alcohol, on his part, obviously had something to do with it, but it'd been brewing for a while for lots of reasons.

The real reason behind Sheri Jones leaving, I think, was the money was starting to dry up by the summer of 1998, and I guess she figured she wasn't going to make enough managing me to make all the bullshit worthwhile. As far as she saw it, I was turning my back on everything that had made me successful in the first place, which was probably true.

In spite of the way our relationship ended, I have nothing but good things to say about Sheri and all she did for me. She took me under her wing as a naïve kid and gave me a foot in the door of the music business. She saw I had the talent to succeed in a very difficult industry if I just got the chance, and she made sure I got it.

So, that was that; I was on my own again. After parting company with Sheri, I worked with a couple of interim managers just to get me through the rest of that tour and to line up some gigs for me down the road. Sam Feldman, the Chieftains' manager, helped me out a bit, as did Brookes Diamond from Halifax. Finally in August of '98 I hooked up on a more permanent basis with Jeff Rogers, who I had met earlier when I toured with the Crash Test Dummies, who he also managed.

Then 1998 drifted into '99 without me really noticing. I was so far into my addiction by then I was only aware of the time passing because my record company was on my ass constantly because it'd been over three years since I'd made a new studio album. But I was becoming less and less capable of putting a record together with each passing day.

The year started off with a bang for me and ended with an absolute explosion. Early in January, my record company got snapped up. I'd been in the business for a good few years by then, but A&M Records was the only label I'd ever known. I'd signed with them in May 1994. But in January of 1999, Universal Entertainment bought up A&M, or they merged or something, and Universal Music was the result. So, just like that, I had a new boss you could say.

Unfortunately, the good relationship I'd enjoyed, for the most part, with A&M, didn't survive the merger. I picked A&M originally over offers from bigger labels because it had a more personal, less corporate way of doing business, and Sheri and I both thought that would probably be the best environment for an artist like myself. Overnight though, my label became this huge music money machine that didn't have a lot of time or patience for a drugged-up Cape Breton fiddle player.

I had, in fact, released a record since 1995. That was *fine® thank you very much,* which came out in 1998, but the record company really put that one out on their own with leftover, more traditional recordings from the *hi™ how are you today?* sessions. I'd done lots of one-off, "guest appearances" too, on records by other people like Big Rude Jake, David Byrne, the Chieftains, Bruce Hornsby and Mary Jane Lamond. I'd also contributed tracks to various compilation CDs and to original soundtracks for the movie *The Hanging Garden* and for the TV show *Due South.*

What the record company wanted though, was "the next big Ashley MacIsaac record." A&M had been prodding me to do something, but not too hard, because I think they sort of knew I was a bit "fragile" shall we say. Universal couldn't care less; the heat was on for me to get into the studio from the minute they took over.

The truth of it was, I wasn't in any shape to make a record in the first half of 1999, either emotionally or financially. I was using pot and acid regularly, and cocaine and crack probably a couple of times a month. My real problem though, was that I just couldn't afford to stop touring for two months or so to make a record. First of all, I had to pay for my living accommodations and my drugs, plus Revenue Canada was after me with this huge tax bill and I was still trying to keep my house.

It all came to a head in July of '99. I convinced myself that Universal was ruining my career by forcing me to make a record when I wasn't ready to make one. I eventually broke ties with Jeff Rogers because he didn't agree with me about it. Finally Universal and I both decided that we didn't want to work together anymore and I was out of my recording contract. We basically just went our separate ways and the media called the split "amicable."

That left me with no manager, no record company, and practically no money. But I still had my house in Belle Cote, and I still had my fiddle, and the drugs hadn't killed me, so I figured I still had a chance to pull out of my nosedive. And that chance came in the form of Loggerhead Records.

Within weeks of leaving Universal, I signed a three-record deal with Loggerhead, a small label run by Paul Church and Andrew McCain.

McCain was one of the frozen food McCains, so he was the money man while Paul ran the show. The Loggerhead thing started out very positive in the beginning. They were all behind me and very supportive of my career, but they only had one stipulation: I had to get off the drugs.

"Fine. Whatever," I thought; I wasn't really in a position to argue because the labels weren't exactly lining up. Anyway, to tell you the truth, at that point I would've signed a record deal with the devil himself if he was willing to give me some money to pay my tax bill.

The Loggerhead deal got me back on my feet and things seemed to be looking up again, for a while anyway. I signed with Loggerhead at a time when drugs had actually taken over first place in my life over my career and I was in big financial trouble. Then, magically, within just a few weeks of the split with Universal, Loggerhead Records was there with money in their hand.

Loggerhead was a pretty low profile "boutique" label based in Toronto that was actually distributed by Universal, funnily enough. Signing me gave them a big-name act and I got cash up front to get my ass out of tax hock. I really had no choice.

But the Loggerhead deal wasn't a few weeks old before I started regretting it. I knew I was in trouble as soon as I realized the guys behind the label were greedier than I was.

The guy from Loggerhead who actually signed me was the vice-president of the company, Paul Church. When we made the deal, of course, everything was beautiful and exciting. In a press release about the deal, Church said he considered me "the world's greatest fiddler," and he called me "an icon" and "a Canadian treasure." But you know what they say about one man's treasure being another man's trash. I found that out when I met the moneyman behind Loggerhead, company president Andrew McCain, or "French-fry Man" as I called him.

I remember walking into McCain's office in Toronto and him meeting me at the door and saying, "Hey, Ashley, how ya doin'?" and taking me by the hand and leading me into his office to sit down.

We shot the shit for a while and I thought things were going along nicely, until he said to me, "You know, I don't know you very well, but from what I hear, you're a bit of an asshole. And I hear you have a drug problem. So, I think we should set things straight before we go any further. If you're gonna work for me, this is the way things are gonna be…"

He then proceeded to serve me a big, 30-minute bowl of brown verbal diarrhea about how I was going into rehab, and I was going to stop swearing in interviews, and I was going to stop talking about my sexuality, and I was going to do this and that.

Meanwhile, I just sat there and took it, mostly because I needed the money, but in the back of my head I was saying, "You bastard. I'm the biggest artist this label has ever had. I've already sold hundreds of thousands of records in my career and I could make a lot of money for you and you're talking to me like I've never sold a record in my life."

It was so fuckin' stupid. Here was this french fry salesman telling me to stop being the very person the public thought Ashley MacIsaac was. I almost said to him, "Excuse me, I'm Ashley MacIsaac. You know, the 'wild-man' fiddle player who you want to make records for you?" But I didn't. I just basically shook my head and listened, but I had already decided that this guy was exactly the kind of stupid prick I could never work with.

But I had a contract, and Loggerhead had given me money, so I made a record for them.

I had no clear idea of what I wanted to do, but I did have hours and hours of digital audio tapes and cassette recordings I'd done dating all the way back to before *hi™ how are you today?* Some were from recording sessions in professional studios, some were made on mini-disc recorders on tour buses and in hotel rooms. There was all kinds of shit there: techno beats, scratching, samples from TV show themes, hip-hop rhythms, heavy metal guitar solos, you name it. What essentially happened was, I handed all that noise over to the sound engineers to play with while I laid the fiddle tracks over it. Loggerhead left me alone for the most part while I was making the record, except for chopping out the F-word from a few tracks, "so we can sell the record at Wal-Mart."

When it was done, in October 1999, I didn't really care about how it turned out one way or the other. I didn't care about anything much at that point, except getting money and getting high. I was feeling shitty about my life and my career, and about the music business in general. If you look back now at the press clippings from that time, it's obvious that I'm just a totally drugged-out mess. It's amazing how often I answered questions in interviews about the new record and my career in general with "I don't care," or "It doesn't matter." I just didn't give a shit about anything anymore. Music was just a way to make money, and with money I could eat KFC and smoke drugs.

I compared myself to Brian Wilson. I said I was an egomaniac. I said I hated the press, then I said I didn't hate the press, then I said the press could go "suck my fuckin' arse." I said that I hoped that I had lost all my integrity and professed my faith in the power of witchcraft.

Then I came out and admitted that I became addicted to crack in 1997, but said that I'd kicked it earlier that year. That, of course, was a lie, because by the fall of 1999 I was still smoking crack regularly, plus dropping the occasional hit of acid and smoking my usual daily quota of pot. I was such a mess it's a wonder I could concentrate long enough to just lay down the fiddle tracks for the record.

Then it came to the title. I had this crazy idea about putting a picture of me on the cover sitting in the middle of the produce section of a grocery store and calling it *Ashley MacIsaac: Just Me and a Bunch of Fruits*. I also thought about *Ashley MacIsaac: My Root Is Showing*, because Natalie MacMaster had put out a record called *My Roots Are Showing*. *Pickled Walnuts* was another name I started using in interviews before the thing even came out.

But the boys at Loggerhead were adamant; they wanted to call the record *Helter's Celtic*. They said they liked that title because "it played on my image."

"What the fuck image is that?" I asked. "Fuckin' crazy man, Charlie Manson, on the fiddle?"

I knew the answer of course. That's when I snapped I guess; it hit me that I'd really become the madman that the press had always said I was, and now I was so desperate to survive and get high that I couldn't run away from that image then even if I wanted to. I was reduced to selling a caricature of myself, and that pissed me off. I guess I was really mad at the world, but I needed to take my frustration out on something, so I directed my anger at the record and at Loggerhead.

In the record business, if a recording doesn't sell enough copies, the artist can be fired by the label. Well I *dreamed* of being fired by Loggerhead. When I realized Loggerhead wanted to take advantage of all the negative shit that had gone on in my career to that point just to sell a record to make money for themselves, I went out of my way to make sure that record didn't sell any copies. I went to the press and told them point blank that I didn't think the record was very good. I did "promotional" interviews where I said things like, "Please tell people not to buy my record. I don't want anybody in the world to buy this record. I'm sick of the sight of it and I don't want it sold."

Needless to say, my relationship with Loggerhead deteriorated rapidly after that. But I didn't care. If I was as greedy as that label, and as much of a monster as they wanted to portray me, I could've just gone with it. I could've got behind the record and promoted it and sucked whatever money out of the thing I could get. But it wasn't as simple as that, because I was trapped in a three-record deal, and if the experience with the next two records was going to be as bad as my experience with the first record, I didn't want any part of it.

Meanwhile, in spite of the best efforts of my new record label, my family and what friends I had left, my drug use was as constant as ever. I was getting a little pissed off though about everyone being on me about it. I just wanted people to give me some space. I even started to say as much, admitting in some magazine and newspaper interviews to using drugs to escape the pressures of fame and the music business. All that did was piss off people even more.

Then, near the end of October, when I was on a trip to Las Vegas for a bit of a holiday before the record came out, I sort of lost my mind at an auto auction. The object of my affection was a beautiful 1975 Cadillac Seville that, so the story goes, Elvis had bought for his manager Colonel Tom Parker. Well, I do have a thing for big cars from the '70s going back to my beloved Parisienne. So, I saw it, I liked it, and I bought it. Final bid: $75,000 … U.S.

The press, of course, had a field day with that one. Still, it grabbed us some great publicity with the record coming out: "There's crazy Ashley up to his old tricks again." We even planned to use the car in the video for the first single off the record, a remake of Hank Snow's "I'm Moving On."

We never got around to that though. See, the problem was I never had a hope of paying for Colonel Tom's old Caddy — not $75,000 U.S., not $75 U.S. I worked out a payment schedule with the seller, but I think I started defaulting on my second payment.

In November the record came out and the music press ripped it pretty good. They called it a "mish-mash" of sounds and styles that sounded like it was thrown together in a couple of days. Well, it *was* a collections of styles and samples, but that's what I was fuckin' shooting for. I'd been experimenting for years with hip-hop, funk, techno, dance and hard rock, as well as traditional Celtic music, and in *Helter's Celtic* I tried to bring it all together. Anyway, I figured the press ripped it not because they didn't think the record was any good, but because they just didn't like me very much, especially the East Coast press, and it didn't matter what I did.

By that time, Loggerhead was really getting on my nerves. They were at me all the time to stay off the drugs, and not say anything stupid, basically treating me like a kid again. Plus, they were giving me a hard time about money, and that was making it harder and harder to buy my drugs and do what I wanted to do. Just to spite them I continued to crap on the record in interviews, saying it *was* just thrown together in a couple of days and that I didn't really like it much. I started to really try to live up to the "jerk" label the press had hung on me by giving one-word answers in interviews and missing promotional events. Course, that didn't do anything for the relationship either.

Finally, in December, I was in New York and did an interview with *New Yorker* magazine. I was pretty stoned when I did it, and you could say I gave a "classic." Ashley MacIsaac interview, complete with cursing and gay sex talk and drug talk. I pretty much trashed Loggerhead as well, and the record. I think I must have said "It doesn't matter" a hundred times during the course of the conversation. I got a little upset at one or two stages and smashed a lamp or a chair in the hotel room. I think I was just really having fun with the writer; I even said at one point that I was weirder than Michael Jackson.

Anyway, the article came out and the upshot of the whole thing was that Ashley MacIsaac was nothing more than a promiscuous, gay drug addict.

You can imagine that put me in a great frame of mind for New Year's Eve.

Friday, December 31, 1999 — another day that will live in infamy. While every computer geek on the face of the Earth was up the wall worried that planes would start falling out of the sky at the turn of the millennium, not one of them could have guessed that the one thing that really would stop functioning that night was Ashley MacIsaac's brain.

Looking back on it now, the two months or so leading up to my scheduled New Year's Eve gig at a club in Halifax were, in a word, crazy. It's not that my schedule was crazy, it was more like I was. And considering the way I was behaving in the time leading up to that gig, it's a wonder anyone was surprised by the way it turned out.

At about 4:00 in the afternoon on New Year's Eve, 1999, I was smoking pot in a hotel room in Halifax and looking at myself in the mirror. I was pretty fucked up at that point, but I remember saying to myself: "You are a mess. What the fuck are you doing here? Did someone actually offer you $10,000 to play a gig tonight?"

Well, someone did offer me $10,000 to play a gig that night, a rave actually, to welcome in the new millennium. But I'm not sure that person knew exactly what he was buying that night.

A few weeks earlier, my unlisted phone rang out of the blue, and it's this guy I went to high school with who I hadn't said two words to the whole time I knew him. It turned out, lo and behold, he was in the music business in Halifax, working as a promoter and he was looking for a big act to play a rave on New Year's Eve. I still don't know how the fuck he got my number.

"I don't think I'm interested in going out to Halifax just to do a traditional fiddle show," I said to him. That was the truth. After all, my new record had just come out and it was loaded with hip-hop and techno samples and all kinds of different stuff.

"No, that's why I think you would be perfect for this show," he assured me. "It's a rave, and it's the millennium; people will be looking to have a good time, but they want to see something different and memorable as well."

"OK," I said. "But I hope you don't expect me to go out there and do a nice, friendly, Dick Clark, ring-in-the-New-Year thing. Because my shows just aren't like that."

No, no, he insisted, he wanted a hard-chargin', classic Ashley MacIsaac show, and he said he understood that I could be a bit vulgar and stuff like that but that didn't matter. "It's a rave," he said again. "There isn't going to be anybody there that's going to be offended by some swearing.

"Besides," he added. "It's an Ashley MacIsaac show; people are going to expect something like that."

"Well, true enough," I said, and that was it, I was booked to bring in Y2K in Halifax.

Nothing happened that night that was particularly out of the ordinary. Halifax was rocking that night, just like every other city in the world. But unlike your average New Year's Eve, this one had a bit of an edge to it, like everyone, including myself, was just a little nervous that all the shit the computer experts said was gonna happen actually would happen. It was like, "Hey, maybe this really will be the last New Year."

That sort of underlying feeling that something really bad could happen was also making people think about who they were inside and where they were in their lives. You always do that in a way on New Year's, I know, but the change of the millennium made it a bit more important. People really wanted to mark the event, do something or experience something that would make that night special for the rest of their lives. I know that's what I wanted to do.

Well, being an entertainer, I was marking the millennium by working a gig. But just because I was working didn't mean I didn't intend to have a hell of a lot of fun and make the event a memorable one for me as well.

The evening started off with a live TV performance I was booked to do on a New Year's Eve special for CTV. By the time I got to the TV studio at about 8:00, I'd already been celebrating, so to speak, for several hours in my hotel room, so I was already pretty wound up. I did a few tunes and made a few comments in between, but nothing that I thought would offend anybody. Then, while me and my band were playing "I'm Moving On" off of my new record, I started to make some more comments and the next thing I knew the director walked up waving his arms and saying, "That's it, we've gone to commercial. You're done." So that was it; I got cut off.

"No problem," says I, "Fuck ya if ya can't take a joke." I just packed up my fiddle and me and the band headed off to the next stop, my gig at the rave club called The Underground.

Now I wasn't exactly sure how I wanted the gig to go, but I did know that I didn't want it to be just a standard show. After all, it was the end of the century, and the end of the millennium, and maybe the end of the fuckin' world for all we knew, so I wanted the show to be really memorable for me and for everybody else there.

I'd been thinking for a while leading up to it about a rave I'd been to at a small gay dance club when I was in New York in 1994. That was back when raves were just beginning to happen in London and in some cities in Europe and the whole scene was very underground and cool. That rave in New York was kind of a combination of music and poetry and theatre, with people going up onstage between songs and making statements or reciting poems or whatever. I decided I wanted to try to recreate that feeling that night in Halifax, rather than just go up and play "Sleepy Maggie" for the millionth time.

I got to the club just before 11:00 P.M. and the party was really going good by then. The DJ was spinning dance and hip-hop tunes and the crowd was dancing and really getting into the whole "millennium" excitement.

I was feeling pretty good myself, because I'd smoked a couple of joints in the car before I went in, and I might have dropped some acid but I don't really remember. I know I dropped half a hit of acid at my hotel earlier in the evening, and I did take a puff of a joint before I went onstage.

Anyway, I had to go on no matter how fucked up I was; I was the big headline act who was gonna take everybody into the next century, even if we all exploded at midnight.

The "performance" that night is a bit of a blur, but I remember I started off: "And for my next number ... Oh, by the way, is anybody here drunk or high? Because if ya are, you're not gonna be in about five minutes because I'm gonna show ya what drugs really do."

Now people who use drugs regularly know that saying something like that can really crush your buzz, especially when there's a really good vibe happening, like there was that night because the DJ was good and the music was pumpin'. People started getting pissed off from that moment on because they thought I was going to go on some kind of anti-drug rant. Right away people started yelling at the stage: "C'mon man, why are you bringing us down," and "Chill out Ashley, you're screwing things up for everybody." They wanted to see the wild man, but the wild man who made it OK for them to be happy stoners for the night.

Then I remember I played a few notes on the fiddle, and everybody kind of perked up because they thought I was getting down to it as last.

But I stopped again and said, "OK, now you saw me play the fiddle; you all wanted to see that. Now here's the rest of the show. Hey you over there, the girl with the short hair. Are you a lesbian?" And it just sort of snowballed from there.

For the first few minutes of my "performance" the crowd was kind of laughing because they didn't really know what the hell I was up to. Then as I rambled on and maybe said a few things that might be considered harsh, the crowd started to take on a kind of a stunned look. I told the audience they were the ugliest bunch of losers I'd ever laid eyes on. A few minutes later, as I slipped into full vulgarity mode, people in the crowd started to yell back at me and a few even threatened me physically, which got me going even more.

I started picking people out in the crowd for special treatment. There were a couple of teenaged girls in the front row, stoned for the first time, and they were freaking out because I called them lesbian bitches. The straight guys in the audience were freaking out because I was talking about being gay and having gay sex and the gay guys were freaking out because I keep using the word "faggot." I was freaking out everybody; I didn't leave out anyone I could imagine.

People said afterwards that I used offensive racial slurs and kept asking people in the audience to come up onstage and blow me. It was a show to remember or forget, that's for sure.

Finally the manager of the place walked on to the stage and grabbed the mike out of my hands and said, "OK, you're finished."

I just looked at him kind of stunned myself and said, "Are you sure? Do you want me to finish now, because you paid me already, but I'll leave right fuckin' now."

"No way," he said. "You're finished. It's over. Get out."

Then I got my back up again. "Well I'm not leavin'," I said. "I'm gonna hang around and see what happens. You paid me for 70 minutes, so I'm gonna hang around here until the 70 minutes is up so you can't say that I wasn't here. And you just try and get me out of the building."

With that I went backstage and I just sat there on a chair listening to the crowd booing and yelling. I sat there for the next half hour with the manager, the bouncers and a bunch of upset patrons screaming at me trying to get me to leave. But no fuckin' way I was going then.

The manager went back up onstage and started cursing me out to the crowd, telling them that the club paid me $10,000 to do a one-hour set of music and that they didn't know that I was gonna go up and go on a rant insulting people for 15 minutes. He called me an asshole. He called me an idiot. He said my career was finished.

Meanwhile, I just sat in my chair backstage laughing at them all.

Finally, after I figured I'd been there long enough to satisfy my contract, I decided to leave. I stood up and said, "OK, if none of you bastards is man enough to throw me out, I'll just have to leave on my own." By then the place was practically empty and nobody was dancing anymore. The manager and the bouncers were threatening me then, saying I better give back the money they paid me or they'd fuckin' kill me.

"Happy New Year," I yelled as I walked out the door.

I didn't feel bad about how the show had gone, not one bit. At that point, I felt I was totally justified. I was contracted to do a 70-minute show, and 15 minutes into the show they decided they didn't like the way it was going. Well that was just too fuckin' bad for them, I thought. I gave them an intense show, without any blood or gore, and at the end of the day it was all just words. That's all it was. Shit, guys like Allen Ginsberg and Lenny Bruce used to do the exact same thing and people revere them.

To be honest, after it was all over, I actually thought I'd done a pretty good job of recreating that underground New York rave scene I remembered. Plenty of other people, on the other hand, didn't see it that way. In fact, "offensive" and "scary" were words I heard a lot afterwards. My memory of that night is little clouded, to say the least, but people in the press who were there say the whole show was just a rant of "profanity, sexual comments and racial epithets." Apparently I was using bad words to describe people's sexual orientation. I was calling lesbians dykes when I shouldn't. I even bent over a few times, it seems, and told the audience to suck my anus.

Well, going by the way the show was described in the newspapers afterward, it's quite understandable that people were offended and were calling me a racist or whatever. But to me, the whole thing was ridiculous, because I didn't mean anything that I said that night to be offensive; I was just an artist doing a very hard-core show at a rave, for Christ's sake. It wasn't a square dance at the community centre in

Creignish, after all. Oh yeah, that and I was ADDICTED TO DRUGS at the time, but I guess that was a minor point.

I didn't get to do as long as I would've liked either. I was only on stage for about 15 minutes, and only 10 minutes of that was the actual performance, while the other five was me arguing with the management of the place about why they should let me continue. I was scheduled to do over an hour.

The only thing the press didn't have anything bad to say about that night was the music, but that was because I only played about two or three notes. I would have played more music, but, like I say, I never got the opportunity to continue. In a 60-minute set I usually do about 50 minutes of actual music and the rest is me talking to the audience. In the case of the New Year's Eve show, I just started off with a lot of talking. They might have heard some good music if they'd have let me go.

No doubt about it, I was rude and I was vulgar and I was intense, but so is Dennis Miller.

To be honest, the show turned out a lot tamer than I'd planned going in. I don't know if it was my problems with Loggerhead or the way the record had been ripped by the music press, but I obviously had a lot of anger inside me at that time and I had plans to vent it at that rave in a really big way. I mean, I thought about bringing a dead rabbit onstage and cutting it up. I was looking for blood, gore; I wanted the whole thing to be a crazy gore fest. At one point I thought it would be a good idea to string a clothesline across the stage and hang a few cats from it so they could howl while I played — a real Alice Cooper–type vibe.

I even warned the people who booked me that I had a pretty wild show in mind and they agreed to let me do it. They may have thought I meant the standard wild Ashley MacIsaac show, with the kilt and the step dancing and the crazy solos, but anyway they agreed to it.

But, as the show approached, I started to think that getting animals involved would be a little complicated, not to mention against the law probably. I finally said to myself, "Why the hell am I thinking of doing this?" First of all, all it was gonna do was gross people out. On top of that, because it was a rave and it was New Year's Eve, most of the people there would probably be high on ecstasy or something, or they'd be drunk, so a gore fest show would definitely freak a few of them out. I definitely didn't want any little girls on E throwing up or passing out. I might have liked to see that, but I'm pretty sure their parents would-n't have appreciated it. Whatever I did, I just knew it couldn't dissolve into chaos.

But still, I wanted to freak people out that night. I wanted to give them an experience they'd never forget at the turn of the millennium. So, I tried to accomplish that with just a microphone. And you know what? With just that microphone I managed to create two years' worth of chaos — mostly for myself, unfortunately.

Still, I accomplished my goal of giving those people an experience they'll never forget, and I'm quite proud of that. They went there expecting a nice little Cape Breton hootenanny and within two minutes I was telling them, "I'd like to cut your face off, faggot," "I'd like to take a knife and cut your uterus out, you dyke."

Looking back now, I still find it unbelievable that people were so surprised at the way I behaved. Imagine people finding Ashley MacIsaac being vulgar unusual, especially at that low point in my life. All they had to do was look at the three years of crack-addicted media I'd offered to the world up to that point and they might've expected I wasn't going to lead the crowd in the Lord's Prayer.

I don't blame that night entirely on the drugs though. Sure I was high before I went onstage that night, but what the hell else is new. I smoked a joint right before I went onstage, which is something I'd done a thousand times before. But it wasn't as if the whole act was random. I'd planned to do an intense, vulgar, nasty show that would frighten those little Ecstasy girls right out of their panties. I didn't set out to come off like a racist, hate-mongering, anti-Christian homophobe, but if that's what I had to do to shake people up, I was willing to do it. But shouldn't it have been obvious from about three words into it when I made fun of somebody in the audience for being gay — as if — that there was a show going on?

A couple of people did cop that. There were a couple of girls in the front I remember who were shocked at first, then started to really laugh the more other people in the audience got upset and started to come back at me. Also, about 10 minutes into it, I noticed this huge guy in the middle of the crowd standing head and shoulders above the rest of them and I realized it was a guy I knew from my hometown. Now this guy was the toughest, meanest hockey player to ever come out of Creignish, but I picked him out anyway and let him have a dose of his own. He reacted like anyone from Creignish who knows me at all would react: he laughed. He caught what I was doing. Then he yelled back, "Yer really lettin' em have it tonight, Ash."

The people who got it, they had great fun for those 15 minutes. That wasn't true of most of them though. By the time the manager came on to pull me off, quite a few of the girls were leaving. And why not? They'd gone from being high, and dancing, and having a great time to being yelled at, and called whores and dykes, and crying, all in a matter of 15 minutes. But that was my exact point: Whether you think drugs are nice or not, the good trip you're on can turn into a nightmare all of a sudden. Drugs had taught me that much by then.

I don't deny that I said some pretty vulgar stuff onstage that night, but I always go back to the fact that it was a rave. I probably wouldn't say some of the things I said at a regular show, but I felt what I said was appropriate in that context. I also felt that it was appropriate that I was commenting on the dangers of the rave scene. I think that's what was the scariest part for the people there.

Well, luckily the millennium bug didn't blow up all the computers and the media was able to come down on me like a ton of bricks the next day. All I could do was go back to my apartment in Toronto, lock the door and pull the covers over my head.

Just about the first one to chime in and say what an asshole I was was my very own record label. On January 5, Loggerhead Records put out a press release with a statement from Andrew McCain that said, "We are offended by Ashley's recent behaviour. We signed Ashley for one reason only, his musical talent." He was offended by my behaviour, apparently, not just as the label president, but "as a father."

Paul Church joined in the next day, telling the *National Post,* "I hope Ashley gets some help."

The same day, the *Halifax Chronicle-Herald* ran an open letter to my mother, criticizing her for not spanking me more when I was a kid. Well, that brought me out of hiding right away. I called up the *Chronicle-Herald* and told them I was filing for bankruptcy that week when I knew I wasn't. They ran a big story about it and ended up looking stupid. I didn't feel too bad about it though, because it was only really a half-lie; I knew I was going to have to go bankrupt eventually, it just didn't really happen officially until a few months later. And actually, because I'd planted that story out of spite after New Year's, it kind of softened the blow that came in the press when I finally did file for bankruptcy. I knew when I went bankrupt that it would be in the press again, but they couldn't really do as much with it as they wanted because they'd already cried wolf four months earlier.

Anyway, the only reason I lied like that was because they picked on my mother for the New Year's fiasco. So you bet I jerked them around; I mean, say what you like about me but leave my mother out of it.

I tried to defend myself a few days later in an interview with the CBC: "I don't think anyone should have any concept in their minds that what I did was how I was musically going forward," I said. "Obviously I don't think so. I thought it was a one-off, I didn't think it was a story. I thought I was speaking to the children who were there."

I told a reporter from some newspaper that I was trying to deliver "an Allen Ginsberg–style, stream-of-consciousness rant.

"It was the turn of the millennium," I said. "I was having fun. I figured I should be able to have fun and maybe I have fun in a weird way, but gosh, I think everybody knows that already, don't they?"

Nobody seemed to believe I had any kind of good intentions though, and in the days and weeks that followed, the floodgates just opened. First, CBC Radio dumped me from a scheduled performance on their "Kitchen Party" series. In the announcement, the show's executive producer said, "Overall he has become very unpredictable, and we're not prepared to cope with that."

Not long after, CTV started making noise about not paying me for the New Year's performance they pulled the plug on. The show's executive producer told the *Halifax Daily News,* "The payment is under review because of the performance and because of contractual obligations — what was expected and what was received." He added that all kinds of people had called in to complain about my performance, using words like "pathetic," "embarrassment," and "disgrace."

Later that same week, the annual Scottish Festival of Music, or Scotia Fest, in Halifax dropped me from its list of artists-in-residence. I was booked to give two performances and teach some master classes in fiddling at the festival that coming May. The organizers of the event told the press, "We can't risk Ashley not showing up and not doing what he has been asked to do. It is also not the image Scotia Fest needs." It came out afterwards that the organizers were under pressure to drop me from the festival's big sponsors, Sable Offshore Energy (the gas company) and the Bank of Montreal, because they didn't want to be associated with my name in any way. They even reprinted all the brochures for the festival just to get my name out.

After that the gigs started to fall like dominos. I was supposed to start the East Coast leg of a national tour to promote the new record with three nights at the Marquee Club in Halifax, but they quickly disappeared. At that point, it started to become obvious that I wasn't going to be welcome anywhere on the East Coast for a while, so the entire East Coast leg of the tour went in the shitter.

I was really stung by a stunt at the East Coast Music Awards that year. It was just a couple of months after the whole thing happened and "Ashley's millennium meltdown" was still big news in Halifax, where the awards show was being held. I didn't attend that year primarily because I had a gig to play in New York, but I was just as happy to stay away from Halifax just then.

Of course, that didn't stop the show organizers from poking fun at me by wheeling that guy dressed up to look like me with tape over his mouth out on to the stage strapped to a dolly like Hannibal Lecter. Everyone there had a good laugh over it I was told.

The ECMAs were on the Saturday night and I didn't really hear about the joke until I flew back in to Halifax from New York on the Monday. That was when someone showed me a picture in the paper of the pretend-Ashley out on the stage.

"OK, that's fine," I thought to myself. "Fuck 'em, they'll never get anything else from me." I felt I was completely justified in feeling that way at that point, after all I'd done to help make that show a national event. As if I didn't have enough people turning on me in the couple of months following the New Year's show, the ECMAs has to do it on national television?

Still, I wasn't completely without friends after my little New Year's celebration. My friend Rob Cohn, who was acting as my business manager at the time, tried to stick up for me in the press, although I told him not to say anything. He said I probably got "pushed over the edge" because of my "troubled love life," financial troubles, professional pressure, and "a lot of Catholic guilt for being gay."

My good friend Gerry "Spoonman" Deveau, who built my house in Belle Cote and played the spoons with me on *hi™ how are you today?* called me and talked me into playing a traditional ceilidh with him and my fellow Cape Breton fiddlers Brenda Stubbert and Jackie Dunn at the Doryman Pub in Cheticamp, "to get your mind off your troubles," he said. Then he told the Halifax *Herald,* "I always welcome Ashley with open arms. He was very good to me: I've toured with him and built his house, and now I look after it for him."

It was great to know not everyone hated me, especially at home in Cape Breton. I think the people who have stuck with me the most through the years, regardless of what the scandal of the day happened to be, have been musicians, musicians from Cape Breton and the East Coast especially. I've had relatives who decided they didn't want to talk to me for one reason or another over certain periods of time, but that was partly jealousy. But I can't remember any musician I knew who ever refused to talk to me. The reason for that, I think, is because only professional musicians understand what the pressure to perform to a certain standard is like, and what it's like to be in the public eye. The ones who've made it big, of course, understand even more what it's like to be in the fishbowl of celebrity — the fans, the groupies, the media, the industry bloodsuckers.

The acts from Cape Breton who've made it big share a really special kinship because none of us ever expected to have the kinds of opportunities we did have. We were all just born into the same Cape Breton Scottish culture and grew up playing music because we loved it and it was just inside us to do it. We all started out the same before we were famous; none of us had any idea how really big it could get, or how overwhelming the media and the music industry can be when it does get big. Plus we all know where the other one comes from, so you can't put on airs with your own. It's like, "Yeah, he's got a nice suit on him now, but I remember when the arse was out of his jeans."

The Rankin Family were really the first ones from Cape Breton to make it big on a national level. I actually came with them, I think in '94 or '95, and played a few shows when they went on their first "tour" into Ontario. I remember we played at the Mariposa Folk Festival and I got introduced to a guy named Richard Flohil who I found out later is a big wheel in the Canadian music industry. Richard was there to meet the Rankins and he was really excited about them and wanted to help them move their careers along in Canada. I remember sitting there listening to him talk about the industry and what the Rankins needed to do to move to the next level. Me and the Rankins just looked at each other in amazement. Both the Rankins and myself were well-established acts in Cape Breton and throughout the East Coast really by that time, but we still didn't have a clue how big it could get.

The Rankins and me sort of grew up together, in Cape Breton and in the music industry. That's why it just knocked the shit out of me when it came across the news January 16 that John Morris Rankin had died in a car crash in Cape Breton. Apparently he'd been driving his son and a couple of friends to their hockey game early that morning in Margaree Harbour when his truck swerved off the icy road and into the Gulf of St. Lawrence. The boys got out, but John Morris didn't make it. He was only 40.

With the state I was in emotionally from the drugs and the pressure of the fallout from the New Year's fiasco, the news of John Morris's death was just the last straw. I was supposed to start my national tour in Windsor, Ontario, on March 2, then move right across the country, wrapping up in Nanaimo, B.C., on March 20. But the thought of doing so many shows when things were just so bad was too much to face. I cancelled most of the western dates on the tour and kept less than half the shows I was originally scheduled to do. I took a hit in the wallet over that but my financial situation being so bad anyway it probably didn't make much difference in the end.

As for the new record, by the beginning of February 2000, it was pretty much dead in the water. I had basically no contact with Loggerhead after the New Year's shit hit the fan, but I didn't care because I figured I'd gotten as much money as I was gonna get out of them, unless they sold a lot more records. There wasn't much chance of that though, because they'd fucked up the promotion of the thing right from the get-go by going out of their way to put a negative spin on the record. After all, it was them who insisted on naming it *Helter's Celtic* after Charlie fuckin' Manson. Goes to show you what they thought of me.

The thing is though, everybody kind of did think that I was that insane, and that's why they did it. New Year's just confirmed it. I knew I was in trouble too, but I couldn't bear the thought of my record company deliberately trying to make money off my problems.

I mean, think about it: here I was, struggling with cocaine and crack addiction, just one step ahead of the taxman, facing bankruptcy, persecuted because of my sexuality and ripped regularly by the press for my lifestyle, and here they come along and try to link me with one of the world's craziest, most notorious mass murderers just to sell records.

Right from the beginning of our relationship Loggerhead was always telling me how they wanted the release of my next record to be a positive thing, to get something positive going in my career and my life, and I was all for that. So I worked hard on the record. I pushed all my problems to the side so I could get it done. Then, when all the hard work was done and I thought we had something positive to release, Loggerhead says, "OK the record is great. Now let's put together a nice marketing campaign starring Ashley as a madman and sell this thing."

My reaction to that, of course, was, "Well, no thank you." So no, I didn't get behind the record and I did bad-mouth it in the press and started making noises about getting out of my record deal. Then comes New Year's Eve.

Just think of how stupid Loggerhead was. Here they are trying to sell a CD using a dark, negative marketing campaign to take advantage of the artist's notorious reputation. So the artist goes out and does a dark, negative, insane performance that gets all kinds of press and is just tailor-made for the image they're trying to promote. You'd think they'd have the brains to just say, "Thank you very much, Ashley," and go with it. But no, instead they decided to turn on me.

In the days and weeks following the New Year's Eve show, the people from Loggerhead took every chance they got to distance themselves from me. They were saying that I needed psychiatric help and that they tried to get me straightened out but I was out of control. Of course, the marketing campaign for the record was all my idea by then. It was like they were the pure, well-intentioned businessmen who didn't know what they were getting into and I really *was* Charlie Manson. I felt really betrayed and started saying publicly that I had no intention of honouring my contract with them.

"If these people are going to be this stupid, then fuck 'em," I figured. I gave them a good product that they said they liked, and they got it pretty cheap because I needed the money. Then they decided to sell it on the negative image thing and link it to a convicted mass murderer against my wishes. Then finally, when I do something that plays up the negative image, suddenly they have nothing to do with the whole thing.

For fuck's sake, they'd given the first video from the record, the video for "I'm Moving On," to MuchMusic just a few weeks before New Year's and it was in rotation. Then after New Year's they call up Denise Donlon and tell her, "You see Denise, it's like this. That artist that we've been promoting and pushing you to get on the air, well, we really have nothing to do with him."

When I found out about that, I called up some music journalists I knew to tell them that I didn't want people to buy the record because I didn't want Loggerhead to make a penny more off the negative publicity they were now running from.

"Fuckin' bastards," I thought. "They don't want the good Ashley MacIsaac and they don't want the bad Ashley MacIsaac either. Well they don't have to have Ashley MacIsaac at all then."

That was pretty much that with Loggerhead, although they didn't release me from my contract right away. Oh, Loggerhead had no problem shitting on me publicly after the New Year's thing, but no fuckin' way were they going to wash their hands of me legally. In fact, they even said I owed them money on the production of the record because it hadn't sold enough copies to cover the cost.

Then, after Andrew McCain telling the press "we'll never work with Ashley MacIsaac again," they tried to tell me I couldn't make records for anyone else. Basically, Loggerhead was saying that because they had a deal with me for two more records — never mind the fact they didn't want to work with me anymore — they were still entitled to money from any record I might make for another record company. And to add insult to injury, I was told that if I came around the Loggerhead offices, I'd be arrested (which, come to think of it, probably wasn't a bad idea on their part, considering the nasty thoughts that were going through my mind concerning certain principals at the company).

It would take another year and a half before I managed to pull myself out of that shit pile, and I went bankrupt in the process. But at least I got out of that record deal, and I didn't kill anybody and I didn't go to jail, so score one for Ashley.

After the New Year's Eve thing, Loggerhead didn't seem think it was necessary to try to sell the record anymore and it just sort of slipped beneath the waves. But that will happen to any record, no matter who releases it or how good it is, if both the record company and the artist aren't behind it 100 per cent. *Helter's Celtic* sold about 20,000 copies in the first two months after it was released, and that was with the press bashing it, and then me bashing it because I was pissed off at Loggerhead. It could have sold a lot more in the months following New Year's if both Loggerhead and me had got behind it. But Loggerhead fucked it up because they panicked over the press reaction to one bad show, instead of figuring out how take advantage of the scandal it caused.

My *Helter's Celtic* experience'll never be over for me really, because I'll see that record for the rest of my life with that title on it and all that that means. Am I bitter about my Loggerhead experience? I can say today that I hold no grudge. I know that, because today I can sit and eat a nice McCain's Deep and Delicious chocolate cake, with white frosting and chocolate sprinkles, and it doesn't upset my stomach. I couldn't do that for a long time after. I couldn't even look at them; they disgusted me. When I saw a McCain's frozen pizza in my fridge one time, I threw it out on the road. But not anymore. I mean, why should I take my frustrations out on McCain's fine frozen foods and baked goods, just because that family spawned the evil youth that owned the record company that screwed me around for a year and a half.

✳ ✳ ✳

It took a while but things started to get slowly back on track as the New Year's incident faded into the past. My old friend and mentor Philip Glass gave me a hand up once again by inviting me to play at the annual Tibet House benefit concert at Carnegie Hall in New York, the scene of so many good times for me in the past. That show came at the perfect time and gave me a shot of confidence when I needed it the most.

I'd been through a hell of a lot in the previous six months or so, so when I arrived at Kennedy Airport on a cold Thursday morning in early February 2000, I wasn't in the mood to party like I usually was when I hit New York. I knew the press back in Canada was going to be watching me like a hawk after what happened in Halifax, just waiting for me to embarrass myself on the biggest stage in the world. I wasn't going to give them the satisfaction though, and I was never going to do anything to embarrass Philip after all he'd done for me.

The line-up of stars on the bill was amazing, of course. There was Philip as well as David Byrne, Patti Smith, Rufus Wainwright and Trey Anastasio from Phish. I came out and played a couple of tunes by myself and then David Byrne came out and joined me onstage for one. Throughout the rest of the night I sat in here and there with the other performers, just playing a background role and keeping my mouth shut.

In fact, the only time I did speak to the audience was when someone in the crowd shouted, "Yo, Cape Breton," and I went to the mike and answered, "Hello, Father Stanley," and crossed myself.

Philip took care of me throughout the whole show, introducing me to the audience and to any of the performers I didn't know already. Robert Thurman, the head of Tibet House (and Uma Thurman's father), also went to great lengths to make me feel welcome, and I really appreciated that.

In the end, it all worked out exactly like I hoped it would, with nothing but positive vibes all round. The *Globe and Mail* said I comported myself "like a perfect Boy Scout," and "behaved like a repentant man in front of a parole board." I don't know about the repentant part, but I think I did prove that I could mind my manners when I wanted to.

With that solid performance under my belt, I set out over the course of the next couple of months to win back the confidence of the booking agents. I followed up the Tibet benefit with a visit to the very scene of the crime, a series of shows around Nova Scotia, including a couple in Halifax itself, with my old friend Howie MacDonald backing me up on the piano. I packed pubs and clubs wherever I went, although lots of the people who bought tickets only showed up because they were hoping I'd have another meltdown. In fact, on more than one occasion I had people shouting at me between tunes, "Ashley, do somethin'," and

"Hey Ashley, Happy New Year." I just kept my head down though and played my fiddle.

After Nova Scotia I did three sold-out nights at an Irish pub called the Medieval Room in Montreal, of all places. Demand for tickets was so big, the club ended up putting four bouncers on the door to keep the gate-crashers out. I played with my cousin Wendy on piano, and the press said I was "the soul of professionalism," during those Montreal gigs, in spite of the fact everyone was still waiting for the next explosion.

But, against the odds, I was keeping it together and building momentum for what I hoped would be the big "comeback" performance that would put the New Year's debacle to bed forever: a sold-out show on March 3, 2000, for more than a thousand people at the George Weston Recital Hall in Toronto.

The build-up to the Toronto show was so crazy it was like the Super Bowl or something was being played. But when you consider the fact that Toronto is the centre of both the music and the media industries in Canada, I guess you could say, for me, it *was* the Super Bowl. The Tibet thing was a good start, but I wasn't the headliner there. And a string of successful gigs at small clubs in Nova Scotia and Montreal was great, but Toronto was the big time. The rest of my career, if I was going to have one, depended on how I performed at that show — at least that's what the experts said.

Denise Donlon, the head of MuchMusic, said that after what happened on New Year's I had to demonstrate "creative consistency." She told the *Toronto Sun,* "We all know his genius level and all of that, but he needs to restore some faith in concert-goers, and the industry in general, that he's the guy to bet on."

Larry LeBlanc, the Canadian editor of *Billboard* magazine, said that if I didn't prove that I could deliver onstage again, I'd never get the chance to do another record. "That's the least that's expected of you — not to screw up your shows," he said.

My old manager Sheri Jones even got into the act. She was quoted in the *Sun* saying, "I think every show Ashley does is very very important. I think that after everything that went on in January, the only way he can really re-establish himself as a great musician and performer is to go out there and do it."

I hadn't talked to the people at Loggerhead at all, basically, since before the New Year's show, but I was still under contract with them, and they actually showed up at the Toronto show, telling the press they just wanted me to "come back and have fun," and "prove that he's the artist that we all know he is."

"Well, thanks a lot," I thought when I read that. "Where the fuck was that support when I really needed it — in January?"

I did the show with Howie MacDonald and my sister Lisa and a couple of other musicians and the whole thing came off without a hitch. We basically stuck with a playlist of traditional tunes with a few of the more well-known contemporary songs, like "Sleepy Maggie," thrown in for flavour. I stayed seated for most of the show, which was not like me at all, but I just didn't feel like stomping around that particular night. I was more interested in concentrating on the music.

Once again, I didn't say much, but I couldn't resist saying into the mike at one point, "We sound pretty good considering we haven't really had a good rehearsal since New Year's."

That prompted one of the guys in the band to chime in: "How was that show?" he asked, smiling.

"Good rehearsal, bad show," I said, and that was the end of it.

That show in Toronto was nothing special really, just a solid, traditional fiddle show like I'd give at a square dance on Cape Breton on any given Saturday night before I was ever famous. But that's exactly what it needed to be — solid. The next day, one Toronto paper described the show as "a traditional two hours of reels and jigs, expertly performed without any fooling around." As for me, "the constantly seated headliner would have been an appropriate and welcome guest on the old *Don Messer's Jubilee.*" Well, as any Nova Scotian will tell you, you can't get any better than that.

So I was back again, as a professional touring musician anyway. But, though I could at least feed myself and pay my rent, I was still a long way from being the "recording star" I used to be. My success in Toronto and in the gigs leading up to it led to a string of solo gigs all over Ontario as well as a series of shows with the likes of Stuart Cameron, Jimmy Rankin, the Barra MacNeils, Lennie Gallant, the Mahones, the Colour of Soul, and the Chieftains. Still, no matter how often I worked at that point, I was never going to be able to make enough to stave off the inevitable.

By April of 2000, all the drugs, and all the room service, and all the partyin', and all the fiddling while Rome burned finally caught up with me. When I officially declared bankruptcy in April of 2000, it was really just an anti-climax. The bankruptcy had been coming for almost a year or more by that point. Christ, in the summer of 1999, before I left Universal and signed with Loggerhead, I was well on my way to not being able to pay my taxes. I would've filed then if the advance I got from Loggerhead for *Helter's Celtic* hadn't pulled my ass out of the fire.

By April 2000, I'd sold close to half a million records and played, at a conservative estimate of about 200 shows a year, something like 1,400 shows in the previous seven years, going back to when I was 18. After all that, at the time of my bankruptcy filing, my assets were valued at $119,000. They included my house, valued at $100,000; a '49 Dodge valued at $2,500; a '72 Olds valued at $4,500; a '69 Olds valued at $1,000; furniture and household items valued at $10,000; and musical instruments valued at $1,000. I had no cash, no stocks or bonds, no RRSPs, no gold, no jewellery, no winning lottery tickets.

On the other side of the scale, I had liabilities totalling $305,633.68. My creditors included Revenue Canada, which was looking for $180,000 in back taxes; the Royal Bank, which held my $100,000 house mortgage; and Royal Bank Visa, which was owed another $13,000 on my Visa card. Only two of the three showed up at my hearing in Halifax.

I happened to be touring in the States with the band Seven Nations at the time — making money for someone else — so I was represented by my trustee. It was all over in a matter of 15 minutes, I was told. Thanks to an exemption for personal belongings related to your profession, I was allowed to keep my fiddles.

It's funny, but when you have a lot of money, you don't even think about how much little essential things like food and shelter cost, because you're too busy thinking about all the non-essential things you wanna buy, in my case dope. But after I went bankrupt, that's when it hit me just how much money I'd pissed away on living the high life — literally. After I "took the cure," as they say, I was still working but I didn't have money for any fancy shit anymore. I was down to the bare essentials: some food to eat every day; a reasonable place to live; and, just for sanity's sake, a little bit of pot.

After the bankruptcy came out in the papers, someone asked my old manager Sheri Jones, the person who was with me at the very beginning, what she thought about it all. "He made the decision and did what he had to do," she said. "I think it is really sad that it's come to this."

No shit.

~ 10 ~

Poor and Famous

Fame came to me pretty early in life, probably too early for my own good, but it was still late enough that it was a shock to my system.

There's no real trick to being famous, no way you've got to act or talk. That's because who you are as a person doesn't really have anything to do with why you're famous most of the time. People are famous because they can shoot a puck, or throw a football, or sing, or play the fiddle, and their particular personality doesn't necessarily have anything to do with their talent. Actors, meanwhile, are famous because they're good at *not* being themselves.

Still, once their particular talent takes that average person and turns them into a famous person, the process almost always has an effect on their personality. Just look at Madonna: she speaks with a bad English accent now, and she spent the first, what, 30 years of her life at least living in the States. So being famous, for the most part, is about putting on an air at the right time so someone hears you or gets it on tape. Then you can go back to being yourself. I bet when Madonna's on the can she's as Detroit as she was when she was 16.

I got a small taste of fame when I was just a kid. When I was a champion step dancer, I travelled all over Nova Scotia and to other provinces in the Maritimes to competitions and festivals, so I knew what it felt like to perform in front of an audience and to have people cheer for you and applaud what you were doing. It was the same when I started playing my fiddle at square dances and such.

I don't think I started to actually want to be famous until I first saw the show *Fame* on TV when I was a kid. It was then that I realized some people have special talents and some people don't, and it's the ones with the special talent that become famous. I knew I was a pretty good fiddle player because people I respected, like my music teachers and other musicians, told me I was, and lots of people liked to listen to me play. So even as a kid, I started to think of myself as being someone kind of important, or at least unique.

I got a greater sense of what it was like to be famous when I started playing the fiddle for money all around Cape Breton. But that was like being famous in my own backyard. Fame, I found out later, was when somebody walks up to you on the street in Vancouver and asks for your autograph. Stardom, on the other hand, was when that same person in Vancouver offers to sleep with you.

I never had a problem with that aspect of being famous either — people walking up and just talking to me or asking me for an autograph. (I never had a problem with them asking to sleep with me either actually.) I'm polite, generally, like I think most Cape Bretoners are bred to be with strangers, and under the right conditions I can be a golden boy.

In the last little while though, with all the shit I've been though, I admit I probably haven't been as nice to fans as I once was. For a long while there, I'm sure I was as nasty as any other drug-addicted celebrity.

If I had to pick a time when I really felt the most famous, I'd have to say it was when I played those three shows in one day and made $40,000 doing it. It just amazed me that I could make that much money — as much as most people in Cape Breton make in a year — in one day. It amazed me that there were that many people interested in booking me on the same day. And, finally, it really amazed me that I could walk away from it all with basically nothing and not give a shit because I had my dope. How many people can do that? There had to be something bigger than me as a person, going on around me, I figured, that would allow me to experience a day like that, and it just had to be fame.

Another thing about fame is, not only does it alter your personality, it alters the personalities of almost every person you meet. People who you've never met in your life start kissing your ass as soon as you shake their hand. They kiss it even more if you're just a little bit nice to them, and they kiss it even more if you're an asshole.

Now in my case, I couldn't get enough of that. In fact, I needed all the people around I could get who were willing to do things for me without getting anything in return, because I already had a whole bunch of people around me getting paid to do things for me.

But if people do things for you and expect to get paid, I'm fine with that. What I can't stand are the people who hang around and do nothing and expect to get, or take, things from you just because you're famous. People like that, whether they're groupies or just leeches, have the attitude, "Ashley won't mind if we order room service, he's got lots of money," or "Let's smoke Ashley's pot, he's got lots of it." It never crosses their mind that you might have bills to pay just like they do, and a lot more besides because you are famous and actually provide employment for a lot of people.

Some people just assume that because a person is famous, even just a little famous, that they somehow eat better or live in a massive house. Let's say you see some guy on the street and you recognize his face because he's an actor you've seen in a few TV commercials — that does-n't mean he's going to have any more money in his pocket at that moment than you do. Likewise, just because there may be 10 people hanging around my dressing room after a gig, they shouldn't assume that I could afford to order Chinese food for everybody. I may only have 20 bucks in my pocket at the end of the day.

But I didn't understand that at the time. At 20 years old, I was famous *and rich*. I didn't pay my own bills; I didn't even think about bills. I didn't have a cheque book or a bank book. I just didn't have to deal with that shit. Of course, I wasn't living in any particular place at that time. I was living mostly in hotels, so I didn't accumulate the monthly bills that most people deal with and that I have to deal with now, like rent, phone, cable, groceries, whatever. Even when I was 16 and 17 and 18, and living in my parents' house, any time I wanted to buy anything I just got the cash out of the pile I had in my dresser. It didn't matter what it was, a car, a leather jacket, a vacation; if I wanted it, I bought it.

When I was famous *and rich,* my concerns when it came to money mostly revolved around having enough to buy the dope I wanted. And I was pretty generous about it then too: I wouldn't just buy a pound of dope for myself; I'd buy a half a pound for me and give a half a pound away to other people. That's when you know you're famous *and rich,* when you have such a seemingly endless flow of money you don't even worry about giving away stuff you're addicted to. Try talking a homeless crack addict out of his last rock of cocaine and you'll know what I mean.

When the money flows like that for one year, then two years, then three years, and year after year, you really do begin to think it is endless. It's like you can't spend it all. It fact, you stop thinking about money and what things cost altogether. I never even knew how much money I had at any given time. I suppose if I'd gone out and paid cash for a Ferrari out of the blue one day I could've gone through all the cash I had on hand in a couple of weeks. But, as a 19-, 20- or 21-year-old, to have two or three hundred thousand dollars at your disposal at any given time, that's pretty fuckin' rich.

That's all I'm missing in my life now, the rich part. I've still got the fame, such as it is; people know my name and most know my face if they see a picture of me, in Canada at least. I can still play the fiddle, so I can make money and pay my bills. But I don't make so much these days that I can run around buying fancy cars and buying Chinese food (or pot, for that matter) for 20 people after every show.

So I'm not exactly destitute. People think, "Oh there's Ashley MacIsaac; he's addicted to drugs; he went bankrupt; he's had all these problems in his career…" and they make things out to be really bad for me. But I don't. I'm not crying the blues because I'm not living the "rock star" lifestyle anymore or blaming anybody for stealing my money. I'm not playing that game. It's just a simple fact that I once worked hard enough and had enough money to drive around in a nice, new S-Class Mercedes and now I don't. But that doesn't mean that I won't have enough money to drive a car like that again. For Christ's sake, I'm still in my 20s.

The good thing is, now I won't have to work as hard to have that kind of money because I know so much more than I did when I was 19. I don't expect to ever play 300 dates in a year again, the way I did when I first became famous. Back then it was a case where the record company needed me to put my name and my face and the music out in front of people so they would get to know me and might buy my CD. All that work is done now — most people in Canada and a lot around the world already know who Ashley MacIsaac is and they know, basically, what to expect from me musically.

Plus, I've been through a lot of shit in the last couple of years that I don't expect to ever have to go through again. It's like that old saying: what doesn't kill you makes you stronger.

I had a lot of highs at the beginning of my career, maybe too many highs. And I might be stupid to think so, but I think I've had more than my fair share of lows in the last two or three years. If you believe life goes in cycles, as I do, then you'll agree that I'm on the upswing now and on the road to a pretty healthy lifestyle and a pretty healthy bank account. But if I'm going to go on doing what I do, I have to think that I can have the things I had at 21 when I'm 30 and older. If I didn't think that, I probably wouldn't bother fighting to stay in the music business.

I know that it's more than partly my fault, but I've had to eat a lot of shit in the last couple of years and I'm just about fed up with the taste of it. My career went higher than I ever dreamed it would in the space of a year and half, but it came down one hell of a lot faster and I've had to get my head around that. Imagine playing for the Queen herself and having her shake your hand and tell you "you're just fabulous," then, inside of four years later, you're dodging drunks in some fuckin' bar called the Eight Ball in Chatham, Ontario.

Obviously, I didn't take the gig at the Eight Ball because I wanted to; I took it because I needed the $1,200 to make a mortgage payment on my house in Cape Breton. So to Chatham I went, and I thought I was playing a good show, at least good enough that I didn't deserve to feel threatened. Still, I turned around at one point and there's some guy with a beer bottle in his hand dancing on the stage no more than four feet from me, drunk out of his mind.

All I could think of that second was, "Oh great, he's going to hit me with the bottle." But I didn't wait around to find out; I got right the fuck out of there and right the fuck out of Chatham.

Now the guy didn't hit me or anything — in fact, he was loving me — but I was still scared. Was I right to leave? I think any musician who considers themselves a professional, or, God forbid, an "artist," reaches the point where they're no longer prepared to put up with drunk ass-holes dancing onstage while they're trying to play. I don't think that's a lot to ask. I was there doing a show for not much money, and me an international recording artist with gold records and Juno Awards, so I figured the least they could've done was not let anyone yell, "Heeeeeyyyy Ashleeeeyyyyyy! You're fuckin' greaaaaaaat maaaaaan," in my face while I was working.

Now if I wasn't convinced by that point, in late 2001, at 26 years old, that the initial tidal wave of fame and fortune that I'd been riding since I was 19 had petered out, that night really brought it home to me. On the ride back to Toronto I thought to myself, "Holy fuck, I've played for the Queen, for the Pope. I've played in Carnegie Hall. Now I'm playing in Chatham for $1,200 for a bunch of drunks in a club called the Eight Ball. How much lower can ya go?" Well, as it turned out, a little lower yet.

About six months after my "Eight Ball" experience, and in no better financial condition, I took a gig against my own better judgement, and it's exactly because of gigs like that one that I don't tend to trust anyone in the music business, including my manager or agent, with my personal well being. I was booked, believe it or not, in a strip club.

I was on tour in Western Canada and I'd been playing lots of clubs and Irish pub–type places almost every other night. Because of my financial situation at the time, my manager was right on me about spending money. He even told me, "Don't go out and spend $50 or $60 on dinner. You can eat McDonald's just as easy." Then, right in the middle of this "bargain basement" tour, I land in Victoria, British Columbia, the very place where I had performed for the Queen on one of her Canadian visits only a few years earlier.

At first the agent who booked the gig in Victoria wasn't really straight with me about what kind of club it was, and he kept it a secret right up until about 5:00, just three or four hours before the show. When the agent finally told me it was a strip club, I wasn't going to do the show at first. Then my manager got on the phone and informed me that if I didn't take the gig I wasn't going to have enough money to make my mortgage payment (again) and I would lose my house. "You have to play it," he said simply. "You have no choice."

Not everyone gets the pleasure in life of experiencing what it's like to be really desperate for money, and they should pray to God they never do, because it sucks. You can get all upset about it and throw a fit if you want to, but you still have to get to the point where you can say to yourself, "Well, ya gotta do what ya gotta do." Once you can say that to yourself, then you can put your discomfort or disgust out of your mind long enough to get as much money out of the situation as you can.

Actually, the gig in the strip club in Victoria didn't turn out so bad after all. Unlike any other stage I ever played on before — including Carnegie Hall, funnily enough — I had a brass pole to lean on while I played, which made things a lot easier on the back. I think the people in the crowd liked that show; I mean they clapped and shouted and sounded like they liked it. I have to say, though, I never looked at any of them, mostly because I was too ashamed.

To tell you the truth, I probably haven't looked at an audience in about four or five years anyway, ever since the *Maclean's* scandal turned me into a sex-crazed child molester. I think it pissed me off then, and still does today, that people enjoy my music and will pay money to come and hear me play while in the back of their mind they have this totally negative image of what kind of person I am. But that's fine, if they pay their money they can think what they like about me. It's just easier for me if I don't look at them. If that makes me "remote," that's just too fuckin' bad.

I wasn't always that way though. When I first made it big the press used to make a big deal out of how friendly and down-to-earth I was with everybody. Even *Maclean's* pointed out back in '96 that I had no trouble saying "Hi, how ya doin'?" to "interviewers, club-goers, taxi drivers, busboys, cameramen, hotel clerks, chauffeurs, even strangers on the street." Not anymore. Now people get out of my way when I walk down the street, even the homeless guys. I think in my heart I'm a nice guy, but fame and all the shit that goes along with it has made me learn to be not such a nice guy. What matters in this business is that my *music* is nice — and profitable.

So, you might ask, what happens to a professional musician when their music is no longer profitable? Well, they're fucked, simple as that — fucked at least on any kind of major level, any level involving record companies and national tours or anything like that. A good musician who knows how to entertain people will always be able to make some kind of living off of it, as long as the music is enduring. There will always be people willing to pay to hear good jazz music, or classic rock tunes, or Celtic music in my case; a guy like Buddy MacMaster is a perfect example of that. The artists that have a problem are the ones who get famous on a fad, like those Spanish guys who did the Macarena song. I bet nobody would pay money to see them sing that in some shitty bar in Chatham now.

I hope to continue touring and I'll put out CDs as long as people buy them, but I won't hit my head against a brick wall for the sake of my music career. If the day ever comes when I can't sell tickets to a performance in a big club on the other side of the country or I can't sell CDs anymore because the record companies don't want me, I guess I'll have to quit the "big-time" music business and go back to playing square dances and funerals in Cape Breton. It wouldn't be all that bad: I'd have a hell of a lot more time to lie on the beach for starters, and I'd be able to eat all the lobster I want.

If worst came to worst and nobody even wanted to hear me play even in Cape Breton, I suppose I could get a regular job like everybody else in the world. Either that or I could go on welfare. With a thousand dollars a month I could sit in a hotel somewhere for $20 a day and go back to smoking crack. Sometimes I think that there's quite a few people out there who wouldn't mind seeing that happen. At least they'd prefer to see that than to see me with a new hit record, and lots of money, and off drugs, and in a loving, committed relationship.

Think that's an exaggeration? Well think again. Ask around. Ask people what they think of when they think of Ashley MacIsaac. I bet you'll get more than a few who'll say, "That Ashley MacIsaac is evil. I wish that queer would just crawl back into his crack-smoking hole and never come out again."

I know that that feeling is partly my fault for sure. But I also believe the media had a hand in creating the Ashley MacIsaac "monster" as well, though you'll never hear anybody in the press admit that.

When you get right down to it, all I ever did was offer two things to the world: one was my music, which isn't the kind to offend anybody; the other was a personality, which is, admittedly, more colourful than most. That's all it was in the beginning: lively, friendly, happy music from an energetic young guy in a kilt with crazy hair who loved to step dance all over the stage when he played — just a positive, positive, positive vibe.

Some people have said to me, "Ashley, your problem is you're too colourful for Canada." It's one thing, they say, to experiment with traditional music and to have the crazy hair and the crazy clothes and the wild performances, but you throw in the gay sex and the drugs and it's just too much.

I don't know if I buy that. I guess I am unique, for a Cape Breton musician certainly, but I think there've been colourful performers like me before in Canada. Well, maybe not many exactly like me, but it hasn't all been Don Messer and Anne Murray, I'm pretty sure.

So ask yourself, did seeing my image in the media go from something totally positive to something totally negative in the space of a year have a negative impact on my personality and my feelings about the business? Well, I guess it did. I was angry about it then and I still am, because the bottom line is my image didn't change in the media because I was a bad guy. It didn't even change because I smoked pot. It changed because I was gay and I talked about being gay, and that's a no-no. And once I was tarred with that negative brush, there was sure as fuck no going back; I had to make the best of it.

So as far as being Canadian is concerned, well let's just say Canada is not the best place to be a bad-ass, prima-donna musician. There's just not that many people to piss off in this country. If you think about it, there's only a couple of people who run the music business and a couple more who run the media in Canada, so an outspoken guy like me can run out of friends pretty fast. Throughout my career people have told me, "Watch it Ashley or you'll burn too many bridges." Shit, by the time I was just 21 the media had branded me a sexual deviant and I figured there wasn't another bridge I could burn.

It's funny to look back now at the press I used to get before my sexuality became such a focus. Before the media knew what I did in my spare time with my significant other, they all thought I was a great guy, doing so many amazing things to bring traditional music together with contemporary music. Then, all of a sudden, you can see a sort of clear dividing line where the media stops talking about my music and my performances and starts talking about my "dark" private life. And there was only one reason for the change I figure, and that's a deep-rooted fear of homosexuality that still grips this country.

My reaction to that change wasn't the best I suppose. I got so frustrated with the negative press and the obsession with my private life at times that I would vent to whoever was around. Even as I continued to perform all across Canada and tried to keep my cool publicly, I told my managers and record company executives and the people in the music press I could trust not to make things worse exactly what I thought of my native country and its attitudes towards gay people. As far as I was concerned then, and still am, once you get outside the biggest cities, and there's only about four or five of them, Canada is basically full of ignorant, hung-up, redneck homophobes and racists.

The crazy thing about it is, lots of ignorant homophobic rednecks (oh yeah, and Catholics) love Celtic music. So the dilemma for me, and for my record company, is how to sell the rednecks the music they like if the music is coming from a faggot who they don't like. The only way to do it is to cast me as an "evil" gay person with a "dark" private life and punish me publicly for my "sin." See, the homophobes will agree to come and see me play and they'll buy my CDs just as long as we all agree — the media, the record company, the public and me — that what I do in my private life is wrong.

The problem is, if you tried to go the other way, and sell my sexuality as a positive aspect of my personality, that would turn me into a strictly "gay" act, and most gay-fearing Canadians wouldn't go near me anymore. I'd be like the Indigo Girls or Melissa Etheridge. Sure they're both popular acts, but not nearly as popular as they'd be if they weren't "lesbian" acts. Besides, I'm a guy. How many straight guys do you think buy tickets to shows being put on by openly gay guys?

At the end of the day, then, those open-minded Canadians will buy gay artists, but their image has to be "gay negative" not "gay positive." Therefore, you work with what you've got and you go with it. So when I go into Montreal and I see the headline in the paper that says, "Lock up your sons, Ashley MacIsaac's in town," there's no point in me getting pissed off and sayin', "Well fuck you, Montreal, I won't be coming back here any time soon." You just have to go with it and figure, "Hey, any publicity is good publicity."

And when the Montreal division of my record company —

Universal at that time — set up an interview with the very newspaper that ran that headline in the fuckin' bathroom at the club where I was playing, there was no point in getting all upset. I had to just go with it.

There was no point in me screaming at the record company people, "Why the fuck can't you set up the same kind of interview for me that you set up for other artists? Why do mine always have to be about smut?" I already knew the answer: because that's what people expect from Ashley MacIsaac. So if smut is what people expect, and they'll pay for it, you give 'em smut. And there's no better man for the job than me.

I don't consider myself smutty actually. I'm just a person with a rather large sexual appetite who's comfortable with their sexuality to the point where I'm not ashamed to talk openly about it. Unfortunately, my brand of smut is a bit much for a lot of people sometimes, in Canada anyway. It can be a real Catch-22: I'll be the evil, dangerous, smutty fiddle player because that's what people expect; but I've got to be careful, because if I'm a bit too evil, or too dangerous, or too smutty — like I was on New Year's Eve in Halifax — people turn on me. It's a fuckin' joke: even when people know what to expect, and I'm encouraged all the time by the press and the record company and the promoters to be at my crazy best, they still get all taken aback and offended and weirded out when I behave just that way.

That's exactly why I didn't want anything to do with Loggerhead Records after that New Year's Eve show. I thought, here's a bunch of people, using my name and my music to make money for their record company, telling the press that I'm a bad person and I'm sick after they just released a CD of mine that *they* called *Helter's Celtic*. I mean, goddamn it, they want Charles Manson, but when they get Charles Manson they don't want him anymore. How the fuck was I suppose to feel about that anyway? In a few short years I went from releasing a CD called *hi™ how are you today?* because that title reflected my happy and friendly music and personality, to releasing a CD called *Helter's Celtic*. Why *Helter's Celtic*? Because that title reflected what? My insanity? And I was supposed to be OK with that?

Jesus Christ, do people not think that it has some effect on you when you're constantly portrayed in the media as awful and rude and vulgar and so much the "villain"? It becomes a chicken and egg thing: was he an insane vulgar bastard before the press started portraying him as that, or did he become an insane vulgar bastard because that's what the press said he was? Once you're in that trap though, it doesn't matter which came first anymore. Like I say, you just have to play the hand that's dealt you and make the most of it. Unless I wanted to chuck the music business completely right after the *Maclean's* scandal, after working so hard to make it in the first place, I had to not only continue to play the villain, I had to be the villain, because no one was going to let me go back to being the nice, innocent, friendly, happy little fiddle player from Cape Breton they all thought I was when *hi*™ *how are you today?* took off in 1996.

To tell you the truth, I probably should have seen the fallout from the *Maclean's* scandal coming a long way off. Back a couple of years before the scandal, before I even released my first record and I was still shopping for a label, I actually refused to sign a recording contract with one record company (I won't name them) because they had some weird ideas about "marketing" my sexuality. I remember the guy from the record company was at the recording session when I was recording "Sleepy Maggie" for the first time and he was really hot to sign me.

"That song is going to be a huge hit, guaranteed," I remember him saying to me. "That song is going to sell a ton of CDs for you. And once the record's out and you have a hit on the charts, we can go to the press and you can come out publicly, and the publicity from that will sell a whole pile more CDs."

"Let me get this straight," I said to him. "First, I can sell records because you figure people will like my music. Then I can sell even more records when I tell people that I'm gay?"

"Right," he said, nodding.

I couldn't believe it. What shocked me the most about what he said was that he was so just positive I could use the fact I was gay to sell records. I was stupid enough then, back in 1994, to think nobody would give a shit that I was gay, but the record company executive knew better. He knew that the public was gonna find out one way or another, so I had to try to get the most positive spin out of it that I could.

My career was just getting started then, and to the record company guy my sexuality was like a card I could keep back and play when it could do me the most good. Until then though, it was implied, I should just keep my sexuality to myself and try not to make it obvious to anybody through what I did in my personal life that I was gay.

"Some people might suspect and some might even know," he said. "But until you say it publicly, it's all just speculation. And once the cat's out of the bag, it's no use to you anymore."

Well, with that advice in mind, I thought I played it pretty good right up until the *Maclean's* thing. Most people in Canada, at least outside the Maritimes, had never heard of Ashley MacIsaac until *hi™ how are you today?* came out in 1995, and it was well into 1996 before the record started to get big attention nationwide. By the end of '96, the record was doing well, the single was doing well, I was in demand for concerts and appearances. I guess I figured my popularity was strong enough at that time that it would be safe for me to talk openly about my sexuality. Of course, I was wrong.

First, the mainstream media bashed me for being too gay and talking openly about it, then the next thing I know, I'm on the cover of a gay magazine under the headline, "Would Ashley MacIsaac quit being so butch." As far as the gay press was concerned, I wasn't being gay enough.

Meanwhile, I've got my record company and my manager and promoters all around me saying, "Don't worry about it Ashley. This is 1997; people don't care if you're gay anymore. We can still sell you." And that was the bottom line really, as far as the music business was concerned: it didn't matter if I slept with sheep, as long as they could still sell me.

They could still sell me all right. But the whole vibe around my career had changed. Suddenly, I had all these new "requirements." I had to start working with promoters who were used to working with gay artists. I had to start playing gigs in gay-positive places and at gay-positive venues. I had promoters telling me, "OK Ashley, you have to do this interview to promote the gig, but try to stay away from the whole gay thing, OK." It was really weird; it was like there was a mystique about the whole gay thing that they knew they could sell, but you couldn't shove it in people's faces.

Make no mistake, people can't take their eyes off anything that has sex attached to it, be it gay, straight or otherwise. It was then that I really got the true meaning of the phrase "sex sells." I remember seeing an ad in the newspaper when I was about 13 that read: "SEX, SEX, SEX — Now that I've got your attention, Car For Sale…" Well I was now, "SEX, SEX, SEX — Now that I've got your attention, Fiddle Tunes For Sale."

Prior to the *Maclean's* scandal, I'd developed this image as a high-energy performer with wild coloured hair and a kilt and army boots. I was the punk-rock, heavy metal, whatever you want to call it, fiddle player. It was different, for sure, and that's what attracted people to my fiddle music in the beginning, but it wasn't a negative thing at all until the "pee" article. After that, my image included all the things it did before, but it also took on this dark, deviant, even evil undercurrent that was the direct result of my being gay and having a teenaged boyfriend.

So from then on, in the public consciousness, it was no longer "One night only: Ashley MacIsaac, fiddle player," it was "One night only: Ashley MacIsaac, EVIL DOER." Talk about your "axis of evil," all the time the U.S. has spent looking for Osama Bin Laden and they could've just grabbed me and made just as many people happy.

For example, that headline that greeted me when I arrived for that gig in Montreal: "Lock up your sons, Ashley MacIsaac's in town" — I just didn't know how to react to shit like that. Here I was, just arrived in town; the show was sold out; I was all excited about it and ready to put on a great show for the people who bought the tickets and the first welcome I got was a slap in the face.

What bothered me most about that headline, and many others like it, was I knew it wasn't meant in fun, not like the old Elton John "Don't let your son go down on me" jokes. The press *was* really saying, "The heavy-metal, crazy man, gay sex maniac fiddle player is in town," and there was nothing funny about it. One writer once described me as "violently gay." Well what the fuck does that mean? Did he think I knock on people's front doors and try to drag their teenaged boys outside to rape them?

Anyway, that's the kind of fame I've had to deal with since the end of 1996, and the fact I got addicted to cocaine didn't help improve things, you can imagine. But while I may not exactly have liked the way my image was twisted by the press, I still had to make a living. I had to sell CDs and have people come to see me play. I couldn't just stop working because some people wanted to see me, not because they liked my music but because they saw me as the gay version of Gene Simmons.

So in order to keep people coming to my shows, I had to make people curious enough to want to pay to see the crazy sexual deviant fiddle player, but not nervous enough to think I'll spread STDs to them without actually having sex with them.

* * *

Obviously, I've been through a lot, both good and bad. I've been at the top, and I've been at the bottom, both financially and professionally. I know what it's like to have every agent, every record company, every music journalist and every promoter in the country calling trying to get a piece of you. But I also know what it's like when nobody in the industry wants to touch you with a 40-foot pole.

My experience came at a high price, but I've learned a lot about the music industry. And if I had to sum up what the music industry is all about in just a couple of words, I know exactly what those words would be: Fuck everybody. That's it, plain and simple.

I know it sounds cynical as hell, but the people who'll help ya get ahead in the music business, they'll cut yer throat just as quick. I've had people who told me they loved me like a son or a brother, and said that they'd stick with me no matter what. Then, after parting company with that person, I've read in newspapers or magazines not too long after where they called me an idiot and wouldn't care if I ended up in a ditch somewhere. And I made a ton of money for those people too; funny how they forget that.

So "Fuck Everybody" has got to be your motto. If I learned anything from all the shit I've been through, it's that if you really want to have a successful career in the music business, you have to take control of your career by fuckin' anybody that stands in your way. And if you have to get fucked by people that you trusted a couple of times in order to learn what can happen to you, then it's worth it if you learn the lesson.

I know that sounds bitter, and lots of people will say, "Well, any problems that Ashley MacIsaac has had he created for himself." And that's true to an extent, but not in the beginning. In the beginning, when I first hit it big and started to make some serious money, I was just a kid for fuck's sake, and people took advantage of that. Now, I don't think I ever got taken advantage of in a real bad way. I mean it wasn't like some of those boy bands where the managers and promoters were literally stealing all the money while they ran the band ragged. But I'd say if you start out as a teenager and you make $10-million in three years and end up with nothing to show for it, I think it's fair to say you were taken advantage of. Someone made the money — figure it out, do the math.

I was just a stupid kid from a little town on Cape Breton Island and I was having fun. I wasn't thinking about how much management and travel and musicians and accommodation and promotion and everything else were costing me. And it never really sunk in with me, as an 18, 19-year-old, that all the people being so nice to me, from the various record company suits to the promoters and all their flunkies, were all dependant on me for a paycheque. 'Course, it didn't have a hope of sinking in once I started smoking $300 worth of pot a week. What's that? Over 52 weeks a year, that's around $15,000 a year just on pot. For seven or eight years, that's over a hundred grand on pot. That's not cocaine, or crack, or acid, or mushrooms or anything else. Funny, but there was always money enough for my dope.

And people always ask me, "Ashley, you had parents, a brother and a sister, all kinds of relatives and neighbours back home, you had lots of friends in the music business, musicians and whatever, did no one ever try to give you any guidance when you first broke into he music business as a teenager so you could avoid all the shit?"

Well, the answer to that is easy: no. The only direction anyone ever gave me after my career took off and I suddenly had all this fame and money was directions to the next gig.

Yeah, my family was back in Creignish, but they weren't equipped to help me handle the big-time music business. They gave me all the support and encouragement they could with my music up to the point when it just outgrew them, just like it outgrew Creignish and Cape Breton for that matter. My parents bought me my first fiddle, and they paid for my fiddle lessons, and my dad drove me all over hell's half acre on Cape Breton to gigs until I could drive myself. But once we started talking about recording contracts and cross-country tours, they were in over their heads. All they could do was stand back and put their trust in the people who were getting paid to handle all that.

Besides, you have to remember too that just around the time my career took off I was also coming to terms with my sexuality. By the time I made my big splash at the East Coast Music Awards in 1994, I'd already been to New York a couple of times and I'd pretty much moved to Halifax full-time and I was living the gay lifestyle. But my family and everybody else in Creignish — my relatives, the neighbours, school friends — they didn't know that. They may have suspected it. Some of 'em may have even been sure of it. But I hadn't "come out" publicly yet and I sure as hell hadn't told my parents. Because of that I did everything in my power to avoid my family around that time.

But a couple of years later, when the pressures of my career and fame and the press and my sexuality drove me to look for an escape in hard drug addiction, my family were the only ones who were a real comfort to me. Everyone else who was calling me wanted something from me, but they called me just because they were my folks and they cared about my welfare.

But, just like the big-time music business and homosexuality, hard drug addiction was something else in my life that my family was just not equipped to deal with. I mean they knew about drugs from TV, but there just weren't any crack addicts they knew around Creignish they could compare me to. They couldn't relate to the pressures I was experiencing, so they didn't really know what to be saying to me. The best they could do was just let me know that they were there if I ever needed them. I remember my mom saying to me on the phone, "Look, if you ever need to just get away from the whole business, just come home."

So I knew I always had that there, but that didn't mean it would've been easy for me to drop everything and go home. Even though I knew my family loved me deep down, I knew that they were struggling with the whole sexuality thing, and they continue to struggle with it to this day. I think 99 percent of parents would struggle with something like that, but if you grew up in an isolated, deeply Catholic environment like my parents did, you can imagine how much harder it would be. So on the one hand I was reaching out to my family because they were the only people who really cared for me, and on the other hand I was hating them because of their torturous beliefs about how bad it is to be gay.

It's been a struggle for me and them, no doubt about it. But the pain of our struggle to come to terms with my sexuality still doesn't compare to all the wonderful things my family has done for me throughout my life. That's been especially true during the last couple of years, as I've tried to get over my drug problems and my financial problems and get my career back on track.

Shit, they even loaned me a car to get around in after I went bankrupt and the car dealer came and repossessed the new truck I was driving. I'll never forget it: I was playing a gig in Antigonish and the repo man hooked the fuckin' truck up right there in the parking lot while I was inside playing. I had to ask one of the guys in the band for a ride home that night. Then I had to go ask my parents to lend me a car for the next couple of weeks so I could drive to the store to buy toilet paper.

Still, things didn't change that much for me when you think about it, in spite of everything I went through. When I was 16, I had my fiddle and my own car and a roof over my head. Then, after I went bankrupt nine years later, I had my fiddle, which they couldn't take because I make my living with it, a (leased) car and a roof over my head.

That's quite a long way to go to end up where you started, but I got through it all. And I learned that most of the worrying and fretting I'd done in my life had been about money. All the other shit really just rolled off me. I found I could deal with anything — the fame, the pressure to sell records, the media — as long as I was in a positive cash situation. But once I wasn't in a positive cash situation, all that other shit got really bad. And it's the same for anybody with the problems and pressures they have in their life.

It's true: money changes everything. Shit, when things were going good and the money was flowing in and everybody was making enough, I was able to live my life the way I wanted and it didn't matter what kind of negative crap happened onstage or what came out in the press. When I was making money for them, the record company and the promoters were happy to buy my dope for me. When I wasn't making enough money for everybody though, then I had a "drug problem."

That was the way it was for me, basically, from the age of 18 to about 25. I was a young adult being used by the music industry because I didn't know any better and I didn't have anyone looking out for me like most young stars do in music or movies or TV or sports or whatever. And the people who did take advantage of my ignorance can't say they didn't know they were doing it, because part of my whole marketing appeal that the record company used to sell records was that I was this cute bumpkin from this little town in Cape Breton.

Now, no one put a gun to my head or anything to get into the music business, I know that. When I started to get a taste of the big time, I admit I liked the money and the freedom that a career in music offered and I was willing to do whatever it took to get there. I also admit that I found drugs, well pot anyway, on my own before I hit it big. But after I did finally have a hit record and I'd made it to where I always thought I wanted to be, the pressure to stay there made drugs a necessity for me. I needed the drugs to continue to perform at the same insane level night after night.

In the back of my mind, I knew that's why I was doing it. I'd say to myself, "OK Ashley, if you need drugs to do a show, if that's what it's gonna take for you to want to do it, then that's what you'll do." The drugs made it possible for me to make the money to pay the musicians, to pay my managers and whoever else needed to get paid, to pay for my hotel room and my room service. Without the drugs, I probably would've only been able to play half the number of shows I did play between 18 and say 25. If I kept a good buzz on though, it was all just mindless, gung-ho, having fun.

Now lots of musicians will argue that they play as many shows as I did per year during the height of my career and they don't need drugs to do it, and that may be true. I'm not saying every musician is the same; we're all human beings after all, aren't we? And I also know that I played as many as 200 or 250 shows a year as a teenager before I became famous and I wasn't on drugs then, but it was different then. When I was a kid, I didn't play for the money really, and I wasn't trying to sell records; I was just playing because I was good at it, I liked the attention and I was bred to it anyway. But when playing the fiddle started to become a job, I started to like drugs more. I still like to play the fiddle today, but I like to play on drugs a lot more than I like to play not on drugs.

The drugs also made it possible for me to ignore the lack of control I had over my career. When I was stoned I could say to myself, "Well Ashley, you played all these shows for all these years and sold records and made all kinds of money and you've got nothing to show for it. But that's OK, 'cause you had a party doing it." At that point it wasn't about love nor money; I was literally playing for the drugs. And I enjoyed it. I enjoyed smoking crack, at least until I became addicted and it got to the point where I was so physically and mentally screwed up that it threatened to end my career and maybe my life.

Actually, my story should be a warning to all those young aspiring musicians and singers and bands out there working their asses off to "make it." If you do make it, well good for you; when it works out, it can be a fabulous experience. But just keep in mind that fame doesn't always work out exactly the way you want it to. And when the president of the record company tells you he thinks it'd be better for your career if you wore pink bell-bottom pants and covered disco tunes instead of playing the music you want to play, you better think long and hard about just how bad you want to make it. Because they won't just ask ya to sell your soul to the devil, they might ask ya to *be* the devil as well.

By and large, people I've met in the music industry, whether artists or record company people, are generally pretty nice people. You get the odd prick, but you don't mind a prick if they're really good at what they do. But now that I'm older and wiser, if I have to deal with someone in my professional life who's a prick and is stupid at the same time, that person's gonna have a problem with me.

Unfortunately, there are a fair number of people like that at the top level of the record business, people who are running mega-international record companies and don't know their ass from a hole in the ground. Either that or they're just such huge greedy pricks that they couldn't care less if an artist that is making all kinds of money for them can't pay their own bills. If you want to be in the game though, you have to learn to deal with it.

Before they actually make it anywhere in their careers, most serious artists spend about 99 percent of their time thinking about one thing and one thing only: the record deal. How do they get one? Who do they have to meet? What do they have to play? How are they supposed to look? It's a goddamn full-time job just thinking about it. The thing is, artists who don't have recording contracts with record labels tend to think that the hard part is getting the deal, rather than actually living up to the terms of the deal and making any money for yourself.

A recording deal is actually a very flimsy agreement between the label and the artist that essentially says, "If you do this, this, and this, then we'll do this — maybe." The label never actually guarantees that it'll do anything for the artist and, at the end of the day, the contract really has no binding effect on the record company. So, even if a year or so goes by and the artist has done the "this, this, and this" in the contract — put together material for a record, put together a band, toured the music from the record, recorded the material, done promotion — that doesn't mean the label has to get behind the record necessarily. The label may have soured on the artist by then, or they may decide they want to put their resources behind another record. Lots of things can change between the day you sign a recording deal and the day you finish your record.

The thing is, a record deal isn't like a simple business transaction where one party is selling something and the other party is buying. In fact, the musician may not even have the music for a record ready to go when they sign a record deal. Often a musician, singer or band is signed by a label simply on the strength of their talent, or their potential to become a recording artist. But that raw talent often has to develop and mature, and be polished and packaged appropriately before the artist is ready to put out a recording. All that nurturing requires time and money, and that time and money has to be invested in the artist long before they ever see a dime back from record sales.

Where does the money to develop an artist come from? Most of the time the artist raises that money themselves through performing for years in small venues, the way I did. Sometimes money comes from an investor, maybe a family member, who believes in the artist. In the rare cases where an artist is lucky enough to have a record company pay their bills for a year or two while they polish their act and get together material for a record, all the money invested is deducted from the artist's end anyway when they finally do start selling records, so they end up paying in the end.

So what the record company is really saying to the artist when they sign them to a recording deal is, "We like you. You might have what it takes to be big. If you can get yourself to the point where you're ready to make a record, we'll help you make one. Then, if the record sells, and after we've got back the cost of making the record and promoting it, we'll give you some money."

As you can see, it's a long way from "We like you" to "We'll give you some money," and lots of things can go wrong on the way. Maybe when it comes time for the artist to go into the studio, they might disagree with the record company over what songs to record or how they want the finished product to sound. Maybe the record company wants to package the artist in a certain way that the artist isn't comfortable with. Or maybe the artist turns out to be gay, and that just wasn't in the original marketing plan.

So there's any number of reasons why the record company might turn around at the last minute and say, "Sorry, but you're not the product we thought we were getting. Deal's off."

On the other hand, if the artist does everything they need to do to get themselves to the point where they're ready to make a record, and the record company is happy with the content and the image and they're still convinced they can sell it, then the artist will actually get to make a record. That's when the real pressure starts, because the record company usually doesn't have much of its own money invested in you, if any, until you make the record. Once the label's money's invested though, they want it back — and fast. That means the artist has to get out there and play, and tour, and promote, and do media, and be the image that the record company is trying to sell.

If it all works out and the record sells, the label gets its investment back and then some and the artist makes money too. If the record doesn't sell like the label expected, the artist might get dumped after making little or no money off the project. Worst-case scenario: the artist might end up owing the record company money.

See, it's not like going into a hardware store and buying ten 2x4s. The record company doesn't hand me money and say, "We'd like one Ashley MacIsaac record please, with ten tunes on it, five traditional and five contemporary." Nope, it's a hell of a lot more complicated than that.

I say owing the record company money is the worst-case scenario for an artist, but on second thought, maybe it's not. The worst case scenario for the artist just might be when they're tied by a contract to a label they don't want anything to do with, and that's exactly what happened to me when I got into bed with Loggerhead Records.

I think I've been around the music industry long enough now that I can safely say I know a thing or two about how it works. And one thing I've learned for sure is that, whoever comes out on top in a record deal often comes down to who's the bigger asshole. So, I've learned the hard way to be a pretty damn big asshole when it comes to my business dealings. Because I'm not gonna let people fuck me upside down and backwards every day the way I used to when I was a kid and when I was on drugs. OK, I got myself into most of it, but at least I learned a lesson or two from my bad business experiences.

Obviously, I didn't think I was getting fucked in the beginning because I was too naive to know better. I thought all the people who were being so nice to me were really just trying to be nice to me, and not looking to get something out of me. In the first four years of my career, all I could see was how much money could be made in the music business. I didn't think about how fast I was spending it, especially since other people were spending it for me.

It wasn't until I realized that I'd burnt through all the money I made at the beginning of my career that I woke up to the fact that there are people around you in the music business who can be really dangerous. It took years, but I eventually learned that if you're gonna be in the game and be around those kinds of people, you have to have your wits about you all the time. If you're a kid, of course, you're at a big disadvantage. If you're a kid on drugs, you can forget it.

I wasn't prepared for stardom, that was obvious. I wasn't like Britney Spears or Celine Dion, who were groomed and managed for a career in music from the age of 12. I got myself to the level I did through pure dedication to my instrument. I just practised and practised and practised, and eventually got so good that the world came calling. But I didn't really know what I was getting into, and my parents couldn't help me because they didn't know anything about the music business either. I was a lamb to the slaughter.

Still, I have to admit that I did get a lot of fun out of being in the music business and lived the kind of life that most people only dream of — fame, drugs, parties, sex, travel, hotels, room service, limousines. But in spite of the fact that I made a lot of mistakes, and I went from the bottom of the mountain to the top and then all the way back down to the bottom again financially, I'm still in the music business and making a living off of it. I'm not living the way I used to, not yet anyway, but I'm still alive and I have a nice place to live. I lost all my money, but

I managed to keep myself out of the gutter at least, although I had one foot in it for sure.

I think anyone from the music business who knew me back when I was riding high would realize I'm not the same artist today that I was in the beginning. I'm not a wide-eyed kid anymore and I'm not a coked-out zombie either. Now I just show up at my gigs and do my job. I'm a professional musician, rather than a pop star. I perform, I entertain, and I expect to have more than a bag of dope to show for it afterwards. And if anybody I deal with now doesn't like it, then they can suck my arse.

Epilogue

My house burned down.

Can ya believe that? Is that the final insult or what? After all the work I did, and the endless touring, and all the bullshit I had to deal with over being gay, and the *Maclean's* bullshit, and the drugs, and the New Year's Eve thing, and the bankruptcy, you'd think the good Lord woulda had enough of pilin' shit on me. But no way.

On February 12, 2002, less that two weeks before my 27th birthday, I was in New York recording some tracks for a demo CD I was putting together for my new manager, David Bluestein, and my new record company, Decca. Things were really looking up; it finally seemed like all the trouble of the previous couple of years, financial and otherwise, was behind me. I was in a stable relationship; I had a new project on the go; I had some money in my pocket. Then I got a phone call.

It was my manager. "Ashley, you're not gonna believe this," he said, kind of sheepishly.

"Blue, if something shitty happened, of course I'm gonna believe it," I said. "Don't you know who you're talking to?"

"Well, OK," he said, "but your house burned down this morning."

"Of course it did," was all I could say. "Of course it did."

Blue got the news from my old friend Gerry Deveau, the guy who played the spoons with me on *hi™ how are you today?*. A contractor by trade, Gerry built my house for me in Belle Cote in Inverness County on Cape Breton, and he still took care of it when I was on tour or staying in Toronto, which was most of the time. It was a big, beautiful place, two and a half stories and covered in sky-blue siding. It sat on one hectare of land on a hill overlooking the ocean and the Margaree River. It was the perfect summer place, but it was a lot more than that to me. That house represented all I had to show for all the gigs I played and all the records I sold going right back to 1994.

Anyway, it seemed that Gerry was in the house that day checking up on it when he discovered that the pipes in the upstairs bathroom were frozen, so he decided to plug in an electric space heater to thaw them out. Now the second floor of the house was not completely finished, and there was still a lot of exposed framing and construction materials up there. Gerry told Blue he went back downstairs to do something else and then he started to hear a strange noise coming from the second floor.

"By the time he got back upstairs," Blue said, "the place was engulfed."

Gerry said he figured the heater must have tipped over and fell against the plastic vapour barrier on one of the frame walls, which could've easily sparked the fire. It didn't take long for the whole second floor to flame up, and the place was in a remote enough location that it never had a chance. By the time the Margaree Volunteer Fire Department showed up, the house was "fully involved," as they say. Then they had to hack through the fuckin' ice on the river to get water to fight it, if you can believe that in this day and age.

Gerry called me that night to apologize, but I didn't blame him; he was just trying to help me out.

Let me tell you, you might think you've got problems in your life, and you might think that things aren't going well for you, but the only way to really know how low you can feel is to have your house burn down. I know it wasn't my "permanent" home exactly, but I did build it with my own money, and it was "mine." I hadn't even had it that long, but I had grown attached to the place. I was mostly in it in the summertime and at Christmas, so my memories of the house are happy ones for the most part. I smoked lots of dope there and watched the sunset, and had campfires outside, and had friends over for barbecues.

When I went bankrupt in 2001, the court forced me to try to sell it for the appraised value of $68,000, in spite of the fact I still owed the bank $100,000 on it. I was happy, though, when they couldn't find any takers, even at that price. So God took it. Or fate. Anyway, it's not there anymore, and that's all there is to it. Nice birthday present.

Well, you might think that that was the end of it, but you'd be wrong. It could never be as easy as that for me. Within a couple of days of the fire, Gerry Deveau called me up to tell me that the RCMP was investigating the cause of the fire and that he had to go in for an interview. "I think they want to talk to you too," he said.

Sure enough, the next day I got a call from the RCMP detachment in Inverness County asking me if I could come to Nova Scotia and swear out an affidavit testifying to what I knew about the facts surrounding the fire at my house. My insurance company, apparently, was demanding that the police explore the possibility that the house was burnt down, shall we say, "conveniently" for financial reasons. Before I knew it, they were asking me to give them permission to check my phone records. I was forced to bring my lawyer into it.

Now it was bad enough having my house burn down, but being accused, even in a roundabout way, of setting up a whole conspiracy to do it was just too much to take. I remember shouting into the phone from Toronto at some guy from my insurance company, "You idiot arse-holes, I shouldn't have to deal with this nonsense! I worked my ass off trying to get the money to build that house, and to keep it, at such a young age. Do you honestly believe that after all it took for me to have that house that I'd just burn it down?"

People say you have to have insurance when you have a house, but having insurance can sometimes cause as many problems as it solves. If I never had insurance, the house would just be gone and that would suck. With insurance, the house was gone, it still sucked, plus I had to deal with all the other shit. I mean, what are the odds? I never in my life knew anybody who had their house burn down on them. Besides, the only reason Gerry was there checking up on the place was because the goddamn insurance company told me I had to have a "caretaker" coming in if I wasn't living there full-time. I tell ya, the insurance people were nothing but perfect pricks.

The insurance company was one thing, but the rumours in the press in Cape Breton and in Nova Scotia pissed me off even more. First off, the day after the fire my mother called me to tell me there was a picture of the house burning on the front page of the biggest newspaper in Nova Scotia under the headline, "Fiddler without a roof."

"Very funny," I thought, "very nice."

Then three weeks later, just about the time I started to get over the fact my house was gone, my mom called me again to tell me the same paper had a story on the front page saying the police were calling the fire "suspicious."

"A suspicious pile of baloney," I told her.

I mean, I've been called a lot of things in my time — drug addict, cradle snatcher, sex maniac, mental case, bankrupt — but I didn't mind so much because they all had an element of truth to them, depending on how you looked at it. But to be accused of arson and insurance fraud was almost worse, because there was no truth to that at all. I was so mad about the whole stupid mess that I even threatened never to go back to Cape Breton again.

"Why should I go back to that fuckin' place," I remember saying to a friend from home on the phone, "if they're going to blame me after all these years. All I ever did was go back there and go into schools to teach the fiddle, and teach step dancing and perform all over and promote the place. I bet over the years I'm partially responsible, indirectly anyway, for millions of dollars in tourism money coming to Cape Breton."

I would've stayed away too, if doing that wouldn't have made so many of the sons of whores in the press there happy.

The joke of it is, even with my house burned down, I'm still a freaking tourist attraction for the place. There's just a pile of black rubble now where my house used to stand, but the local authorities won't let me go in there and hire someone with a backhoe to clean it away for some reason. Apparently it's still "under investigation." So now people can get in their cars and go on a nice drive down by the Margaree River and say, "Hey, that's where Ashley MacIsaac's house burned down." It's enough to make me want to rip my head off, or somebody else's.

Still, that's the price of fame I guess: if you're willing to let people kiss your feet when you're on top, you have to expect them to piss on you a bit when you fall down. Looking back on it now, I'd have to say that in terms of the East Coast in general, and Nova Scotia in particular, I was probably too famous for my own good. At certain points, for sure, like just before the *Maclean's* thing when my popularity was just crazy, then after the *Maclean's* thing, and then after the New Year's thing, and then during my bankruptcy, I'm sure people on the East Coast were sick to death of reading about me in the paper. The coverage was so overwhelming sometimes that it got to the point where I'm sure if I had farted in public it woulda been on the news.

When the New Year's thing happened, it was all over the newspapers Down East for weeks and weeks, in Halifax especially. It was on the front page, on the editorial page, in the letters to the editor, in the entertainment section; you couldn't get away from it. I mean, I know I say any publicity is good publicity, but you reach a point where enough's enough. I was sick of it after a couple of weeks, and I'm sure it started to drive everyone else down there crazy as well.

The Nova Scotia press, particularly, lived off my bankruptcy for a while too. They made a real meal out of the fact that on the day of my bankruptcy court hearing I happened to be at Disney World in Florida.

Aside from the fact I was on tour in the States then anyway, another reason I happened to be in Florida at the time was because my trustee had told me that the terms of my bankruptcy were already agreed upon by all the parties involved. All the court was going to do was rubber stamp it, so there was no need for me to be in Halifax for that. Besides, all my being there was going to do was stir up more bad publicity. "The best thing you can do right now," he told me, "is get out of town."

So that's what I did. My partner and I both wanted to go Florida, and it seemed appropriate to me to be enjoying fantasy land at Disney World while a bankruptcy court was carving up my real life back home. All I could think of was how the press always asks football players after the Super Bowl, "You've won the championship; what are you gonna do now?" and the player says, "I'm going to Disney World!"

I was dying for some reporter to come up and ask me, "Hey Ashley, you've declared bankruptcy; what are you gonna do now?" just so I could say, "I'm going to Disney World!"

The *Chronicle-Herald* in Halifax didn't think it was so funny though. I made the front page again that day: "Bankruptcy looms; Ashley at Disney World."

Although I often did get sick of reading negative stories about myself in the paper, I never really got tired of reading the letters that people wrote in to comment on the stories. Of course they covered the whole spectrum, from people who'd say "Why can't you leave Ashley alone and let him play his music?" to the ones who'd say, "I wish that guy would end up in a ditch somewhere."

More often than not, what I heard in the letters was jealousy:

"That guy's had more luck…"

"That guy has more money…"

"Why doesn't that spoiled brat quit complaining?"

"What's Ashley crying about now?"

"He doesn't know how good he has it…"

That kind of resentment is natural coming from Maritimers. It's the same kind of resentment Maritimers feel for people in Ontario. They tend to think they have a harder life Down East than people in the rest of Canada — and in a lot of ways, they do. Maritimers get pissed off when they see someone with money and success making a fuss about anything. It's like, "Shut up and eat your cake, for fuck's sake." Well, I get a lot of that.

The music always seems to bring them back though. Just when people in Cape Breton, or anywhere in the Maritimes, think they've heard way more about Ashley MacIsaac than they ever want to hear, they hear a fiddle tune on the radio and the music brings 'em back. Maybe they think they're putting on a particular CD but push the wrong number and end up playing one of my CDs by mistake and end up saying to themselves, "Hey, this music is pretty nice. Maybe that Ashley MacIsaac isn't a total idiot after all." Then, just like that, they're a fan again — until the next time I piss them off.

Still, it's not like I get no respect at all back home for the things I've accomplished. In Cape Breton, for example, I think people appreciate what I've done for Cape Breton music. I think that people there do give me credit for bringing the music to a broader audience, and for adding some elements to it that were never there before that will help the traditional music survive.

How do I know the people of Cape Breton feel that way? Well, it's not because they're giving me ticker-tape parades down the main street in Sydney, I'll tell ya that. Basically I know the people there have some respect left for me because they haven't literally run me off the island. Oh, I've been given the finger and called a "faggot" plenty of times, but nobody has thrown rocks at my car windows or run me off the road — yet. That's what amounts to respect in my case. But I still sleep with a tire-iron when I'm there, let's put it that way.

I also think the East Coast music community respects me as a musician, if nothing else. I mean, I know so many musicians out there and I've played with a lot of 'em. Christ, they're not stupid; while they may not like me personally, they know enough about the business to know what it took for me to go from Cape Breton to Carnegie Hall. It's not every day that an East Coast musician does that. Plus, they know that by making Cape Breton music popular right across North America and around the world, I helped pave the way for other East Coast artists to get their music out there.

How does the East Coast music community show that respect? Sort of the same way Cape Bretoners in general do: by not turning their back on me when it seems everybody else is. For instance, it's not like I can't put a good Celtic band together when I need to to do a show, and I still get invited to play shows with other big East Coast acts.

Shit, the East Coast Music Awards still calls me up every year and invites me to attend. I didn't go for a few years because it took a while for me to get over the "Hannibal Lecter" stunt they pulled after the millennium New Year's thing. That's all in the past now, though, and I've since made up with the ECMAs. So much so, in fact, that I opened the 2003 show in Halifax with a song off my new CD.

Dorothy was right: there is no place like home. I've made records in various places and played my music all over the world, but when I take up my fiddle and close my eyes, in my mind I'm back in Cape Breton. When I still had my house there, I went back as often as I could.

Because Cape Breton is such a huge part of my life and my music, people often ask me if I hope to move back there one day to stay. It's strange, but when I think about that now, after everything that's gone on in my career and everything I've been through personally, I'm loaded with conflicting feelings. The first 17 years of my life revolved around Cape Breton — so much so that I was truly immersed in the people and place on every level, musically, personally, emotionally, psychologically. I was really torn for a long time: wanting to leave, not wanting to leave;

wanting to grow up, not wanting to grow up. Facing up to my own personality and needs and the desire to fulfil my potential as a musician put me at odds with the very place that created me. But fate took over and I did finally make the break, and I've found the years since I left Cape Breton have been just as relevant in my life as the years before I left.

But Cape Breton is always with me. To be honest, the link to that place and that culture was the only thing that kept me grounded at all when I was at my lowest point personally. No matter what was going wrong, be it my addiction to drugs, or my problems with the media or with money, I always had Cape Breton. I can close my eyes and the culture and the musical tradition that I learned is still with me, and no one can take it from me. I couldn't even get rid of it if I wanted to. Even on those dark days when I wasn't sure exactly who I was, I always knew what I was at heart, and that's a traditional Cape Breton fiddle player. And not just any Cape Breton fiddle player; maybe, on my best days, the best Cape Breton fiddle player in the world. Once I got hold of that, I could always find my way back to who I was as a person.

So even if I'm not living there, I believe me pedigree is still strong enough to qualify me as a genuine Cape Breton fiddle player. It may get buried at times, but I don't think I'll ever lose that feeling I had as a 14-year-old kid, hungry to play and learn my instrument and practising and practising just to see how good I could get with it. No matter how far I get away, both physically and psychologically, I think my roots are imbedded deep enough that I'll always have the ability to play the traditional music the way it's always been played.

And as the culture of Cape Breton grows and evolves over the course of my lifetime, however long that is, I think I'll be able to grow and evolve with it. I'm like a bridge I guess, in a lot of ways, between that traditional, Cape Breton Scottish culture that has evolved for centuries in isolation and a culture that is strong and distinct, yet aware of the outside world and willing to go out and meet it. It's kind of sad, but I think in order to become that bridge, I had to leave.

I'm really a citizen of the world now. In fact, I believe I could make my home anywhere in the world I'd care to choose. I could live in another culture and enjoy all the wonderful new experiences it has to offer. I have the ability to learn the music of other cultures and incorporate it into my music, and I've been known for doing that in my career. But at the end of the day, I know where my true musical home will always be. And when your musical home is a place, rather than a style or an era, it's tough to stay away for long.

I always feel a pull to go back to Cape Breton, and sometimes that pull is stronger than at other times. At this point in my life, the pull isn't that strong because I have other needs that are greater. To put it on the most superficial of levels, I have a strong need at this point in my life for good Chinese food, and the Chinese food you can get in Toronto is a hell of a lot better than the Chinese food you can get on Cape Breton — simple as that.

On a professional level, I'm living in Toronto because I need to work here. When it comes to the Canadian music industry, all the movers and shakers are in the big smoke. So are the best recording studios, and producers, and technicians, and agents, and publicity people, and the record company offices.

Finally, and maybe most important, I'm not in Cape Breton because, like every other human being, I need to have love in my life. My partner wants to be in Toronto at the moment, so that makes my decision to live in the city all the more simple. Other than my career, my partner is the biggest part of my life, and right now those two things aren't in conflict with one another.

As if work and love aren't enough to make a person choose one place over another, there are probably a hundred other reasons I would choose the city over Cape Breton at this point in my life. But there's nothing unusual about that; I think most any young person would choose to live in a big bustling city rather than spend 24 hours a day in a small island village, no matter how beautiful the ocean and the beaches are. I tend to think of Cape Breton as a holiday place now, rather than a permanent home. After a while there, I even think it begins to become too peaceful and too picturesque. I start to miss the noise and the action and even the filth of the city.

That's now though. I'm still young and still exploring and finding out about myself and the world. Someday, when the attraction of the city and the world has worn off for me, Cape Breton could be enough for me again. I think I could live there the rest of my life. I know I could work there the rest of my life — leave the record industry behind, all the deals, travel, media, and just be a Cape Breton fiddler again.

It's tempting to think of living full-time in a beach house on Cape Breton, growing my own vegetable garden in the back, having fresh deer and rabbit meat in the winter and the best lobster in the world in the summer.

But even if I want to return, I wonder sometimes if my childhood home will have me back. I've had some bad experiences there. It wasn't anything big, just little disturbing events that made me feel like I wasn't in the right place. Things like people I've known my whole life pretending not to see me when I wave at them from the car, or teenagers screaming "Faggot" at me as I'm walking down the beach with my partner. Nobody wants to live with a baseball bat under their bed, even if they do get to listen to the ocean waves crash on the shore as they drift off to sleep.

I still go back to Cape Breton regularly, to see my family and to go to the beach and to play a gig if I want to. But I set my life and my music up around my heart. And if my heart is with somebody, and that somebody can't live in a certain place, then I have to move my life and my music to a place where they're comfortable. I'm very comfortable where I am right now. I enjoy the convenience of living in the city; you're really close to restaurants and clubs and theatres and cool shops. I also really like the view from my 22nd-floor window. Of course, it's not all excitement and nice views; when I walk down the street, seeing the dealers and the homeless people sometimes really gets to me. But that's the trade-off of the big city.

At the moment I'm happy to say I only have positive shit going on in my life right now. The most important part of that is my new record. It's great to be involved with a good record label again, after all the crap I went through with my last label. The record company I'm with now is wonderful, and big, and it's full of lots of smart and talented people who really know what it takes to make an artist famous and to make a record a success. God almighty, when I think now of the situation I got myself into the last time I signed a record deal, I'm just amazed I didn't end up in jail for the rest of my life over it. It was all just such a waste that it took two years and a bunch of lawyers to bring an end to something that should've never happened in the first place. But that's all in the past, I hope.

I'm back playing gigs regularly as well. I still love performing, although I do think my playing style may be mellowing a bit with age. Plus, doing shows lets me keep my hand in with the fiddle so I'm in top form when it comes time to record. It keeps my hand filled with money as well. Two or three shows in a month gives me more than enough money to pay my bills and buy my weed, which is all I really need at the moment. And I'm still a big enough draw that my agent doesn't need to make too many calls before he can get something for me.

It's strange to say so, but I think the whole experience of losing my money, and getting off drugs, and then losing my house has had some really positive elements to it. It's made me take stock of my life, for sure. I think more about certain things now than I did when I was a drugged-out rock star, things like my family and my friends and my health. I don't think I'd go as far as to say I've undergone a personality transformation in the last couple of years, although I know there's plenty of people out there, lots of them in the media, who have prayed for that. Everyone has a unique personality; it's just that my personality is a little more intense than most. I know that I'm not like most people in a lot of ways, and I've come to terms with that, as have my family and friends.

I'm also smart enough to know that my personality is one of the things that makes me a unique performer, so I've got to be who I am onstage — an intense, energetic musician. But that doesn't mean because I'm Ashley MacIsaac the fiddle player, I can't be Ashley MacIsaac the regular person, able to maintain a life, and a home, and have a relationship, and even smoke the occasional joint, God forbid. It used to be that way; because my image and my behaviour was so abnormal, there was no way I could maintain anything resembling a "normal" life. The hype was my life. But now that the hype has died down, a real life is getting a chance to emerge, and I like it a lot.

Actually, there's no better life than the life of an artist, if you can strike that balance between what's real and what's "image." Big-time recording artists I've met and played with, like the Tragically Hip and the Barenaked Ladies, all love to spend their days writing songs and creating music in the studio and playing gigs to thousands of people. But those guys have partners, and kids, and homes of their own, and they love eating apples and oranges and enjoying all the regular things in life too. So they love making art for a living, but they're not artists 24 hours a day, and they're certainly not "rock stars" 24 hours a day. Some artists, I think, fall into the trap of trying to be a famous person all the time and they end up forgetting who they are, or were before they became famous. I mean, do you think Madonna could hold a conversation with someone she went to high school with for even two minutes today? I lived like that for a while, and it almost killed me.

It's just a hell of a lot easier, both mentally and emotionally, to be an artist than it is to be a rock star. It's such a gift as well, one that people who aren't artists don't understand. As an artist, I can read about war in the newspaper or go to see a sad movie or go to the park and look at ducks swimming in a pond and I can take in all that beauty and feeling and emotion and then pour it out again in my music. The same thing goes for any kind of artist — a painter, an actor, a sculptor, a singer, a musician. It's just fantastic to be able to express your feelings in some kind of creative way, and I'm really grateful for that. And if people will pay to hear or see you express your feelings, that's even better.

People have been reading about me for so long now, and reading nothing but negative, terrible stories about fights, and drugs and financial problems, I think most of them don't realize I'm still a pretty young person. I'm only in my 20s, after all. I'm an established professional musician, and I expect I'll be a professional musician 10 years from now, and 20 years from now. It may not be on as big a scale as it once was, but I expect there'll still be people listening to Celtic music in 10 years' time. It has survived for centuries already, I figure it can go another 20 years at least.

I can imagine myself at 45 years old playing at a square dance just like Buddy MacMaster, but I don't know if many other people can. I don't think the public who read about me, or the media who write about me, think of me as someone they'll still be dealing with in 10 years' time, let alone 20 years' time. I guess that's because the first 10 years or so of my career were so intense that neither I nor the media are gonna be able to keep it up at that rate for another 10.

But then again, there are a lot of artists in that boat. Back in the '60s, when it seemed everyone in music was on drugs and into "free love" and the whole scene, I bet lots of people thought none of those artists would be around very long. Of course, lots of them proved that theory right; Jim Morrison, Jimi Hendrix, Janis Joplin, that guy from the Rolling Stones, they all flamed out under the weight of the whole thing. But there were a few who survived it and are still making music. Just look at the Rolling Stones; they're all pushing 60. Can anyone picture me playing my fiddle at 60, I wonder?

To be perfectly honest though, I've got no interest in being 65 years old and being Don Messer, if that's what people expect a 65-year-old fiddle player to be. I've got no interest in being 65 years old and being Buddy MacMaster. What I'd like to do when I'm 65 is be Ashley MacIsaac. And that's the guy, in my mind, who worked his butt off to take Cape Breton music to the rest of the world and sold a whole pile of it to make loads of money for other people, and got chewed up and spit out by the media and the music business in the process.

Still, none of that will bother me if, in the long run, I can play my fiddle, and make a living, and live my life the way I need to live my life. If I can just do that ... well, I'll be the golden boy again.

Discography

2003: *Ashley MacIsaac*
2001: *Cape Breton Fiddle Music NOT CALM*
  (with Howie MacDonald)
2000 *Fiddle Music 101*
  (with Dave MacIsaac)
1999: *Helter's Celtic*
1998: *fine® thank you very much*
1996: *hi™ how are you today?*
1993: *A Cape Breton Christmas*
1992: *Close to the Floor*

Compilations and Other Artists' Recordings
Edie Brickell — *Picture Perfect Morning*
David Byrne — *Feelings*
Big Rude Jake — *Blue Pariah*
The Chieftains — *Fire in the Kitchen; Water from the Well*
Bruce Hornsby — *Spirit Trail*
Mary Jane Lamond — *Lan Duil*
Celtic Colours International Festival:
 Cape Breton Island — The Road Home

Soundtracks
The Hanging Garden
Due South
Nabbie's Love

Index

A

A&M Records, 85, 96, 207
Acadian heritage, 30–31
  influence on musical style of, 31–32
acid (LSD), 128–29, 150
Adams, Bryan, 111–13
adolescence, 44–45, 178
  musical career during, 60–61, 65
  sexuality in, 66–68, 177, 178–89,
  192–93
Advocate, The, 160
agents, 73–74, 254. See also Jones, Sheri
AIDS, 165, 187–90
Akalaitis, JoAnne, 7–8, 12–13, 97
alcohol, 62, 145–46, 147, 154
Antigonish, 27, 52, 252
artists, 270
Atlantic Distributors, 76–77

B

bands
  playing in, 82–83
  playing with, 115
  putting together, 84
bankruptcy, 119, 232–33, 261
  media and, 221–22, 263–64
Barenaked Ladies, 102–4
Beaton family, 57–58
Beaton, Harvey, 34
Beaton, Joey, 64
Beaton, Kinnon, 51, 58
Belle Cote, Nova Scotia, house in, 121,
  122, 208
  burning of, 259–62
Bingo, 40, 41
bisexuality, 177–78, 199
black people, 11–12, 14, 22
Bluestein, David, 259
Boden, Brigid, 204–5
Bono, 174
Boy George, 180

Bramalea, Ontario, 44
Brickell, Edie, 88
Byrne, David, 97, 98, 229

C

Cameron, John Allan, 100, 109
Cameron, Stuart, 100, 109, 231
Canada, 142, 157
  celebrities in, 169, 173–75, 243
  drug laws in, 153–54, 155–56
  homophobia in, 159, 161, 164, 166,
  244
  music business in, 83–84
  outspokenness in, 170–71
  pride in, 172, 173
Cape Breton Island, 27, 173, 264, 265,
  267–68
  Acadian heritage of, 31–32
  Catholicism and, 178–79, 181, 183
  culture, 23, 58–59, 62, 266
  homogeneity of, 11–12, 14, 15, 22
  homosexuality and, 69–70, 196–97
  music of, 31–32, 54–56, 71, 96
    competition and, 61–62;
    genealogy and, 57–58
  Scottish heritage of, 29, 55, 107
career, 68–69, 71, 72–73
  decision to turn professional, 73,
  241–42
Carnegie Hall, 97–99, 160, 228–29
car, 45–46
  effect of ownership of, 46, 66–68,
  193
  Elvis's, 212
Catholicism
  guilt and, 139, 182, 196
  sexuality and, 178, 181–82, 183,
  197–98, 251
CBC, 222
CDs (compact discs)
  sales of, 76–77, 78
  See also fine® thank you very much;
  Helter's Celtic; hi™ how are you
  today?; recording
celebrity, 98, 174. See also fame

Celtic music wave, 106, 108, 132, 270
Chapman, Stan, 20, 51–56, 58–60
Chatham, Ontario, 239–40
Chieftains, 82, 100, 105, 114, 194, 203–4
childhood, 30, 32–33, 41
    moneymaking in, 40–41, 43–44, 62–63
    musical development in, 33–34, 39–40, 41, 53, 60. *See also* fiddle: lessons
    sexuality in, 33, 178
    traumatic events in, 48–50
Christians, born again, 155, 198, 199
Church, Paul, 208–9, 221
Cleveland, Ohio, 163, 201, 202–3
cocaine, 139–40, 144, 201, 205, 248
    effects of, 133–35, 143
    first use of, 129–30
    money and, 134, 141
    See also crack cocaine; drugs
Cohn, Rob, 223–24
coming out, 17
    to family, 102, 192, 193, 194–96, 251
    publicly, 102, 159
    to self, 184, 187
competition, 61–62
Corner Brook, Newfoundland, 80–81
Cote, Dwayne, 52
crack cocaine
    addiction to, 124–25, 131, 133–34, 135, 136–41, 143–44, 145
    effects on musical performance of, 123–25, 131–33, 210–11
    first use of, 130
    media and, 133, 211
    See also drugs
Crash Test Dummies, 105, 114
Creignish:
    after New York trip, 24–26
    location of, 28–29
    move away from, 48, 68–70
    See also adolescence; childhood
Crow, Sheryl, 114
CTV, 215, 222

D
Decca, 259
decriminalization, 155
DeGeneres, Ellen, 166, 198

detoxification, 141
Detroit, 43–44
Deveau, Gerry, 224, 259–60, 261
Diamond, Brookes, 207
Dion, Celine, 173, 174
discipline, 36, 42
Donlon, Denise, 230
Doucette, Marcel, 77
Dowling, Adam, 100
Downie, Gord, 114
drugs, 148, 253, 254
    addiction to, 133–36, 152–53, 218–19, 251
        treatment for, 141–42, 210
    attraction of, 17–18, 79–80,
    legality of, 153–54, 155–56
    money and, 118, 134, 141
    in the music business, 80
    use of, 145, 205, 221, 253–54
    See also alcohol; cocaine; crack cocaine; marijuana
Due South, 208

E
East Coast Music Awards
    in 1994, 90–94, 95, 194
    in 2000, 223, 265
    in 2003, 265
East Coast music community, 224–25, 265
Elizabeth II, Queen, 109, 172
Elvis' car, 212
EMI, 96
Etheridge, Melissa, 114
Europe, 199

F
fame, 101–2, 167, 248, 254, 262–63
    advantages of, 113–15, 238–39
    disadvantages of, 117–18, 194
    effects of, 235–37
    See also media; publicity
family, 27–28, 29, 164, 195
    drug addiction and, 135, 251
    extended, 30–31, 32
    music business and, 250
    and New York trip, 8–9, 10, 23–24
    sexuality and, 192, 193, 194, 251–52
Feldman, Sam, 207
Festival of Lights (Charlottetown, PEI),132, 133

Fiddle Music 101, 64
fiddle, 34, 38, 39, 51, 147
  Acadian style of playing, 31–32
  as crutch, 147–48
  lessons, 39–40, 51–56, 58–60
  Scottish style of playing, 31–32
fine® thank you very much, 125, 208
Fort Erie, Ontario, 163, 206
France, 105

G
Gaelic, 29, 31, 57, 106
gay
  club scene, 17–18, 186
    music in, 18
  community, 18–19, 67, 68, 165,
    166, 189, 191
  lifestyle, 90, 165, 166, 251
  pornography, 67
  press, 160, 247
  See also coming out; homophobia;
  homosexuality; sexuality
genealogy and music, 57–58
Ginsberg, Allen, 98–99
girlfriends, 193
Glass, Philip, 7, 9, 19–21, 86–88, 97,
  98, 228–29
  Cape Breton and, 20
Globe and Mail, 167
Governor General's Awards, 109
Gzowski, Peter, 96, 194

H
Halifax, 67, 74, 194, 251, 263
The Hanging Garden, 208
Helter's Celtic, 210–13, 225–27, 228,
  245
hip-hip music, 130, 132, 205
hi™ how are you today?, 85, 108, 125,
  194, 201
  recording of, 95, 127, 129
  tour for, 99, 101–2, 104–5
HIV/AIDS, 189
homophobia, 198–99
  in Canada, 159, 161, 164, 166, 244
homosexuality, 17, 18, 33, 45, 67, 166,
  179
Hudson, Rock, 198
Hynes, Ron, 78–79

I
insurance, 261
Inverness County, Nova Scotia, 29
Ireland, 106

J
Japan, 116–17, 203
John, Elton, 174
Jones, Sheri, 77, 78, 84, 88, 95, 203
  Ashley's drug use and, 135–36
  departure of, 206–7, 230, 233
  first meeting with, 74–76
Judique High School, 26, 42–43,
  46–48, 72
Juno Awards, 201, 202

K
Kitchen Devils, 132

L
Lamond, Mary Jane, 106
lang, k.d., 167
Late Night with Conan O'Brien, 167–69
Lennon, John, 156
lobster, 32–33
Loggerhead Records, 213, 227–28,
  230–31, 256
  drug use and, 142, 209–10
  Helter's Celtic and, 210–12, 225–27,
  245
  New Year's Eve 1999 show and, 221
  record deal with, 208–9
Los Lobos, 114
lottery win, 36–39

M
Mabou, Nova Scotia, 29, 57, 58
MacDonald, Dougie, 52
MacDonald, Howie, 229, 231
MacDonald, Mary Janet, 34
MacGillivray, Kendra, 52
MacGillivray, Troy, 52
MacIsaac, Angus (father), 28, 34, 42
  lottery win by, 36–39
MacIsaac, Carmelita (mother), 28
MacIsaac, Dave, 64
MacIsaac, Geraldine (aunt), 34
MacIsaac, Henry (brother), 28, 30, 35
MacIsaac, Lisa (sister), 30, 38, 231

MacIsaac, Wendy (cousin), 34, 47, 52, 60, 230

Maclean's magazine
honour roll, 160–61, 174
interview with, 161–62, 163
"scandal", 159, 175, 247, 248
effect on relationships of, 167–68, 192
fallout from, 164, 165, 166–67, 202, 219, 241, 246, 247

MacMaster family, 57–58

MacMaster, Buddy, 20, 35, 45, 52, 58
influence of, 56, 65

MacMaster, Minnie Beaton, 57

MacMaster, Natalie, 29, 52, 57, 60, 61

Manheim, Camryn, 13, 16–17, 86

marijuana, 128–29, 250
legality of, 153–54, 155–56
medical use of, 155
in music industry, 145, 151–52
musical performance and, 103–4, 144, 148–51, 152, 202, 204–5
possession charge for, 154
touring and, 79–82, 143

Mariposa Folk Festival, 224–25

McCain, Andrew, 208–10, 221, 227, 228

McDermott, John, 100

media, 101, 102, 162, 171–72, 247
dealings with, 164, 210–11, 242, 243–44, 244–46, 261–62
East Coast, 263–64
sexuality and, 162–63, 164–65, 246–47

Messer, Don, 51, 103, 164

Mexico, 134, 139, 140

money, 252, 255
drugs and, 140–41, 151, 238
earnings as a teenager, 40–41, 44, 60–61, 62–63, 65, 237
earnings as a professional musician, 73, 125, 152, 238, 240–41, 249–50
from record sales, 120
from tours, 118–20, 120–21
liquor licence laws and, 60–61
from lottery win, 38–39

Montreal, 230, 244, 248

movies, 115–17

MuchMusic, 113, 227

Murray, Anne, 103, 109–11, 170

music, 115

industry, 74, 78, 145, 151, 211–12;
in Canada, 83–84, 143–44, 173, 243, 249–50, 254–58
drug use in, 79–80, 124, 131–32
influences, 34–35, 66
practice, 40
style, 31–32, 41–42.132

musicians
drugs and, 131–32
sexuality and, 190

N

Nabbie's Love, 116–17

Nelson, British Columbia, 149

New Year's Eve 1999 performance, 213–21
effect on career of, 222–23, 230–31
media reaction to, 221

New York, 71, 79, 86, 184, 186, 193
1992 sojourn in , 11–12, 14–16, 72
gay community in, 17
music and, 17, 22

New Yorker magazine, 213

Nyanza Monster Bingo Players, 132

O

O'Connor, Wayne, 206, 207

O'Donnell, Rosie, 198

P

pedophiles, 197

performance, live,
first, 53
for Pope, 54
onstage behaviour, 132–33, 205–6, 218–19

piano, 35

playing in a band, 82

Pope John Paul II, 20, 54, 197, 198

pornography, 67, 68

Port Hawkesbury, Nova Scotia, 28–29, 30–31, 53, 132, 133

pot. *See* marijuana

professional career, 46, 65–66, 71
beginnings of, 73–76

promiscuity, 190–92

promotion, 78, 245–47

public image, 242–43

publicity, 102, 164, 168–69, 222–23
East Coast Music Awards and, 95
Paul Simon and, 88–89, 90

pubs, 60

Q

Queer As Folk, 166, 199

R

Rankin Family, 29, 57, 58, 79, 114, 224–25
Rankin, John Morris, 44, 58
    death of, 225
record company, 84–85, 94, 95, 256
    deals, 95–96, 254–57
recording, 63, 64
    first independent, 63–65, 74–75
        re-release of, 84
relationships, 74, 183, 186–87, 192
    touring and, 101, 187
Riverdance, 85, 204
rock star, 270
Rogers, Jeff, 207, 208

S

scabies, 91–94
school, 41, 42
    elementary 33–34, 41
    final year of, 47–48
    secondary, 42–43, 46–47
Scotia Fest, 221–22
Scotland
    fiddle music of, 55–56, 107
    visit to, 106–8
sexuality, 18, 102, 159, 167, 196, 199, 251
    in adolescence, 66–68, 177, 178–89, 192–93
    in childhood, 33, 178
    first experiences of, 44–45, 67–68
    New York and, 184–86
Simon, Paul, 87–89, 90, 97

Skinner, James Scott, 55–56
"Sleepy Maggie", 104, 105–6, 134, 161, 168
Spain, 105
step dancing, 34, 105, 106
swearing, 30, 33

T

talent, nature of, 42
taxes, 120, 208, 209
tobacco, 146, 153, 204
Toronto, 97, 127, 128, 194, 267
    March 2000 performance in, 230
    move to, 97
    three gigs in one day in, 121–22
tourism, 262
tours, 79, 99–101, 104–5, 118–19, 143
    drugs and, 79–82
    first, 44, 46
    first professional, 78–81
    relationships and, 101, 187
Tragically Hip, 114

U

United States, 154–55, 169, 170, 199
    touring in, 100, 105
Universal Music, 84, 207–8, 209

V

Vancouver Symphony Orchestra, 203
Vancouver, 102–4
Victoria, British Columbia, 240–41
Village Voice, 15, 67–68, 192

W

Warner Brothers, 84, 85, 96
Willis, Stephanie, 47
Woyzeck, 7–8, 19–20, 20–21, 21–22, 24